Privileging Gender
in Early Modern England

Habent sua fata libelli

Volume XXIII
of
Sixteenth Century Essays & Studies
Charles G. Nauert, Jr., General Editor

ISBN 0-940474-24-7

Composed by NMSU typographer Gwen Blotevogel,
Kirksville, Missouri
Cover design by Teresa Wheeler, NMSU Designer
Printed by Edwards Brothers, Ann Arbor, Michigan
Text is set in Palatino 10/12

Privileging Gender

in

Early Modern England

Jean R. Brink, editor
Volume XXIII
Sixteenth Century Essays & Studies

This book has been brought to publication with the
generous support of
Northeast Missouri State University

Library of Congress Cataloging-in Publication Data

Privileging gender in early modern England / Jean R. Brink, editor.
    p.   cm. — (Sixteenth century essays & studies ; v. 23)
Includes bibliographical references (p.) and index.
ISBN 0-940474-24-7 (alk. paper)
    1. English literature—Early modern, 1500–1700—History and criticism. 2.
English literature—Women authors—History and criticism. 3. Women and litera-
ture—England—History—16th century. 4. Authorship—Sex differences. 5. Sex
role in literature.
I. Brink, J.R. II. Series.
PR418.W65P75 1993
820.9'9287'09031—dc20   93-5329
                                                                                              CIP

Contents

Acknowledgments

I gratefully acknowledge the continued support of the College of Liberal Arts and Sciences, Arizona State University, for the Arizona Center for Medieval and Renaissance Studies during a time of budgetary constraints. The contributions of the Friends of the Arizona Center for Medieval and Renaissance Studies are also gratefully acknowledged; their generosity makes projects of this kind feasible.

The staff of the Arizona Center for Medieval and Renaissance Studies, particularly Mr. T. Scott Clapp, Dr. William F. Gentrup, Sriram Natarajan, and Patrick O'Callaghan, has been involved in preparing the manuscript for publication. Ms. Melinda J. Holley deserves special thanks for doing the final proofreading of the galleys when I was out of the country. As usual, Dan Brink graciously served as computer consultant for the project.

Finally, I wish to thank Robert Schnucker and Paula Presley of Sixteenth Century Studies for their cooperation and labor in bringing the printed text to fruition.

Introduction

The essays in this volume focus on the issue of gender as it relates to texts written by and about women in early modern England. Among the issues considered are the boundaries between private and public life, the problems of divorcing our understanding of the life from the work of a female author, the bibliographical procedures for charting the intellectual history of women, and the historical difference which obtains between categories of masculine and feminine in the sixteenth century and the late twentieth century.

Taken together, the essays in this collection also illustrate compatibilities among feminist theory, new historicism, and the methodologies of traditional bibliography and old historicism. The contributors engage a variety of theoretical approaches to historical problems and literary texts, but they avoid assuming doctrinaire positions. For this reason, the collection is arranged chronologically, rather than thematically.

Taken as a whole, these essays illustrate that the recent intersection of historical and literary studies has been productive. All of the essays make use of literary and documentary texts, but none of the essays engages in literary analysis as an end in itself.

In the first essay, entitled "The Books and Lives of Three Tudor Women," Mary Erler offers a model for charting the intellectual history of women as readers. Evidence of a dedication to a female patron does not in and of itself demonstrate that a book was intended for women readers. Erler's bibliographical work illustrates the need for painstaking research on the books that women owned and the connections among the women who owned them. Margaret Hannay, in "'Unlock my lipps': the *Misere mei Deus* of Anne Vaughan Lok and Mary Sidney Herbert, Countess of Pembroke," suggests that translation of religious texts afforded women an acceptable means of entering public discourse. Her essay also shows that further work is needed to identify those specific biblical texts that were reread so that they could be used to justify public discourse by women.

The study of "Historical Difference/Sexual Difference" by Phyllis Rackin breaks new theoretical ground by refining our understanding of distinctions between sixteenth- and late-twentieth-century conceptions of sexual difference. Rackin's essay, like that of Jean Howard, illustrates the compatibility of old historicist scholarship with new historicist and feminist approaches to texts. In "The Taming-School: *The Taming of the Shrew* as Lesson in Renaissance Humanism," Margaret Downs-Gamble rereads *Shrew* in the context of Renaissance rhetoric, demonstrating that Petruchio's "schooling" of Kate has affinities with the documentary texts of Renaissance humanism. Her juxtaposition of these texts invites a fresh approach to the decoding of the difficult passages in which Kate is subjected to verbal tyranny.

Source scholarship is given a fresh twist by Catherine La Courreye Blecki in "An Intertextual Study of Volumnia: From Legend to Character in Shakespeare's *Coriolanus*." Blecki argues that an understanding of the intertextuality of Shakespeare's text is essential for an appreciation of the dynamic presentation of Volumnia. In "Domesticating the Dark Lady," Jean R. Brink provocatively traces relationships between patriarchal systems and female characters in three Roman plays of Shakespeare. Like Rackin, she advocates the need for "historicity" in understanding concepts of gender. Jean E. Howard, in "Forming the Commonwealth: Including, Excluding, and Criminalizing Women in Heywood's *Edward IV* and in Shakespeare's *Henry IV*," continues her sophisticated and thoughtful analysis of the intersection between historical contexts and literary texts. Here, she illustrates how social marginalization can also be reread as privileging if understood in its economic context. Comparing Shakespeare and Heywood, figures very different in their handling of the genre of the history plays, she shows that they use the figure of the woman as criminal to manage threats to an ordered commonwealth.

In recent discussions of concepts of privacy, social historians have claimed that early-modern people ignored or conflated the distinction between public and private. Drawing upon a broad range of sources—domestic and religious treatises, journals, correspondence, autobiography—Retha Warnicke, in "Public and Private: The Boundaries of Women's Lives in Early Stuart England," proves that these distinctions existed and offers a valuable description of how women's lives were bounded. This essay illustrates the need for examining a variety of sources in order to assess social constraints. Approaching the issue of public and private from a different perspective, in "Resurrecting the Author: Elizabeth Tanfield Cary," Donald W. Foster compellingly argues that the texts of early women writers should be read in relation to their lives. Using Cary as an exemplary instance, he demonstrates that her life and her works should be read as fictions that recreate each other and that neither her life nor her art was wholly determined by patriarchy.

In "Dictionary English and the Female Tongue," Juliet Fleming calls attention to the connections between the feminine and the vernacular at the inception of the English dictionary. She concludes, however, that even though early-modern anxieties concerning the materiality of discourse were articulated through the register of gender, those concerning a will to knowledge were expressed (and are now expressed) through the register of class. Judith Kegan Gardiner supplies a revisionary essay on Margaret

Askew Fell Fox (1614-1702), author of *Women's Speaking Justified* and an important figure in the history of the Quaker movement. In "Re-Gendering Individualism: Margaret Fell Fox and Quaker Rhetoric," Gardiner reviews the achievements of Fox and her important influence on Quaker rhetoric. Mark S. Lussier, in "'Marrying that Hated Object': The Carnival of Desire in Behn's *The Rover*," examines the interplay of dialogic exchange among competing discourses of sexual and economic politics. His richly appreciative essay throws light on Behn's accessibility to early modern audiences as well as her appeal to twentieth-century critics.

It is highly appropriate that this particular collection should appear under the auspices of the Sixteenth Century Studies Conference and monograph series. Through the years, this conference and its publications have provided a vital forum for interdisciplinary discussion. Moreover, the organizers of the Sixteenth Century Studies Conference have achieved this worthy objective while maintaining a strong commitment to including in their forum scholars who are beginning their careers as well as those who are more established. The same kind of essential ecumenism characterizes this volume.

Jean R. Brink

Saint Katharine, 1519.215X126
[Geisberg XXIV, 12]

ONE

The Books and Lives
of Three Tudor Women

Mary Erler

The history of women's intellectual lives as readers remains to be written. Yet significant cultural weight attaches to female reading, particularly in the early modern period when printing begins in England, and when as a result vernacular and lay literacy increase dramatically. It is in the late fifteenth and early sixteenth century that reading begins substantially to transcend the boundaries of class—and to a lesser extent, those of gender.

Because evidence of women's book ownership is scarce, discussion of Tudor women's reading has been confined for the most part to a familiar group of aristocratic examples: Margaret Beaufort; Cecily, Duchess of York; Catherine of Aragon; Mary Tudor; Elizabeth; and more recently Anne Boleyn and Katharine Parr. Attention to non-aristocratic women readers, however, may offer both broader evidence of women's literacy and more complex ways of viewing this evidence in relation to cultural patterns.

In the Fettyplace sisters we are presented with three able and intellectually acute gentry women whose lives display a range of dispositions. Dorothy and Susan were first married, then widowed; subsequently the former entered religious life and the latter chose the vowess vocation, while the third sister, Eleanor, remained celibate as a nun. All three were connected with Syon abbey, the Bridgettine house for men and women, ruled by an abbess whose wealth, intellectual scope, and spiritual rigor gave it a unique place in English monasticism.

Their intellectual interests are traceable in Susan's bequest of money for a school, in the four books which carry Eleanor's signature, and in Dorothy's provision for book purchases. Members of a wealthy, well-connected, literate family, they were influenced by their family's patterns, both male and female. Susan would perhaps not have endowed a school, for instance, were it not for the existence of the more ambitious foundation initiated by her uncle William; and in fact when the women are remembered, it is principally through their mention in the work of their famous half-brother, Sir Thomas Elyot.

Nevertheless, the spiritual and intellectual connections between women which these lives present are strongly visible. Religiously, for instance, Susan's choice of the vowess vocation follows the example of her grandmother Alice. Intellectually, Dorothy entrusts the procurement of her books to her sister Susan. Personally, Eleanor's bond with another sister Elizabeth is witnessed by the inscription of the latter's death date in Eleanor's breviary. To a substantial extent, these connections between women are made in intellectual terms: through reading and book owner-ship.

The Fettyplaces owned land in Berkshire from the thirteenth until the eighteenth century, when the male line ceased.[1] The sisters were the daughters of Elizabeth Beselles and Richard Fettyplace, who died late in 1510 or early in 1511. Since his will mentions marriage portions only for his daughters Dorothy and Eleanor, it is likely that Susan's marriage to John Kyngeston took place before her father's death.[2] Kyngeston died early in their married life, in 1514. The marriage was childless and Susan lived at Syon thereafter, though the varying amounts entered for board in the monastic accounts indicate that her presence there was not contin-uous. She appears in the accounts, however, from 1514 to 1537 with some breaks, a residence which is registered by the mention of "Lady Kynge-ston's chamber" in a post-Dissolution inventory.[3] Both Susan and her grandmother Dame Alice Beselles were identified in the latter's will as "vowesses," that is, as women vowed to chastity, usually after a hus-band's death.[4] This choice was recognized in an episcopal ceremony which conferred the mantle and ring, but the woman remained formally

[1]J. Renton Dunlop, whose manuscript collections concerning the family are contained in three volumes, British Library Additional M SS 42763, –64, –65, calls the Fettyplaces "a most remarkable family for their ancient descent, aristocratic alliances, acquisition of estates, and public benefactions … " and notes that "their prosperity … lasted for nearly 400 years," Additional MS 42763, f. 3v.

[2]Will of Richard Fettyplace, PCC 1 Fettyplace, Prob 11/17, made August 11, 1510, proved May 15, 1511. According to Stanford E. Lehmberg, Susan's marriage was arranged through the offices of her uncle Anthony Fettyplace, since John Kyngeston was his ward. *Sir Thomas Elyot, Tudor Humanist* (Austin: University of Texas Press, 1960; reprint edition 1969), 191.

[3]Syon cellaress's foreign accounts: PRO SC 6/Hen 8/2214, 2215 (1514–15) through SC 6/ Hen 8/2244 and 2245 (1536–37) show yearly board amounts for Susan Kyngeston ranging from a high of £33 18s. 3d. (she occasionally paid for the boarding of others besides herself) to a low of 55 shillings, the charge for 1536–37, the last year in which she appears in the accounts. The inventory is PRO LR 2/112, quoted in F. R. Johnston, "Syon Abbey" in *Victoria County History* (hereafter VCH) *Middlesex* i.188.

[4]Will of Alice Beselles, PCC 8 Porch, Prob 11/22.

lay, free to arrange financial matters, to travel, even to litigate. Some vow-esses continued their previous patterns of life; others, like Susan Kynge-ston and Alice Beselles, attached themselves to communities of religious women.

Dame Alice Beselles is first recorded in the Syon cellaress's foreign accounts in 1520–21 where she is called "My lady kyngeston her Graunt-dame." Her stay in this year was temporary, but she returned in 1523–24 and continued in the accounts for two subsequent years, accompanied by two servants.[5] The matriarch of a huge clan of Beselles, Fettyplaces, and Yates and the widow of William Beselles,[6] she calls herself "vowess" in her spring 1526 will and asks burial either with her husband or at Syon. The vowess's freedom to come and go is shown in the will's provision of alternative places for burial depending, in Alice Beselles's case, on whether she died at her manor of Beselles Leigh, Berkshire, or at Syon. She is one of a very few women whom the catalogue of Syon's great library records as book donors: her gift, a folio edition of Italian lexicogra-pher Ambrogio Calepino's Latin dictionary (perhaps the first edition of 1502), was clearly an expensive one.[7]

The heir of Alice and William Beselles was their daughter Elizabeth, who married Richard Fettyplace. The family historian, J. Renton Dunlop, believes that Elizabeth was, like her mother Alice, a Syon vowess, but I have not discovered the source of this statement. After Richard's death Elizabeth married a second time, to Sir Richard Elyot, perhaps about 1512. The jurist, who was king's serjeant-at-law to Henry VII and VIII and Jus-tice of Assize on the Western Circuit, was the father of Sir Thomas Elyot.[8] From the latter's preface to his 1534 translation of a sermon by St. Cyprian

[5]PRO SC6/Hen 8/2224 (1520–21); SC6/Hen 8/2227 and 2228 (1523–24); SC6/Hen 8/2229 and 2230 (1524–1525); SC6/Hen 8/2231 and 2232 (1525–1526).

[6]Will of William Beselles, PCC 6 Holder, Prob 11/18, made May 4, 1515.

[7]This pioneering Latin dictionary, which later developed into polyglot form, is dis-cussed by DeWitt Starnes and Ernest William Talbert, who call it the period's "standard work of reference for students of Latin." They note that despite Vives' expressed dissatisfac-tion with its "comprehensiveness, scholarliness, and accuracy" he nonetheless recom-mended its use in his 1523 educational prescriptions for Princess Mary (*Classical Myth and Legend in Renaissance Dictionaries* [Chapel Hill: University of North Carolina Press, 1955], 11–13); Mary Bateson, ed. *Catalog of the Library of Syon Monastery, Isleworth* (Cambridge, 1898), A 38.

[8]For Elizabeth as sole heir of William and Alice Beselles, see *VCH Berkshire*, iv. 456-57. Since Richard Fettyplace was dead by May 15, 1511 (see n. 2), the date of Elizabeth Beselles Fettyplace's second marriage to Richard Elyot falls sometime between the middle of 1511 and the middle of 1514, when in April of the latter year Richard Elyot was named as a trustee in John Kyngeston's will, indicating he had married into the Fettyplace-Kyngeston alliance. For details of Richard Elyot's career, Henry Herbert Stephen Croft, ed., *The Boke Named the Gouernour*, 2 vols. (London: C. Kegan Paul, 1880), i. xxvii-xxxiv.

it seems that he and his Fettyplace stepsisters must by that time have known each other for many years. Speaking to Susan, Elyot alludes to Cyprian's sermon

> which I haue dedycate and sente vnto you for a token: that ye shall perceyue, that I doo not forgeat you: and that I doo vnfayn edly loue you, not onelye for our allyaunce, but also moche more for your perseuerance in vertu & warkes of true faith, praieng you to communicate it with our two susters religiouse Dorothe & Alianour, and to ioyne in your praiers to god for me.[9]

In dedicating a work of piety to a religiously affiliated woman Elyot was adopting a familiar pattern. In 1504 Thomas More translated the *Life* of Pico della Mirandola and dedicated it to Joyce Leigh, a nun of the London house of minoresses near Aldgate, as a spiritual New Year's gift. Joyce and her brother Edward Leigh (Archbishop of York after Wolsey's fall) had apparently been More's friends from childhood. Perhaps a few months after Elyot's translation of St. Cyprian appeared John Fisher was writing, in the Tower, his meditation on Ezekiel ii.10, a *memento mori* dedicated to his half-sister Elizabeth White, a Dominican nun of Dartford.[10]

Elyot's intention in translating Cyprian's work, an exhortation to steadfastness in troubles, has been variously interpreted: as alluding to Thomas More's tribulations (he was imprisoned in May 1534), as echoing More's own writings on Christian fortitude, as offering consolation for the difficult times brought on by the king's treatment of the religious orders.[11] Though Susan, its recipient, has been identified as Elyot's stepsister, until Pearl Hogrefe's biography of Elyot was published her affilia-

---

[9]STC 6157, *A swete and deuoute sermon of mortalitie of man* and *The rules of a christian lyfe by Picus erle of Mirandula*, Thomas Berthelet (1534), A 3v.

[10]More's *Lyfe* was not published until about 1510 (STC 19897.7) by John Rastell; a second edition, by Wynkyn de Worde, appeared about 1525 (STC 19898). For analysis of More's changes to his text, see Stanford E. Lehmberg, "Sir Thomas More's Life of Pico della Mirandola," *Studies in the Renaissance* 3 (1956), 61–74. Pico's twelve rules for the Christian life appear in both More's 1510 translation (in verse) and in Elyot's 1534 sermon (in prose). Fisher's *Spiritual Consolation* was not printed until c. 1578 (STC 10899). It is edited, together with another work dedicated to Elizabeth White, "The Wayes to Perfect Religion," in *The English Works of John Fisher*, ed. John E. B. Mayor. Part 1. EETS ES 27 (London, 1876). See *Humanism, Reform, and the Reformation: The Career of Bishop John Fisher*, ed. Brendan Bradshaw and Eamon Duffy (Cambridge: Cambridge University Press, 1989), 1–24.

[11]For the first reading, see Lehmberg, *Sir Thomas Elyot*, 129. For the second, see John M. Major, *Sir Thomas Elyot and Renaissance Humanism* (Lincoln: University of Nebraska, 1964), 106. For the third, see Pearl Hogrefe, *The Life and Times of Sir Thomas Elyot, Englishman* (Ames: Iowa State University Press, 1967), 212.

tion with Syon had not been noticed, and she had been wrongly called a nun.[12]

It is, in fact, the combination of her lay state with her position at Syon which may account for the privileged status which five family wills accord her. Beginning with her husband's brief 1514 document which says simply, "the ordre and forther Disposition of this I committ to my Wyff Susan Kyngeston," the picture of an unusually competent woman emerges from these documents. In 1523 Susan's uncle Sir Thomas Fettyplace left £400 to be held in trust for his daughter Katherine "by my nece Dame Susan Kyngeston at Syon." In the same year her sister Dorothy's will, made when entering Syon, left £46 13s. 4d. to be disposed as Dorothy specified by her sister Susan Kyngeston, and the care with which both women took this charge is indicated by reference to two indentures, one between Dorothy and her lawyer Thomas Inglefield, and a second between Inglefield and Susan. Three years later, in 1526, Susan was made executor of her grandmother Dame Alice Beselles's will and, with two others, was named to hold in trust for Susan's nephew a large bequest of plate and household stuff. (The three were to judge whether the nephew, when he reached the age of twenty-four, was "towardly and thriving" or likely to misuse the stuff, in which case the bequest was to be postponed until the legatee turned thirty.) Finally, she was one of the witnesses to her uncle William's will of 1529.[13] Her early commitment to a strongly religious vocation is thus coupled with a notably high degree of secular involvement.

These several family responsibilities, in fact, are alluded to in Susan's own will when she found it necessary to stipulate that if her executors should "be in trouble" for any reason concerning her various executorships for others, they must take what monies were needed to defend themselves.[14] She here echoes her grandmother Alice's will, which attempted to shield Susan against the difficulties of an executor's position by specifying that if Susan were "troubilled and besid ... she to haue of this forsaid substaunce to discharge hir self withall."

---

[12]Lehmberg, *Sir Thomas Elyot* 128–29; Hogrefe, *Life and Times*, 212. Thomas Elyot and Susan Kyngeston were probably approximate contemporaries. Although neither's birthdate is known, Elyot's is usually assigned to about 1490. If Susan were already married in 1510 when her father made his will (see n. 2), a birthdate around 1490 or slightly later would appear likely.

[13]Will of Sir John Kyngeston, PCC 23 Fettyplace, Prob 11/17. Will of Sir Thomas Fettyplace, PCC 32 Bodfelde, Prob 11/21. Will of Dorothy Fettyplace Codryngton, PCC 13 Thower, Prob 11/24. Will of Sir William Fettyplace, PCC 6 Jankyn, Prob 11/23. This same material has been summarized independently in Hogrefe, *Life and Times*, 29–30.

[14]Will of Susan Fettyplace Kyngeston, PCC 28 Alenger, Prob 11/28, made June 25, 1540, proved May 11, 1541.

Two elements in Susan Kyngeston's will are striking. First, the document testifies to the assurance with which a number of legal matters, including a family lawsuit, were handled by the testator. Though she employed legal counsel, her grasp of her financial affairs was secure, and she was evidently accustomed to supervising these affairs personally. To support a common pleas judgment favorable to her interests (which she cites by its date), for instance, she alludes to an Act of Parliament dated February 4, 1536—the Statute of Uses which had, in effect, declared previous trusts and family land settlements invalid.

Second, her interest in education was demonstrated by the assignment of eighty marks from the sum the court had granted her to the foundation of a school. Her executors were to find a virtuous priest "to teche pore childern" in Shalston, Buckinghamshire, for twenty years at a salary of four marks per year.[15] In this bequest, which apparently was never implemented, both the educational emphasis of Syon where Susan Kyngeston lived for about a quarter century and a familial tradition of educational patronage may be observed.

Fifteen years earlier, in 1526, Susan's uncle William Fettyplace had established a perpetual chantry for himself and various members of his family, among them Susan and her brother John Fettyplace the elder. The chantry included both an almshouse for three poor men and a school whose elements were carefully specified. Historian of education A. F. Leach points out that Childrey School's curriculum represents perhaps the earliest example of instruction specified in English, to be followed by "Latin if required." Its combination of elementary and secondary schooling, that is, of reading and grammar, is likewise notable,[16] as is the charter's stress on the school's wide-ranging educational mission, addressed not only to the scholars themselves "but for all other families and persons where they [the scholars] resided, in order that they might instruct those who were ignorant in the premises."[17]

---

[15]That Susan Kyngeston's school may have been open to both boys and girls is suggested by the similar will of Syon steward John Morris (PCC 14 Alenger, Prob 11/28), proved in 1540. Morris established a chantry school in Farnham, Surrey, where upon successful recitation before the sacrament of three paters, three aves, and the creed for the founder's soul, boys were to receive 4 *d.*, girls 8 *d.*

[16]A. F. Leach, "Childrey School," in VCH Berkshire ii. 275. The indenture establishing a perpetual chantry at Childrey with almshouse and school is described by John Nichols, *Bibliotheca Topographica Britannica* (London, 1790), iv, pt. 2, 68*–83*; quotations are taken from Nichols' translation of the Latin document. Strickland Gibson discovered a copy of the indenture, made between Queens College, Oxford; John Collysforde, rector of Lincoln College, Oxford; and William Fettyplace, preserved as binders' waste: "Fragments from Bindings at the Queens College Oxford," *The Library* 4th ser. 12 (1931–32), 429–33.

[17]The will of another uncle, Sir Thomas Fettyplace (see n. 13), acknowledges the difficulties incumbent on an Oxford student: it left £20 to provide "to some pour scoler a Cote / to some a gown / or other Clothing or money or suche thinge as shalbe thought moost necessary."

The Syon community was expelled from its monastery on November 25, 1539, according to Wriothesley's chronicle. Susan Kyngeston's absence from the cellaress's accounts after 1537 perhaps means that she left Syon before the Dissolution. In any case she died less than a year after the break, on September 23, 1540, at Shalston, Buckinghamshire, presumably at the home of her sister Anne Fettyplace and Anne's husband Edward Purefoy.

Her brass in the church there, where she is buried, is the second of two such monuments to her: on it she is described as "vowes," and shown in mantle, veil, and wimple, with a ring on her right hand. (Figure 1, reproduced from Lipscomb's *Buckinghamshire*, does not show the ring.) Dunlop says, "The artist has attempted a likeness—the broad face with the prominent dimpled chin is found again in the portrait bust of Sir George Fettyplace" who died in 1743, the last male Fettyplace (Figure 2). Her brass in Childrey parish church, Berkshire, prepared earlier at the death of her husband John Kyngeston (but without her death date) shows her with him, as wife rather than as vowed widow.[18]

Susan's sister Eleanor Fettyplace chose to join the Syon community as a nun. In his will made October 9, 1520, and proved May 26, 1522, her stepfather Sir Richard Elyot says:

> Item I will that my doughter in lawe [i.e. stepdaughter] Elynour, doughter of Richard Fetiplace, Esquier, have after hir marriage celebrate fourty poundes to hir exhibition [support] yerely iii li vi s viii d, till she be professed in religion. And at suche tyme as she shalbe professed to the said xl li as moche as shalbe necessary in bokes or apparell to that entent.[19]

Eleanor's profession date is unknown, but in view of Elyot's will it must be after 1520.[20] A portion of the generous forty-pound bequest may

---

[18]The *VCH Berkshire*, iv. 225 describes her (probably palimpsest) brass, including the ring. Just under two feet in height, it is one of fewer than half a dozen brasses on which the subject is explicitly identified as a vowess, although many women costumed as widows on their memorial brasses may have taken vows. Figure 1 is printed in George Lipscomb, *The History and Antiquities of the County of Buckingham*, 4 vols. (London, 1847), iii. 75. For the pedigree of Purefoy of Shalston, iii. 71. Dunlop's observation comes from BL Additional MS 42763, f. 360v. Figure 2, from Swinbrook church, Oxfordshire, is reprinted by permission of the Royal Commission on Historical Monuments. The joint brass of Sir John and Lady Susan Kyngeston is described in Elias Ashmole, *The Antiquities of Berkshire*, 3 vols. (London, 1719), ii. 211–12; it is reproduced by T. H. Morley, *Monumental Brasses of Berkshire* (n.p., 1924), 77.

[19]Croft, *Boke*, i. 313.

[20]Register Fitzjames, Guildhall MS 9531/9, ff. Cxxviij–Cxxx does not indicate her presence at the abbatial election of 1518.

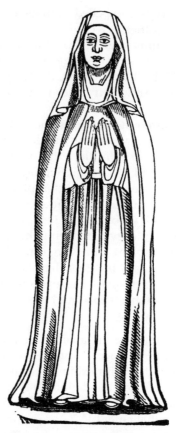

Here lyethe buryed Dame Susan Kynge=
stone, vowes, the eldyst daught' of Rychard
Ffetyplace of Est shyfford in the Countye
of berk· Esquier decessyd & late the Wyfe
of John Kyngeston of Chelrey in the said
Countye of berk· Esquier also decessyd the
whyche said dame Susan dyed the xxiij day of
Septemb' in the yere of our Lord God a
M°ccccc'xl on whose sowle and all crysten
soull' jhu have m'cy amen.

Figure 1. An engraving of Susan Kingeston's vowess brass and inscription at Shalston, Bucks., which omits her ring of profession. Taken from George Lipscomb, *The
History and Antiquities of the County of Buckingham*. 4 vols. (London, 1847), III.75.

Figure 2. Monument to Sir George Fettyplace (+1743), from Swinbrook church, Oxon. A family resemblance to Susan Fettyplace can be observed in the broad face and dimpled chin. Reproduced by permission of the Royal Commission on Historical Monuments.

have subsidized the four books which bear her name: a large and expensive missal, a breviary, a psalter, and a contemporary devotional work.[21]

Two of these books are connected with Eleanor Fettyplace's life after the Dissolution. Although a group of Syon monks and nuns went abroad to Flanders, seven small groups remained in England, many maintaining the monastic observance at their relatives' homes. Eleanor was part of one such community, as was her niece Elizabeth Yate: this group was housed at the manor of Buckland, Berkshire, the home of Susan and Eleanor's sister Mary Fettyplace Yate and her husband James.

In a folio Sarum missal printed at Paris by G. Merlin in 1555 (STC 16217) a handwritten slip now pasted on the inside front cover reads: "Of your charyte pray for the sowle of dame Elyzabethe ffetyplace, some tyme relygious in Amesburye, & also for me Elynor ffetyplace her suster, relygious in Syon, at whose charges thys boke was bought & geven to thys churche of Bocklond, anno domini 1556" (Figure 3). The name of Elizabeth Fettyplace is found in the pension list of Amesbury, a Benedictine house in Wiltshire, where she is recorded as receiving five pounds annually. She and Eleanor, "my Susters," are each bequeathed twenty shillings in the 1543 will of James Yate: hence it is clear that Elizabeth was also part of the group at Buckland.[22]

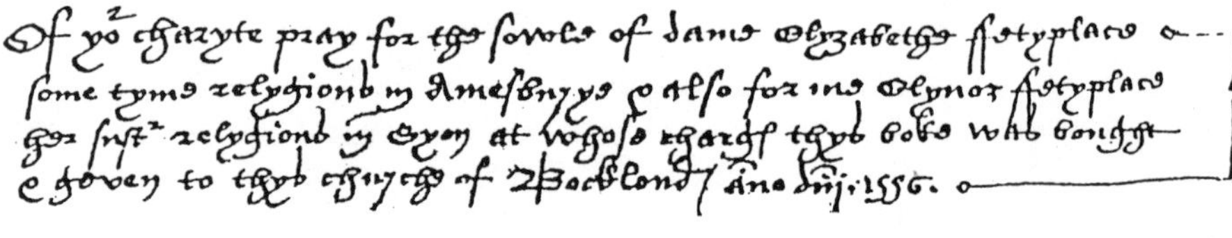

Figure 3. Eleanor Fettyplace's donation inscription in the missal she gave Buckland parish church in memory of her sister (Southwark Diocesan Archives no. 72)

J. R. Fletcher deduces that on Queen Elizabeth's accession Eleanor got back the missal which she gave to the Buckland parish church, since the missal accompanied Syon abroad when the community fled again in 1559, after the queen's dissolution of the restored houses. When G. J. Aungier wrote his 1840 history of Syon the missal was in the possession of

[21]N. R. Ker, ed., *Medieval Libraries of Great Britain: A List of Surviving Books*, 2nd ed. (London: Royal Historical Society, 1964). Andrew G. Watson, ed., *Supplement to the Second Edition, Medieval Libraries of Great Britain* (London: Royal Historical Society, 1987).

[22]For Amesbury pension list, *Letters and Papers of Henry VIII* (henceforth LP) xiv(ii), 646. Will of James Yate, PCC 11 Pynnyng, Prob ii/30, made May 23, 1543, proved July 16, 1544.

the Reverend Joseph Ilsley, vice president of the English college at Lisbon. It subsequently passed through the hands of Canon Daniel Rock, then of Fletcher himself, to the Westminster Diocesan Archives.[23]

Eleanor commemorated her sister Elizabeth a second time, in her breviary of c. 1420 where the obituary of Elizabeth Fettyplace is found in the calendar at May 21 with the date 1556(?), according to the *Bodleian Quarto Catalogue* (Bodl. Auct.D.4.7, formerly Laud misc. 1961). A. Jefferies Collins, commenting on this Bridgettine breviary, says, "We are fortunate still to possess the books from which those two (Eleanor Fettyplace and her niece Elizabeth Yate) seem to have sung their daily Office in banishment"—that is, Eleanor's breviary and Elizabeth's office book, Univ. Coll. Oxford MS 25, which includes a printed Sarum psalter of 1522 (STC 16260), the books which the two nuns used at Buckland.

Eleanor's signature also appears in a late-fifteenth-century manuscript psalter (Brussels, Bibl. Royale IV.481, f. 258). Finally, in a copy of Richard Whitford's 1532 *Pype of Perfection* (STC 25421; Bodley 4o.W.2.Th. Seld.), "Elynor ffetyplace" is found on the recto of the last leaf. This work on the religious life was thus written by one member of Syon and owned by another.

Eleanor Fettyplace and Elizabeth Yate were part of the re-enclosed community when Syon was restored under Mary in 1557, but the restoration lasted only briefly. Eleanor died on July 15, 1565, according to the Syon *Martyrology* (BL Additional MS 22285, f. 46 v). Fletcher says her death occurred abroad "during the time Syon occupied the unhealthy, disused Franciscan house at Zurich Zee."[24]

The third Fettyplace sister Dorothy was, like Susan, a widow, though unlike Susan she became a Syon nun rather than a vowess after her husband's death. Her decision is recorded on her husband's brass at Appleton, Berkshire, which states that John Goodryngton died on December 31, 1518, and that "Dorathe his wyfe ... after his dethe toke relyagon in ye monastary of Syon."[25] That the widow was Dorothy Fettyplace is shown by a chancery suit brought by Sir Richard Elyot and Elizabeth his wife against Christopher Codryngton, esquire. It charges

---

[23]J. R. Fletcher, notebook no. 5, "History of Syon Abbey 1539–63," at Syon Abbey. George James Aungier, *The History and Antiquities of Syon Monastery* (London, 1840), 99, n. 2. The missal is now Southwark Diocesan Archives no. 72.

[24]Eleanor's breviary was presented to the Bodleian by Thomas Manwaring of Brasenose on December 18, 1613, according to N. R. Ker's notes, made in preparation for *Medieval Libraries* (see above) and housed at the Bodleian. For A. Jefferies Collins's quotation, see *The Bridgettine Breviary of Syon Abbey* (Worcester: Henry Bradshaw Society, 1969), v. Fletcher notebook no. 5.

[25]Brass and inscription are reproduced in Morley, *Monumental Brasses*, 23.

that the latter refused to complete the marriage settlement agreed upon because his son John, the bridegroom, had since died (PRO C 1/405/29). Dorothy Fettyplace was probably married for about a year, since the suit dates the marriage settlement in October 1517.

On April 24, 1523, Dorothy made her will, as the community mandated before profession. It reveals both the Syon rule's expectation of book ownership at entrance and a degree of personal interest in reading as well.[26] "Imprimis I will there be bestowed vpon A song booke / and other Inglisshe bookes for my self suche as my Suster Kyngeston will apointe the sum of iij li" (PCC 13 Thower, Prob 11/24). Presumably the first clause refers to the plainsong book necessary for divine office, but what English books Susan Kyngeston bought for her sister we would very much like to know.

Dorothy Codryngton's will was proved on February 16, 1531, with Susan Kyngeston as one of its two executors. Thus she is probably not the person Thomas Elyot calls "our ... suster religiouse Dorothe" in his dedicatory preface to St. Cyprian's sermon, dated July 1, 1534. The situation is unclear, but a number of subsequent references to Dorothy Codryngton, nun of Syon, suggest that a second woman of this name may also have been a member of the community. The name is written in a copy of a devotional tract published October 29, 1535, the *Tree and xij frutes of the holy goost*, and it appears in the Syon pension list of 1539 and the Marian pension list c. 1554. Based on these payments, Fletcher states that Dorothy Codryngton was one of the group of religious housed at Buckland with James Yate. The Syon *Martyrology* records her death on April 26, 1586.[27] Thus it seems doubtful that the Syon nun who wished to provide herself with English books is the same woman whom the Tudor humanist believed would value Cyprian's meditations.

The religious and cultural shifts of the 1530s are mirrored, somewhat differently, in the vernacular reading of these sisters. Though the 1532 *Pype of Perfection* may appear a purely devotional text, Jan Rhodes points

[26]The rule notes that the entrant must arrange for "bokes, beddynge, profession rynge, dyner, offerynge, and suche other." James Hogg, ed., *The Rewyll of Seynt Sauioure. Vol. 4: The Syon Additions for the Sisters ... BL MS Arundel 146* (Salzburg: Institut für Anglistik und Amerikanistik, 1980), 83 (f. 44a).

[27]J. J. Vaissier, ed., *A deuout treatyse called the tree & xij frutes of the holy goost* (Groningen, 1960), xxxviii. The will signature is transcribed in the PCC copy, "Dorathe Cotherington"; the Tree signature "Dorothe Corderynton," according to Vaissier, xxxvii. The 1539 pension list is LP xiv (ii), 581 (or 206). Aungier prints the c. 1554 list (p. 98) from BL Additional MS 8102. For Fletcher's statement that Dorothy Codryngton lived at Buckland, his notebook no. 5 at Syon. Croft's suggestion (*Boke*, cv), that the Dorothy referred to in Thomas Elyot's preface is Dorothy Danvers Fettyplace, widow of John Fettyplace (+1524), cannot be correct, since she remarried and died in 1560 as the widow of Sir Anthony Hungerford.

out that its defense of traditional religious life was conceived by Whitford as a reply to Lutheran attacks. Eleanor's possession of this text may be evaluated in light of Rhodes' comment: "in Syon at least there were women of sufficient intellectual capacity to persevere with a work as lengthy and demanding as this."[28]

Cyprian's *Sermon of mortalitie* too had contemporary resonances. In January 1534, under pressure from John Stokesley, Bishop of London, Syon had signed a document acknowledging the king's marriage to Anne Boleyn, but had been urged to a more conclusive acceptance, which the brethren refused. In May they were visited by Rowland Lee and Thomas Bedyll, Cromwell's agents, to urge that they take the Oath of Succession, and throughout the spring and summer of that year the clergy of the London religious houses, colleges, and parishes were sworn, almost without exception.[29] Elyot's book may have appeared at any time between its July 1 preface and the end of 1534. Though Syon's Richard Reynolds was not arrested and executed until April and May of 1535, for the Fettyplace sisters at Syon Cyprian's counsel to put away fear and sorrow may have been, in 1534, particularly apt.

The books which surface so frequently in these family networks serve several functions. They express personal connection: through them a shared past is recalled and acknowledged, as in Eleanor's purchase of the missal in her sister's memory. They demonstrate shared intellectual interests, as in Dorothy's confident assignment of her book acquisition to Susan. They invoke values held in common: Eleanor's recitation with her niece Elizabeth Yate of divine office from the books they shared in their manor-house community. Men as well as women are participants here: Elyot's open declaration to Susan that "I doo vnfaynedly loue you" recalls their connection, and his gift of the sermon on patience acknowledges a common view of the world. Especially valuable, however, are the glimpses we are afforded of women's intellectual and spiritual exchanges, supported by the ownership and reading of books.

[28]"Private Devotion in England on the Eve of the Reformation," Ph.D. thesis, University of Durham 1974, 18.

[29]Dom David Knowles, *The Religious Orders in England*, 3 vols. (Cambridge: Cambridge University Press, 1959–61), iii. 216–17. Susan Brigden, *London and the Reformation* (Oxford: Clarendon Press, 1989), 226.

David and Bathsheba, about 1526,
by Lucas Cranach,
269 X 196.
Berlin, Kupferstichkabinett [Rosenberg 43]

TWO

"Unlock my lipps": the *Miserere mei Deus* of Anne Vaughan Lok and Mary Sidney Herbert, Countess of Pembroke

Margaret P. Hannay

"**A** Meditation of a Penitent Sinner: Written in Maner of a Paraphrase upon the 51. Psalme of Dauid" by Anne Vaughan Lok (1560) and the meditation on Psalm 51 by Mary Sidney Herbert, Countess of Pembroke (1590s) make an intriguing parallel, for they give us a rare opportunity to compare verse translations by sixteenth-century English women writers.[1] Both women consult Calvin's *Commentaries* on the Psalms of David, but their emphases differ significantly.[2] Lok, like Calvin, stresses original sin and the need for abject penitence. While the countess includes these elements, her version stresses the joy and health that come from God's mercy. Typically, Lok stresses the negative aspects and the countess the positive aspects of the same doctrines. Nevertheless, both women find in the words of the psalmist justification for a public role; like the psalmist, they pray not only for cleansing from sin but also for the education of the soul in God's "hid schoole" so that they will be empowered to teach

---

[1] The Sidney *Psalmes* are cited from Noel Kinnamon's transcriptions of the Penshurst MS for our edition of the *Collected Works of Mary Sidney Herbert, Countess of Pembroke*, Oxford English Text Series, forthcoming 1995. Quoted with the permission of the Viscount de L'Isle, from his collection at Penshurst Place. Lok's sonnets are cited from her *Sermons of John Calvin, vpon the Songe that Ezechias made after he had bene sicke and afflicted by the hand of God* (London: John Day, 1560). I am grateful to the Women in the Renaissance and Reformation Seminar at Harvard University for their helpful comments on a draft of this article.

[2] The original Latin edition of the *Commentaries* was published in 1557; Calvin's own French translation appeared in 1563 and Arthur Golding's English translation in 1571.

19

others. In an age when women were instructed to be silent, they each found a voice through the words of the psalmist.[3]

Meditating on the psalms was a natural activity for these women, both of whom came from families who were active in the English Protestant movement and supported translation of scripture into the vernacular. Anne Vaughan's father had tried to intercede with Cromwell to save William Tyndale from execution.[4] Anne and her first husband Henry Lok were friends and followers of John Knox, who lived in their London home for several months after Queen Mary ascended to the throne. Knox fled to Geneva and later persuaded Anne Lok, with her two youngest children and her maid, to join him there.[5] She lived in Geneva from 1557 to 1559, while the Geneva psalms were being translated. (An early version was published in 1557; the full Psalter was dedicated to Elizabeth in 1559). Her rendering of Psalm 51 was published as an addendum to her 1560 translation of *Sermons of John Calvin, vpon the Songe that Ezechias made after he had bene sicke and afflicted by the hand of God*, a series of four sermons on Isaiah 38 that he had preached in 1557. Lok's twenty-six sonnets, which have just begun to receive critical attention, are important both for their form (they are arguably the first sonnet sequence in English) and for the personal nature of their content. Like Mary Sidney, Lok "*meditated* on the text" and produced highly original poems.[6]

Because the *Sermons* were translated anonymously, there has been some debate over her authorship. The dedication to "the Lady Katharine, Duchesse of Suffolke" is signed "A. L.," traditionally believed to be Anne Lok, an identification reinforced by the Latin inscription written by Henry Lok on a flyleaf of the British Library copy ("Liber Henrici Lock ex dono Annae uxoris suae. 1559."), saying that the volume was a gift from his wife Anne. Parallels with her signed translation, Jean Taffin's *Of the marks of the children of God, and of their comforts in afflictions*, confirm her authorship. (The title page of Taffin states that it was "translated out of French by Anne Prowse"; by 1590 Anne Vaughan, twice widowed, had

---

[3]On the use of religious writings, and particularly translation of male words, to circumvent restrictions on women's speech, see my Introduction to *Silent but for the Word: Tudor Women as Patrons, Translators, and Writers of Religious Works* (Kent, Ohio: Kent University Press, 1985) and "'Wisdome the wordes': Psalm Translation and Elizabethan Women's Spirituality," in "Reconstructing the Word: Spirituality in Women's Writing," a special issue of *Religion and Literature* 23 (1991):65–82.

[4] Patrick Collinson, "The Role of Women in the English Reformation illustrated by the Life and Friendships of Anne Locke," in *Studies in Church History*, edited by G. J. Cuming (London: Thomas Nelson and Sons, 1965), 2:262.

[5] Lewis Lupton, *A History of the Geneva Bible* (London: The Olive Tree, 1977), 4:12.

[6] J. C. A. Rathmell, ed. *The Psalms of Sir Philip Sidney and the Countess of Pembroke* (New York: New York University Press, 1963), xx.

married Richard Prowse.) Both works are dedicated to prominent Protestant noblewomen;[7] both dedications speak of the afflictions of the righteous; both dedications mention David's Psalm 51. Even the signatures are parallel. The dedication of the Taffin translation to the Countess of Warwick is signed, "Your Honors in the Lord, most humble A. P.," as the earlier dedication to Katherine, Duchess of Suffolk, had been signed, "Your graces humble A. L." The works themselves are parallel in that both sets of sermons seek to bring comfort to those persecuted for their Protestant faith, and both the Taffin sermon and the sonnet sequence present David as an example of one who fights against despair. Like Lok's Calvin translation, her Taffin translation ends with sacred poetry, in this case couplets on "The necessitie and benefite of affliction." Both poems, unsigned, end with a simple "FINIS."

We can be quite certain that Lok translated Calvin, but a further complication in attributing the sonnets to her is a heading, possibly by the printer, that prefaces the sequence: "this meditation folowyng vnto the ende of this boke, not as parcell of maister Caluines worke ... was deliured me by my friend with whom I knew I might be so bolde to vse & publishe it as pleased me."[8] Despite this ambiguous heading, internal evidence indicates that the dedication and the poems are by the same hand, since there are verbal echoes of the sonnets in the signed dedication to the Duchess of Suffolk, including the same images of disease, starvation, and horror. Both present God as a physician who brings health. The Suffolk dedication also equates "two moste excellent kinges, Ezechias and Dauid," indicating that Lok herself presented the song of Ezechias and the song of David as parallel.[9] Unless external evidence to the con-

---

[7] Catherine Willoughby, Duchess of Suffolk, was a member of Queen Catherine Parr's circle; both the duchess and the queen were saved from prosecution for heresy by Anne Askew's courage under interrogation. During Queen Mary's reign she went into exile, in Geneva and then in the Polish province of what is now Lithuania. Anne Russell, Countess of Warwick, a close friend of Queen Elizabeth, frequently interceded for the Dudley/Sidney/Herbert Protestant alliance at court.

[8] Charles Huttar attributes the translation of Calvin and the biblical translation to Lok but the poems to Knox, "Anne Vaughan Locke," in *An Encyclopedia of British Women Writers*, ed. Paul Schlueter and June Schlueter (New York: Garland, 1988), 297. Collinson (265) and Lupton (4:21) attribute only the translation to Lok; Roland Green has recently transcribed the sonnets for the Women Writers Project as the work of Anne Lok.

[9] Anne Lok, "Dedication to the Duchess of Suffolk," *Sermons of John Calvin*, sig. A3v. One might also note that her son Henry Lok wrote a parallel work, a metrical version of Ecclesiastes, printed with the corresponding biblical passages on the outer margins, just as the sonnet sequence on Psalm 51 had been printed. Henry Lok, *Ecclesiastes* (London: Richard Field, 1597).

trary surfaces, we are probably safe in attributing the sonnet sequence to Anne Lok.

The prose translation printed on the outer margin of the sonnets indicates her close association with the Genevan psalm translators.Though it may "match no known English prose translation," as Charles Huttar notes, more than half of it is identical to the 1560 Geneva. More significantly, some phrases which depart from the 1560 Geneva text match the exceedingly rare 1557 psalter. For example, where the 1560 Geneva translates the end of verse 1 as "according to the multitude of thy compassions put awaie mine iniquities,"[10] Lok quotes from the 1557 version, "according vnto the multitude of thy mercies do awaie myne offences."[11] She retains the 1557 wording for verse 2, asking for cleansing from "wickednesse" instead of "iniquities" as in the 1560. Verse 5 also matches the 1557 Geneva: "I was shapen in wickednes" instead of the 1560 "borne in iniquitie." In verse 14 she uses the 1557 phrase "God of my health" instead of the 1560 "God of my salvation." Despite these parallels to the 1557 Genevan psalter, her version occasionally departs from both Genevan psalters, particularly in verses 4, 6, and 10. Her translation may well reflect an ongoing discussion with the translators of the Genevan psalms, or some access to their working papers. We know that she did have a copy of Calvin's manuscript on Isaiah 38, since the original French version was first published two years after her English translation. Her protection of John Knox in England, her Genevan exile, and her translations demonstrate her commitment to the Protestant cause.

Like Anne Vaughan Lok, the Countess of Pembroke was active in the Protestant cause. Although the circle of their acquaintances overlapped, differences in age and rank meant that Lok was an associate of Knox and Calvin during the Marian exile while the countess was part of the court of Queen Elizabeth. While the Vaughans and the Loks were middle-class mercers, Mary Sidney's family comprised the powerful Dudley/Sidney/Herbert alliance of Protestant earls; among them, they controlled more than one-fourth of the land under English rule, including Ireland and Wales. The most important literary woman of the Elizabethan era, the Countess of Pembroke is celebrated for her patronage, her translation, and her original works. As "Sister of Sir Philip Sidney," her self-designa-

[10]*The Geneva Bible: A facsimile of the 1560 edition*, ed. Lloyd E. Berry (Madison: University of Wisconsin Press, 1969). Unless otherwise indicated, all biblical quotations are taken from this edition.

[11]*The Psalmes of Dauid, translated accordyng to the verite and Truth of th Ebrue, wyth annotation moste profitable* (Geneva, 1557). The Bodleian copy was saved from Salisbury Cathedral when it was struck by lightning; the bottom margin has been burned but most of the text is intact.

tion, she achieved a significant literary and political role herself when she attempted to carry on her brother's work for the Protestant cause through patronage, translation, publication of Philip Sidney's works, and her own writing.[12]

Philip Sidney had emphasized the importance of the Psalms in his *Defence of Poetry*, praising as the "chief" poets "they that did imitate the unconceivable excellencies of God" such as "David in his Psalms."[13] He had begun writing metrical versions of psalms before he went to the Netherlands to fight against the occupying Spanish army; after his death, his sister translated the remaining 107 psalms. Although they remained unpublished until the early nineteenth century, the *Psalmes* of Philip and Mary Sidney circulated in manuscript and were celebrated by their contemporaries. As John Donne said, they "Both told us what, and taught us how to doe.... They tell us *why*, and teach us *how* to sing."[14] Twenty years ago Coburn Freer could correctly label this "varied and brilliant collection" as "one of the best but most underrated achievements in the Renaissance lyric," but recent studies have established the centrality of Sidneian psalms in the Protestant lyric tradition.[15]

The Countess of Pembroke, a scholar who seems to have consulted virtually every Protestant psalm version in English, French, or Latin, prob-

---

[12] Mary Sidney to Sir Julius Caesar, 8 July 1603, British Library Additional MS 12503, ff. 152.

[13] Sir Philip Sidney, "The Defense of Poetry," in *Miscellaneous Prose of Sir Philip Sidney*, edited by Katherine Duncan-Jones and Jan van Dorsten (Oxford: Clarendon Press, 1973), 80.

[14]Rathmell, ix.

[15]Coburn Freer, *Music for a King: George Herbert's Style and the Metrical Psalms* (Baltimore: The Johns Hopkins University Press, 1972), 73. See also Barbara Kiefer Lewalski, *Protestant Poetics and the Seventeenth-Century Religious Lyric* (Princeton: Princeton University Press, 1979), 241–45, 275–76; Richard Todd, "'So Well Atyr'd Abroad': A Background to the Sidney-Pembroke Psalter and Its Implications for the Seventeenth-Century Religious Lyric," *Texas Studies in Literature and Language* 29 (Spring 1987), 74–93; Gary Waller, *Mary Sidney, Countess of Pembroke: A Critical Study of Her Writings and Literary Milieu* (Salzburg: University of Salzburg Press, 1979) and *The Triumph of Death and Other Unpublished and Uncollected Poems by Mary Sidney, Countess of Pembroke (1561–1621)* (Salzburg: University of Salzburg Press, 1977); Susanne Woods, *Natural Emphasis: English Versification from Chaucer to Dryden* (San Marino: Huntington Library, 1984): 169–175, 290–302; Beth Wynne Fisken, "Mary Sidney's *Psalmes*: Education and Wisdom," in *Silent but for the Word: Tudor Women as Patrons, Translators, and Writers of Religious Works* (Kent, Ohio: Kent University Press, 1985), 166–83, and "'To the Angell Spirit ...': Mary Sidney's Entry into the 'World of Words'," in *The Renaissance Englishwoman in Print: Counterbalancing the Canon*, ed. Anne M. Haselkorn and Betty S. Travitsky (Amherst: University of Massachusetts Press, 1990), 263–275; Rivkah Zim, *English Metrical Psalms: Poetry as Praise and Prayer, 1535–1601* (Cambridge: Cambridge University Press, 1987), 185–210.

ably knew Anne Lok's sonnets.[16] There are several internal hints that she may have done so. First is the repetition of one exact phrase, "O god, god of my health."[17] This idea comes from the Great Bible, "(O God) thou that are the God of my health," but other poetic versions have variant readings.[18] For example, Crowley renders it as "Lord of thy saueynge helth," Sternhold and Hopkins as "O God that of my health art Lord," and Parker, "thou God my God of health."[19] The second hint is a verbal echo. The countess's "filthie fault, my faultie filthines" seems to be an adaptation of Lok, "my filth and fault." The third hint is repeated rhymes, "so/snowe" and "wall/fall," both of which are simple enough to be mere coincidence; the countess, however, has no rhymes repeated from Wyatt, Parker, or even from the ubiquitous Sternhold and Hopkins. The only other repetition I have found in this psalm is the "me/iniquitie" of Crowley. Her "gladness/sadness" rhyme comes directly from Arthur Golding's translation of Calvin's explanation of the paradox at the heart of Christian experience: "verely bicause the sadnes which tormenteth them, openeth them the gate to true ioy … true gladnesse." God has taken away our sin and "is become our frend."[20]

External evidence is equally problematic, but the two Protestant women writers may well have been acquainted, and certainly must have known each other by reputation, despite differences in age and social class. Like Anne Lok, the Dudley/Sidney alliance had extensive connections with the interlocked Huguenot and Geneva communities—including Théodore de Bèze, Anthony Gilby, Philippe de Mornay, and Rowland Hall, printer of the Geneva Bible. Other translators, such as John Field and John Harmar, also dedicated translations of Bèze and Mornay to members of the family alliance, and Golding claimed that his translation of Mornay was a completion of Philip Sidney's work. More direct

---

[16]Seth Weiner is working on the more difficult problem of whether the Sidneys knew Hebrew. See "Sidney and the Rabbis: A Note on the Psalms of David and Renaissance Hebraica," in *Sir Philip Sidney's Achievements*, ed. M. J. B. Allen *et al.* (New York: AMS Press, 1990), 157–62.

[17] Sidney, line 41; Lok, Sonnet 16, line 1.

[18]*The byble in Englysche, that is to saye the content of all the holy scrypture.* [First Great Bible] Revised by M. Coverdale. London: R. Grafton and E. Whitchurch, 1539. See also *The psalter or psalmes of David corrected and poyncted, as they shalbe song in churches after the translacion of the great Byble* (London: E. White Churche, 1549).

[19]Robert Crowley, *The Psalter of Dauid Newely Translated into English metre* (London: R. Crowley, 1549); Matthew Parker, *The Whole Psalter translated into English metre.* Setting by T. Tallis (London: John Daye, 1567); *The whole booke of psalmes collected into English meter by Thomas Sternhold, J. Hopkins and others* (Geneva: J. Crespin, 1569).

[20] John Calvin, *The Psalms of Dauid and others. With M. John Caluins Commentaries*, trans. Arthur Golding (London: H. Middleton, 1571), sig. Cc iiii r–v.

connections may be established through Anne Vaughan's nephew, Sir Julius Caesar, with whom the Countess of Pembroke carried on an extensive business correspondence; with the Countess of Warwick, Anne Russell, the beloved aunt of Philip and Mary Sidney, to whom Vaughan dedicated her second translation; and with Vaughan's second husband, Edward Dering, a Puritan preacher famous for his learning and eloquence. Henry Herbert, Earl of Pembroke, must have known Dering, for he served for a time at Salisbury Cathedral, where the Pembrokes worshipped. Dering died in 1576, the year before Mary Sidney's marriage to Pembroke, but a family connection with the Derings may have continued in later generations, for Sir Edward Dering (grandson of the preacher's brother Richard) owned one of the two extant manuscripts of Mary Sidney Wroth's play *Loues Victorie*.

Although Lok was a generation older than Mary Sidney, their literary efforts in the Protestant cause overlapped. Lok published her translation of Jean Taffin's *Of the marks of the children of God* in 1590, the year in which the countess published her own translation of a Huguenot writer, Mornay's *Discours de la vie et de la mort*. Both works must have been part of the same effort to disseminate the works of Continental Protestants, particularly since Taffin, "Minister of the holie Gospell in the French Church at *Harlem*," included a letter "To the faithfull of the Low Countrie," dated September 15, 1586, a week before Sir Philip Sidney was wounded in Zutphen fighting for Dutch independence from Catholic Spain.

Translation of sermons and commentaries was seen as an act of devotion, but could also be a political activity. Paradoxically, translation was subversive, since it undercut the authority of the established church by enabling even the lower classes to interpret scripture, but it was also a form of control, since the commentaries gave the correct Protestant interpretation. As Gilby says in "The Epistle to the Reader," he is motivated by "loue to his vnlearned countriemen" and by "the excellencie of the worke it selfe," that is, both by concern for the unlearned and by the conviction that he is presenting them with the Truth.[21] Access to commentaries on the word of God was seen as equalizing:

> now euen the simplest poore man for a small peece of monie, may by diligent reading in this Booke of that rare man Theodore Beza, atteine to a better vnderstanding of these holie Psalmes of Dauid, than in old time (by the report of the ancient) the great learned men were able [to achieve].[22]

---

[21]Anthony Gilby, "The Epistle to the Reader," in Théodore de Bèze, *The Psalmes of Dauid, trvly opened and explaned by Paraphrasis, according to the right sense of euerie Psalme,* trans. Anthony Gilby (London: H. Denham, 1580), sig. A5.

[22]Gilby, sig. A5v.

The Countess of Pembroke was praised by her chaplain Gervase Babington for similar efforts to encourage the education of poor believers, probably part of her motivation for translating and publishing Mornay's *Discours de la vie et de la mort*.[23] Her elegant psalm versifications, however, were far more suited for the courtly circle they reached in manuscript than for "the simplest poore man" with his "small peece of monie." John Davies, who transcribed the magnificent Penshurst manuscript of her *Psalmes*, emphasizes the private nature of her work:

> And didst thou thirst for Fame (as al Men doe)
> thou would'st, by all meanes, let it come to light.[24]

Lok must have had a more general audience in mind for her published sonnets, for the Protestant tradition had a dual place for the psalms, both for private reading and for public recitation.

Whether they wrote psalms for publication or for a fashionable coterie, these devout women found an acceptable means of self-expression in a time when women were urged to silence but paradoxically encouraged to speak boldly for their faith like the martyrs Anne Askew and Lady Jane Grey. Translation of godly works provided an acceptable means for a woman to enter public discourse. As Elaine Beilin has observed, in dedicating her Calvin translation to the Duchess of Suffolk Lok draws a direct line of inspiration from God through Calvin to herself: God, "the heauenly Physitan" has taught "his most excellent Apothecarie" Calvin, "and I your graces most bounden and humble have put into an Englishe box, and do present vnto you."[25] That psalm translation was seen as appropriate for a devout woman may be demonstrated by Sir Edward Denny's rebuke of Mary Sidney's niece, Lady Wroth, for publishing a secular work. Wroth, he admonishes, should "repent you of so many ill spent yeares of so vaine a booke" and "redeeme the tym" by writing "as large a volume of heavenly layes and holy love as you have of lascivious tales and amorous toyes." She should "followe the rare, and pious example of your vertuous and learned Aunt, who translated so many godly books and especially the holly psalmes of David."[26]

---

[23]Gervase Babington, "A Brief Conference Betwixt Mans Frailtie and Faith" in *The Works of the Right Reverend father in God Gervase Babington, late bishop of Worcester* (London: Henry Fetherstone, 1615), sig. A4.

[24]John Davies, *The Complete Works of John Davies of Hereford*, ed. Alexander B. Grosart (Edinburgh: Edinburgh University Press, 1878), 2:4.

[25]Elaine Beilin, *Redeeming Eve: Women Writers of thè English Renaissance* (Princeton: Princeton University Press, 1987), 63; Lok, "Dedication to the Duchess of Suffolk," sig. A3.

[26]Sir Edward Denny to Mary Sidney Wroth, February 15, 1622, in *The Poems of Lady Mary Wroth*, ed. Josephine A. Roberts (Baton Rouge: University of Louisiana Press, 1983), 239.

Denny was advocating a particularly Protestant activity. Of course the Psalms have been beloved throughout the entire Judeo-Christian tradition, but the Reformation moved the Psalms out of the chapel into the court and the workplace, and onto the scaffold. So popular had psalms become that Anthony Gilby was concerned that people would read them more "for fashion sake, than for good deuotion and with vnderstanding."[27] The Protestant psalms were thought to be appropriate for all occasions: Coverdale wanted carters and ploughmen to whistle "psalms, hymns and such godly songs as David is occupied withal" and women to sing them as they spin—but they were thought to be especially appropriate for occasions when "the godly," as they called themselves, were in danger.[28] As W. Stanford Reid has demonstrated, they had become "The Battle Hymns of the Lord." Psalms sustained them and psalm-singing gave them "a sense of identity" to the point where they were often called "psalm-singers," or derided in England for their "Genevan jigs."[29] The Countess of Pembroke understood this use of the psalms for political commentary and made the dedication of her own *Psalmes* a pointed statement to Queen Elizabeth about her duty to support the Protestant cause on the Continent, a political content that reflects the nature of her intensely partisan sources and is also present in the sonnets of Anne Lok.[30]

Psalm 51 had gained both doctrinal and political significance in the Protestant tradition. The Seven Penitential Psalms (6, 32, 38, 51, 102, 130, 143) had been of central importance in the medieval liturgy, but had gradually been phased out of daily use in England, since the Reformers saw the purpose of penitence as consolation, rather than discipline. No longer part of the rites for Visitation of the Sick or Burial of the Dead in the 1552 Book of Common Prayer, they were confined to the service for Ash Wednesday. Nevertheless, Psalm 51 had particular meaning for the Reformers, because of its description of original sin and its stress on faith over works, the sacrifice made in the heart rather than in the temple. As Bèze said, "there are ioined in this Psalme also two principal pointes of true religion: the one, of original sinne: the other, of the abuse of sacrifices."[31] That reading of the psalm is apparent in Thomas Wyatt's trans-

---

[27]Gilby, sig. A5.

[28]Miles Coverdale, *Remains of Bishop Coverdale*, edited by George Pearson (Cambridge: Cambridge University Press, 1846), 537.

[29]W. Stanford Reid, "The Battle Hymns of the Lord: Calvinist Psalmody of the Sixteenth Century," *Sixteenth Century Essays and Studies* 2 (1971), 43, 52.

[30]See Margaret P. Hannay, *Philip's Phoenix: Mary Sidney, Countess of Pembroke* (New York: Oxford University Press, 1990), particularly chap. 4.

[31]Bèze, sig. f4.

lation, which, as Stephen Greenblatt has demonstrated, emphasizes "inwardness" when it speaks of "Inward Sion, the Sion of the ghost" and of the "heart's Jerusalem."[32] Lydia Whitehead has recently brought to our attention the centrality of Psalm 51 in Foxe's accounts of the Protestant martyrs in his *Acts and Monuments*. Thought particularly suitable for executions, the psalm had become part of the enforced ritual; the martyrs themselves made it part of the "Protestant iconography" by their recitation in the vernacular.[33] The gesture was well understood. When Dr. Rowland Taylor began to recite the psalm in English as he waited for the fire to be lit, the sheriff struck him. "'Ye knave,' said hee, 'speake Latine, I will make thee'."[34] The Sidney children, who owned a copy of "two books of Martirs" (the two volumes known as *Foxe's Book of Martyrs*) would have been particularly interested in the account of their aunt, Lady Jane Grey.[35] On the scaffold Lady Jane recited "the psalm of 'Miserere mei Deus' in English, in most devout manner throughout to the end," asking the crowd rather than a priest to "assist me with your prayers."[36] Like Wyatt, Lady Jane used the psalm to stress the priesthood of the believer.

The Sidneys also emphasized Psalm 51. In his *Defence*, Sir Philip was probably speaking of this penitential psalm when he said that the psalms are "used with the fruit of comfort by some, when, in sorrowful pangs of their death-bringing sins, they find the consolation of the never-leaving goodness."[37] Mary Sidney's choice of rime royal for Psalm 51 also underscores its importance. The poetic quality of her version of this favorite psalm must have been recognized by her contemporaries, for John Harington included it among the three he copied for Lucy, Countess of Bedford, and it is one of two of her psalms set for treble voice and lute in the fragmentary British Library Additional MS 15117.[38]

---

[32]Stephen Greenblatt, *Renaissance Self-Fashioning: From More to Shakespeare* (Chicago: University of Chicago Press, 1980), 115.

[33]Lydia Whitehead, "*A poena et culpa*: penitence, confidence and the *Miserere* in Foxe's *Actes and Monuments*," *Renaissance Studies* 4 (1990), 294.

[34]John Foxe, *The Acts and Monuments of John Foxe*, edited by George Townsend (New York: AMS Press, 1965), 6:700.

[35]Sidney accounts for 1573, De L'Isle MS U1475 A4/5.

[36]Foxe 6:700.

[37]Sidney, *Defence*, 80.

[38]The Library, Inner Temple, Petyt MS 538.43; British Library Additional MS 15117, f. 4v. See also f. 5v, a musical setting for Mary Sidney's Psalm 130. On this intriguing MS, see Mary Joiner, "British Museum Add MS. 15117: A Commentary, Index and Bibliography," *Royal Musical Association Research Chronicle* 7 (1967), 51–109. On metrical psalms as hymnody, see Robin A. Leaver, "*Goostly psalmes and spiritual songes*": *English and Dutch Metrical Psalms from Coverdale to Utenhove 1535–1566* (Oxford: Clarendon Press, 1991).

Although the Countess of Pembroke translated her version some thirty years later than Lok, she relied heavily on the same Genevan sources. As we have seen, Lok was part of the English community in exile, and apparently knew these works while in preparation, probably through sermons and manuscripts. Mary Sidney consulted the published works of the Genevan community: the annotated Genevan psalms; the commentaries of Calvin in the original and as translated by Golding; and the commentaries of Bèze, dedicated to her uncle the Earl of Huntington, and the English translation by Gilby, dedicated to the Countess of Huntington. To this we may add the metrical psalms begun by Clément Marot and completed by Bèze at Calvin's request. The countess "almost certainly" would have known Wyatt's *Seven Penitential Psalms* in terza rima as another literary model.[39]

The doctrines emphasized in all these versions of Psalm 51 are nearly identical, arising from the traditional attribution of the psalm to David, written as a response to Nathan's rebuke for his adultery with Bathsheba and the murder of Uriah. That context was presented as the first two verses of the Vulgate,[40] emphasized in this Geneva heading, and included in most other English translations, including the Great Bible, the Bishops Bible, Sternhold and Hopkins, and Calvin. Similarly, Wyatt and Lok each supply prefatory verses that deal with David's sins, although Lok does not mention David by name as Wyatt does. In his *Defence of Poetry* Philip Sidney presents Nathan as a poet who brought David to see his "own filthiness" through his fable about the lamb: "the application most divinely true, but the discourse itself feigned." [41] So effective is the tale—and its explication—that David is moved to write "that heavenly psalm of mercy," undoubtedly Psalm 51. The presence of Nathan in the *Defence* raises complex questions about the nature of poetic inspiration, as Anne Prescott has demonstrated.[42] Although the countess does not specifically mention David, Bathsheba, or Nathan, they would have been present for the reader in her text. The circumstances contextualized the psalm, making it a statement about the efficacy of poetry, both in bringing the sinner to repentance, as Nathan did, and in presenting sacred poetry as the true sacrifice of praise sought by God.

[39]Rathmell, xvi.

[40]"Psalmus David, cum venit ad eum Nathan propheta, quando intravit ad Bethsabee." The Bishop's Bible (1568) retains the emphasis on "his great offence in committyng adulterie," as do most other English translations. The Geneva heading does not specify "his great offences," but David's responsibility for the death of Uriah, rather than his adultery, is emphasized in a note to the Geneva version.

[41]*Defence*, 94.

[42]Anne Lake Prescott, "King David as a 'Right Poet': Sidney and the Psalmist," *English Literary Renaissance* 19 (1989), 147–51.

Both women use Calvin as a primary source for their interpretations of this penitential psalm, and may well have worked with his *Commentary* open before them, but their difference in emphasis is striking. Lok, in her "preface, expressing the passioned minde of the penitent sinner," draws on the tradition of the grieving ghosts of Boccaccio and Lydgate, probably derived from the recently published *Mirror for Magistrates*. [43] The "forsaken ghost" of David confesses his "hainous gylt" and "lothesome filthe," and is unable to find the joy available to others:

> Whome cherefull glimse of gods abounding grace
> Hath oft releued and oft with shyning light
> Hath brought to ioy out of the vgglye place.
>
> (Preface, Sonnet 2)

Instead, he remains "in darke of euerlasting light," where like a blind man he must "groape about for grace," yet appears to grope "in vaine." A personified Despair haunts the sonnet sequence, saying:

> In vaine thou brayest forth thye bootlesse noyse
> To him for mercy, O refused wight,
> That heares not the forsaken sinners voice.
> Thy reprobate and foreordeined sprite,
> For damned vessels of his heauie wrath …
> Of his swete promises can claime no part:
> But thee, caytif, deserued curse doeth draw
> To hell, by iustice, for offended law.
>
> (Preface, Sonnet 3)

Lok's speaker falls on his knees and prays for God's mercy in the words of this psalm, even as he dreads death, when he may "damned downe to depth of hell to go." (Preface, Sonnet 5)

No such anguish that the speaker may be foreordained to damnation haunts the lines of Mary Sidney. The difference in tone between the versions of Mary Sidney and Anne Lok may be seen even in their opening lines: Lok begins with a cry for mercy by a speaker who must "dred to take / Thy name in wretched mouth, and feare to pray"; the countess, in contrast, begins with prayer to a "sweet lord, whose mercies stand from measure free." Confident of God's mercy, the speaker can ask that it be applied to "sinnfull mee." Whereas Lok's speaker is pressed down by the "weight" of his sins until he sinks "in fen of depe despeire," the countess's speaker admits his guilt but has complete confidence in God's

---

[43]Thomas P. Roche, Jr., *Petrarch and the English Sonnet Sequences* (NY: AMS Press, 1989), 156.

mercy. Mary Sidney's version also lacks the violence of Anne Lok's imagery. For example, to render verse 4, "Against thee, against thee onely have I sinned, and don euill in thy sight," Lok says "My cruell conscience with sharpned knife / Doth splat my ripped hert," in order to show "The lothesome secretes of my filthy life." In contrast, the countess's speaker acknowledges the sin that "to my sowles eye unceasantlie doth show." In other words, the speaker is fully aware of his sin, without such violence.

The differences in tone are equally striking in their rendition of verse 8, "Make me to heare ioye and gladnes, that the bones, which thou hast broken, maie reioyce." Lok describes the sounds that the speaker hears— not the words of gladness, as one would expect, but "the soundes / Of dredfull threates and thonders of the law" that echo in his "gylty minde" and "with redoubled horror" distract the soul "from mercies gentle voice." The speaker therefore asks that God will "Sounde in my hart the gospell of thy grace" that will bring joy. Then the "broosed bones, that thou with paine / Hast made to weake my febled corps to beare" will finally "leape for ioy." In her rendering God has caused the pain and weakness, even as God will bring the joy. Although the countess, like Lok, has "brused bones" instead of the usual "bones, which thou has broken," she gives an interpretation typical of her faith, one full of confidence and joy:

> to eare and hart send soundes and thoughts of gladdnes,
> that brused bones maie daunce awaie their saddnes.
>
> (11. 27–28)

Nowhere does she suggest that God is the cause of the bruised bones, nor does she suggest that the heart hears the sounds and thunders of the law. Her phrase "daunce awaie their saddnes" is certainly not present in Bèze, in Calvin, in Lok, or in Geneva, which takes out references to dancing even when present in the original Hebrew, as in Pss. 30:13, 149:3, and 150:4.[44] As Freer so aptly observed, in the Sidneian psalms we see "devotion as a joyful game."[45]

Another significant difference, mandated by the poetic form itself, is Lok's expansion of doctrinal emphasis in her sonnet sequence, an expansion impossible in Mary Sidney's fifty-six lines of rime royal. For example, in their rendition of verse 7 ("Purge me with hyssope, and I shal be cleane") both women employ the image of leprosy from association of

---

[44]Although he does see more cheer in this one verse, Gary Waller believes that she portrays "what she saw as the intensely distraught state of mind depicted in the original," a "pathetic helplessness," "horrified self-accusation," and "pardonable exaggeration of a mind revolted by its own depravity." Her version of Psalm 51 is, nevertheless, "a moving poetic expression of a magnificent and challenging original," *Mary Sidney,* 236, 241.

[45]Freer, 25.

hyssop with the treatment of that disease in Leviticus 14. The usual verb is to "sprinkle" with hyssop, as Lok writes ("besprinkle thou my sprite"), but Sidney prays for "thie mercies streames to flow." She apparently found that usage in the Genevan note on Lev. 14:5 (cross-referenced to Ps. 51:7), that explains "running water, or of a fountaine" is to be used in the cleansing of leprosy. Her verb "flow" may imply washing with Christ's blood, as in Calvin's commentaries, but that interpretation is made far more explicit in Lok:

> Not such hysope, nor so besprinkle me,
> As law vnperfect shade of perfect lyght
> Did vse as an apointed signe to be
> Foreshewing figure of thy grace behight.
> With death and bloodshed of thine only sonne,
> The swete hysope, cleanse me defyled wyght.
>
> (Sonnet 9)

Similarly, Lok expands the treatment of the doctrine of atonement, seen by Protestants as implicit in verse 16 ("For thou desirest no sacrifice"), because they believe that the proper response to God's grace is repentance and not penance. As Mary Sidney says, the psalmist does not need sacrifice "to gaine thy grace," for grace cannot be earned. Once again Lok makes the doctrine more explicit—only the sacrifice of "thy swete sonne alone" can save "sinfull man" and "hath repaird our fall." (Sonnet 18)

For the Genevan Protestants, verse 5 ("Beholde I was borne in iniquitie, and in sinne hathe my mother conceiued me") was "a lightsome text for the proof of original sin, wherin Adam hath wrapped all mankynd."[46] Although both women adopt Calvin's discussion of original sin, they choose different metaphors to expand. Lok picks up a reference to the seed of David in Calvin's commentary on verse 13 and carries through the plant imagery. "With sede and shape my sinne I toke also," almost a paraphrase of Calvin, is amplified later in the seventh sonnet: "Such bloome and frute loe sinne doth multiplie, / Such was my roote, such is my iuyse with in." In contrast, Mary Sidney expands the metaphor of heat used in Calvin's explanation that "we be cherished & kept warme in sin, as long as we lye hid in the bowels of our mothers."[47] Yet the countess softens the passage, showing that the mother cherished the child as well as sin and corruption: "as with living heate shee cherisht me." (l. 17) As Beth Wynne Fisken has demonstrated, the countess's translation of this verse is "a striking portrait of frustrated maternal energy

[46]Calvin, sig. Cc iii.
[47]Ibid., sig. Ccii v.

that is not only helpless to save the child from sin, but actually generates the child's fate."[48]

Verse 6, "thou louest trueth in the inwarde affections: therefore hast thou taught me wisdome in the secret of mine heart," is interpreted by Calvin to mean that David has been "taught up by God as one of his household" and has "become a froward scholer."[49] Adapting his metaphor, both women stress the idea of God's school. Although the usual interpretation is that God's wisdom is hidden within the heart, the countess's juxtaposition of the child cherished within the womb implies that the womb itself may be a place where God imparts knowledge, even though the child is stained by original sin. Taught in secret, the "trewand soule" becomes a scholar "in thie hid schoole." (l. 21) Typically one woman gives a negative and one a positive interpretation of that wisdom. Anne Lok identifies God's "secrete wisedom" as the ability "To se my sinnes," emphasized by parallelism with the "hidden knowledge" that is the ability "To fele my sinnes." (Sonnet 8) The countess, in contrast, interprets that wisdom in positive terms, the knowledge of truth and goodness.

Both women emphasize the political content of this psalm, connected to the nature of penance and confession. As one would expect, the Protestant David confesses to God only, his own judge. In both versions there is also the implication that God will give a just "doome," not the unjust doom of the civil courts, an allusion to the persecution of Protestants, particularly in England and France. The treatment of unjust judges is similar to the countess's version of Psalm 82, in God's court that is "pight" above the earthly courts, reminding princes and judges that they are merely God's viceregents, and that they too shall be judged. The necessity for judgment on the ruler is acknowledged, so that all may recognize God's justice is not influenced by rank: "thie doome maie passe against my guilt awarded, / thie evidence for truth maie be regarded."

Similarly, both women emphasize the political implications of verse 18 ("Be fauourable vnto Zion ... buylde the walles of Ierusalem"). Zion and Jerusalem had become synonyms for the Church in the Protestant psalms, so verse 18 was read as a prayer for "the whole Church, because through his sinne it was in danger of Gods iudgement," as the Geneva note states. That is, because of David's position as king, his sin could bring judgment on others. Calvin concurs, explaining "for being anoynted King too the end to gather God and Church together, hee had by his shamefull reuolting dispersed it, so as the vtter destruction of it

---

[48]Fisken, *Silent*, 178.
[49]Calvin, sig. Cc iii v.

was to be feared," a situation that the French and English Genevan exiles applied to their own experience.[50] In Lok's own Genevan exile, she prays that God will "Defend thy chirch," that it "may never fall / By myning fraude or mighty violence" so that "Sion and Hierusalem may be / A safe abode for them that honor thee." (Sonnet 20) Lok's prayer for safety echoes the fervent plea of Calvin "that God should preserue the state of his Church in saftye euen vnto the comming of Christ."[51] As Roche observes, Lok is "very much aware" of the "public concerns," i.e. "that David's sin should be visited on his 'Church'."[52] In Mary Sidney's version political implications are implied with her usual subtlety. She adds to her texts a prayer that God will "embrace" his "loved Sion," that God will "still in peace, maintaine that peacefull place," and that God will turn a "well-accepting face" toward their sacrifices. Writing in the comparative safety of Elizabethan England, the countess presents a loving God who brings peace to his chosen people. Peace is also emphasized in her use of "Salem," which means peace, as a synonym for Zion, perhaps by analogy to Ps. 76:1, which she translates "his restfull tent doth only Salem dignify; / On Syon only stands his dwelling glorious."

Perhaps most significantly, both women also find in Psalm 51 a means of speaking on public issues. When the idea of a woman preaching seemed heretical, Lok could use the ventriloquism of psalm translation to "preach the iustice of thy law." (Sonnet 15) Beilin observes that "as pious writers teaching the faithful," women "could respond simultaneously to the enemies of their religion and their sex."[53] Because building up "the walles of Ierusalem" (Ps. 51:18) had become a code word for active support of the Protestant cause, Anne Lok quotes that familiar expression to justify writing as the only political work that a woman is permitted:

> Euerie one in his calling is bound to doo somewhat to the furtherance of the holie building; but because great things by reason of my sex I may not doo, and that which I may, I ought to doo, I have according to my duetie, brought my poore basket of stones to the strengthening of the walles of that Ierusalem, whereof (by grace) wee are all both Citizens and members.[54]

[50]Calvin, sig. Ccvii.
[51]Calvin, sig. Cc vii.
[52]Roche, 156.
[53]Beilin, 50.
[54]Anne Lok Prowse, "Dedication to the Countess of Warwick," in Jean Taffin, *Of the Marks of the children of God, and of their comforts in afflictions* (London: Thomas Man, 1590), sig. A3v–4.

The psalms made an even more effective persona for public speech than other sacred translations, for in adapting the words of the psalmist to their own condition, they had the weight of Christian tradition behind them, including Athanasius' application of the psalms to specific conditions, a chart reprinted and amplified in Sternhold and Hopkins. Similarly, Calvin compared his own position to that of David in great detail in the lengthy preface to his *Commentary.*

By using the male persona of the psalmist king, Lok and the Countess of Pembroke found a way to offer the sacrifice of praise "with open mouth" (Sonnet 17) despite gender restrictions. Lok uses mouth imagery to demonstrate that the speaker, who prays to be delivered "From gaping throte of depe deuouring hell," will be qualified by "the profe of myne example" to "preache / The bitter frute of lust and foule delight." (Sonnet 15) Once God has opened the lips of the psalmist, that redeemed sinner may preach, teach, or sing God's praises. By attributing the song to God rather than the psalmist, these women justify their own speech. Singing is presented not as a privilege but as a duty, and therefore becomes an act of devotion rather than of self-assertion. Lok's speaker, who cannot even pray without God's help, begs that God will "loose my speche." Once God has heeded this prayer, the psalmist will be empowered to preach:

> Lord loose my lippes, I may express my mone,
> And findyng grace with open mouth
> I may Thy mercies praise, and holy name display.
>
> (Sonnet 17)

Similarly, the countess's psalmist promises God that the result of forgiveness will be public praise: "soe shall my tongue be raised / to praise thy truth, enough cannot bee praised." (l.42) Teaching and song combine in the psalms, as the poet/singer praises God's mercy. When Sidney's psalmist prays, "Unlock my lipps, shut up with sinnfull shame," promising "then shall my mouth ô lord thy honor sing," she echoes her own rendering of Psalm 119:

> Thy speeches have I hidd
> close locked up in Caskett of my hart:
> fearing to do what they forbidd.
>
> (B, 11. 7–8)

But if God will intervene and "make me in thy statutes wise," the psalmist promises, "Then shall my lipps declare / the sacred lawes that from thy mouth proceed / and teach all nations." That is, the natural response to God's empowerment is to become a teacher of God's laws. Similarly, Anne Lok vows

So, Lord, my ioying tong shall talke thy praise,
Thy name my mouth shall vtter in delight,
My voice shall sounde thy iustice, and thy waies ...
God of my health, from bloud I saued so
Shall spred thy prayse for all the world to know.

(Sonnet 16)

Both Anne Lok and the Countess of Pembroke stress the international nature of the psalmist's message, reflecting their involvement with Continental, as well as English, Protestantism. To their originals they add the psalmist's vow to "teach all nations" or spread God's praise to "all the world."

For both women, Psalm 51 becomes a justification for a public role. In the person of the male psalmist, the author can declare that God's mercy necessitates the celebration of public praise. For both women, Psalm 51 is self-reflexive, becoming the praise that it promises. Despite differences in poetic form and tone, both women use this familiar psalm to present Protestant doctrine, to make a political statement, and to justify their own voice. The psalm itself becomes the answer to the prayer that God will "Unlock my lipps."

THREE

Historical Difference/
Sexual Difference

Phyllis Rackin

I originally thought of calling this paper, "Shakespeare and Sexuality: It really *was* different"; but then I decided not to because, of course, we have no way of knowing how "it" really was. The questions with which we approach the past are the questions that trouble us here and now, and the answers we find (even when couched in the words of old texts) are the products of our own selection and arrangement. These difficulties are especially troublesome in the case of gender and sexuality—subjects that tend to be occluded in the historical records of the past, issues heavily fraught with present concerns and present controversies.[1] Moreover, since both women and sexuality were largely unwritten, there is always the temptation to universalize, to assume that because neither has a written history, neither has a history—that both were always and everywhere what they are now and here.[2]

This paper is an attempt to articulate some of the differences between the terms that shaped people's understanding of sexual difference in

---

[1]See, for example, two recent studies of sexual difference in the Henry plays, both published after I had written this paper: Alan Sinfield's discussions of "Masculinity and Miscegenation" in *Henry V* in *Faultlines: Cultural Materialism and the Politics of Dissident Reading* (Berkeley: University of California Press, 1992), 127–42, and Jonathan Goldberg, "Desiring Hal," in *Sodometries: Renaissance Texts, Modern Sexualities* (Stanford: Stanford University Press, 1992), 145–75. Sinfield anticipates my argument at a number of points, emphasizing the ways in which early modern conceptions of male "effeminacy" differed from our own and were "not specifically linked to same-sex physical passion." (134) Goldberg, by contrast, insists upon the linkage, denouncing criticism that fails to discover it as "heterosexist."

[2]This tendency is exacerbated by the fact that current discussions of gender and sexuality are most often framed in psychoanalytic discourse, which itself tends to dehistoricize. As Constance Jordan observes in a provocative unpublished paper entitled "The Best Way to Do Feminist Literary History," "Psychoanalysis, it would appear, functions by reference to a-historical paradigms.... There is always the *stade du miroir*, there is always the *nom du père*. What they mean is universal."

Shakespeare's time and those that obtain today. I have two interests at stake in this project. The first is scholarly: it seems to me that current discussions of the representations of gender and sexuality in Shakespeare's plays are often distorted because they are shaped by anachronistic conceptions of gender and sexual difference. The second is political: to historicize and thus to demystify the assumptions that underlie current discussions of those issues—the beliefs that personal identity depends upon sexual difference and that sexual difference is immutably grounded in the body.[3]

[3]For a similar argument, see David M. Halperin, "Historicizing the Sexual Body: Sexual Preferences and Erotic Identities in the Pseudo-Lucianic *Erôtes*," in *Discourses of Sexuality: From Aristotle to Aids*, ed. Domna C. Stanton (Ann Arbor: University of Michigan Press, 1992), 231–62. Halperin's proposes "to denaturalize the sexual body by historicizing it" in order "to contest the body's use as a site for the production of heterosexual meanings and for their transformation into timeless and universal realities." (241) He shows that in the *Erôtes* homoeroticism is associated with hypermasculinity, while the effeminate man has an "erotic preference for women." (250)

The *locus classicus* for this notion is the passage in Plato's *Symposium* where Aristophanes tells a comic fable to explain the origins of sexual desire and sexual difference. Before the fall, he explains, the world was populated by spherical creatures, each of which had two sets of genital organs: some were male-male, some were female-female, still others had the organs of both sexes. Dividing these happily spherical creatures into two halves, Zeus created a fallen humanity, driven by desire for reunion with their severed halves. The originally female spheres thus became women who desired other women, the originally male became men who desired other men, and the originally androgynous became lovers driven by heterosexual desire:

> Men who are a section of that double nature which was once called Androgynous [he continues] are lovers of women; adulterers are generally of this breed, and also adulterous women who lust after men: the women who are a section of the woman do not care for men, but have female attachments; the female companions are of this sort. But they who are a section of the male, follow the male, and while they are young, being slices of the original man, they hang about men and embrace them, and they are themselves the best of boys and youths, because they have the most manly nature. Some indeed assert that they are shameless but this is not true; for they do not act thus from any want of shame, but because they are valiant and manly, and have a manly countenance, and they embrace that which is like them. And these when they grow up become our statesmen, and these only, which is a great proof of the truth of what I am saying.

See Irwin Edman, ed., *The Works of Plato*, trans. Benjamin Jowett (New York: Modern Library, 1956), 355–56. I am not proposing that Shakespeare derived his conceptions of gender and sexual desire from Aristophanes' fable, but it is worth remembering that the *Symposium* was an influential text in the Renaissance. See, for instance, James M. Saslow, "The Tenderest Lover: Saint Sebastian in Renaissance Painting," *Gai Saber* 1 (1977):61, for its influence on Ficino's analysis of homoerotic love.

Governed by those assumptions, current scholarship on Renaissance gender ideology tends to focus on the body. Failing to discover a stable theory of sexual difference in Renaissance representations of the body, many scholars conclude that Renaissance gender ideology was incoherent and sexual difference indeterminate.[4] What I propose is that although Renaissance gender ideology, like our own, was conflicted and contradictory, it was not incoherent. Instead, it was constructed on different principles and within different discourses. I believe the reason we cannot locate gender difference in Renaissance accounts of the body is that the body itself—male as well as female—was gendered feminine; and the reason we cannot find it in medical texts is that the distinctions that separated men from women, like those that separated aristocrats from commoners, were grounded not in the relatively marginal discourse of the new biological science but in the older and traditionally privileged discourses of theology and history.

I

I begin by citing some Shakespearean passages that challenge modern conceptions of gender and sexuality and assumptions about the ways gender difference is grounded in the embodied experience of sexual desire. One crucial difference is that a man's desire for a woman, now coded as a mark of masculinity, is repeatedly associated in Shakespeare's plays with effeminacy. Romeo claims that his passion for Juliet has incapacitated him for the manly activity of fighting—"O sweet Juliet," he complains, "Thy beauty hath made me effeminate, / And in my temper soft'ned valor's steel!" (III.i.113–115)[5] In *Antony and Cleopatra*, Caesar charges that Antony's passion for Cleopatra has compromised his sexual identity: Antony, he says, "is not more manlike / Than Cleopatra; nor the queen of Ptolomy / More womanly than he." (I.iv.5–8) Cleopatra herself describes a gaudy Egyptian revel which culminated, she recalls, when "I drunk him to his bed; / Then put my tires and mantles on him, whilst / I wore his sword." (II.v.21–23) The same assumption that passionate love for a woman would

[4]The fullest treatment of the subject is Thomas Laqueur's *Making Sex: Body and Gender from the Greeks to Freud* (Cambridge: Harvard University Press, 1990), which concludes that Renaissance sexual theory was based on a one-sex model. For a thoughtful essay influenced by Laqueur's work, see Stephen Greenblatt, "Fiction and Friction," in *Shakespearean Negotiations: The Circulation of Social Energy in Renaissance England* (Berkeley: University of California Press, 1988), 66–93. For a richly documented argument that early modern culture lacked a single normative system by which gender difference could be categorized, see Ann Rosalind Jones and Peter Stallybrass, "Fetishizing Gender: Constructing the Hermaphrodite in Renaissance Europe," in *Body Guards: The Cultural Politics of Gender Ambiguity*, ed. Julia Epstein and Kristina Straub (New York: Routledge, 1991), 80–111.

[5]My quotations from Shakespeare come from *The Riverside Shakespeare*, ed. G. Blakemore Evans et al. (Boston: Houghton Mifflin, 1974).

render a man effeminate, counterintuitive to modern consciousness, appears in Sidney's *Arcadia*, where Pyrocles dresses as an Amazon in order to be near the woman he desires, a transformation that Sidney emphasizes by using feminine pronouns to refer to the disguised lover. As Pyrocles' friend Musidorus explains, "this effeminate love of a woman doth so womanize a man."[6]

By contrast, extreme virility, manifested in Spartan self-denial and military valor, is not only depicted as consistent with erotic desire for other men; it also seems to be expressed in it. In Shakespeare as in Plutarch, Coriolanus is the supreme exemplar of the manly valor the Romans called *virtus*; but when Coriolanus greets his general on the battlefield, he exclaims,

> O, let me clip ye
> In arms as sound as when I woo'd, in heart
> As merry as when our nuptial day was done
> And tapers burnt to bedward!

His general responds with the loverlike epithet, "Flower of warriors." (I.vi.29–32) An even more explicit expression of homoerotic desire between manly warriors occurs when Coriolanus joins forces with his old enemy, Aufidius. Embracing Coriolanus, Aufidius declares,

> Know thou first,
> I lov'd the maid I married; never man
> Sigh'd truer breath; but that I see thee here,
> Thou noble thing, more dances my rapt heart
> Than when I first my wedded mistress saw
> Bestride my threshold.

> Thou hast beat me out
> Twelve several times, and I have nightly since
> Dreamt of encounters 'twixt thyself and me;
> We have been down together in my sleep,
> Unbuckling helms, fisting each other's throat,
> And wak'd half dead with nothing.   (IV.v.106–126)

---

[6]Cf. the description in North's Plutarch of Theseus's excessive lust as "womannisheness," cited by Louis Adrian Montrose in "'Shaping Fantasies': Figurations of Gender and Power in Elizabethan Culture," in *Representing the English Renaissance*, ed. Stephen Greenblatt (Berkeley: University of California Press, 1988), 38. For similar examples taken from a wide variety of texts, see Susan C. Shapiro, "'Yon Plumed Dandebrat': Male 'Effeminacy' in English Satire and Criticism," *RES* n.s. 39 (1988):1–13. See also Winfried Schleiner, "Male Cross-Dressing and Transvestism in Renaissance Romances," *Sixteenth Century Journal* 4 (1988):605–619; and Mark Rose, "Sidney's Womanish Man," *Renaissance Essays and Studies* n.s. 15 (1964):353–63.

Neither Coriolanus nor Aufidius is effeminated by this passion; neither is incapacitated for war, and neither is incapacitated for heterosexual love. Both speeches begin, in fact, by acknowledging the speaker's passion for his wife. The homoerotic passion exceeds the heteroerotic one, but it does not displace it.[7]

Desire for another man, then, fails to compromise these characters' masculinity; instead, it reaffirms it. Desire for a woman, by contrast, incurs the risk of feminization. For women, the situation was more complicated, since to become manlike was often construed, especially in theological discourse, as an elevation, a transcendence of both flesh and femininity,[8] while a man effeminated by passion for a woman suffered a double degradation, the enslavement of his higher reason by his base, bodily appetites, and the subjection of the superior sex to the inferior one. The asymmetry is probably most apparent in the case of cross-dressing, which, then as now, constituted a dressing up for women but a dressing down for men. Shakespeare's only cross-dressed hero is the Falstaff of *Merry Wives*, for whom the disguise of a woman is quite literally a travesty, and also a guise in which he is beaten. A medium for Falstaff's degradation, cross-dressing is, by contrast, a source of empowerment for a number of Shakespearean comic heroines. What remains constant, however, is that in both cases the cross-dressing is associated with heteroerotic desire.

This association is probably most explicit in Shakespeare's *Merchant of Venice* when Portia tells Nerissa her plan for the two of them to disguise themselves as lawyer and clerk. Nerissa asks, "What, shall we turn to men?" Portia's response—"Fie, what a question's that / If thou wert near a lewd interpreter!"(III.iv.78–80)—articulates the connection between turning *to* men and turning *into* them.[9] Portia takes on her masculine dis-

---

[7]Note too that Coriolanus is represented as a father as well as a husband. As Randolph Trumbach points out, "men could be found into the early 18th century who married women and had as well a career of seducing the local boys, without any risk to their status as dominant males." See his "Gender and the Homosexual Role in Modern Western Culture: The 18th and 19th Centuries Compared," in *Homosexuality, Which Homosexuality?*, ed. Dennis Altman et al. (London: GMP Publishers, 1989), 152.

[8]See Margaret R. Miles, "'Becoming Male': Women Martyrs and Ascetics," in *Carnal Knowing: Female Nakedness and Religious Meaning in the Christian West* (Boston: Beacon Press, 1989), esp. 53–62; and Leah S. Marcus, "Shakespeare's Comic Heroines, Elizabeth I, and the Political Uses of Androgyny," in *Women in the Middle Ages and the Renaissance: Literary and Historical Perspectives*, ed. Mary Beth Rose (Syracuse: Syracuse University Press, 1986), 135–54.

[9]For a suggestive gloss on this exchange, see *A Treatise on Lovesickness* (1640), trans. and ed. Donald A. Beecher and Massimo Ciavolella (Syracuse: Syracuse University Press, 1990), 230, where Jacques Ferrand speculates that "it is quite plausible that the genitals of a girl, overheated by the fury of love, would be pushed outside the body, because those parts are the same as the male parts reversed."

guise *after* her marriage, and she does so in order to save her husband's friend. Like the other Shakespearean comic heroines who dress as men, she does so not to repudiate heteroerotic desire but to fulfill it. Rosalind uses her disguise as Ganymede to court Orlando; Viola, disguised as Cesario, serves the man she loves; and so does Imogen, the model of wifely fidelity, who disguises herself as the boy Fidele to follow and serve the husband who unjustly rejected her. Portia's disguise can be seen as an expression of assertiveness, Imogen's as a model of submission, but both are motivated by their love for men.

The connection between cross-dressing and heteroerotic desire is remarkably consistent: it applies to women as well as to men and to bad women as well as to good ones. Joan in *1 Henry VI* is the first of Shakespeare's cross-dressed heroines, and probably the most masculine. She wears armor, she engages in onstage swordfights with male characters, and she leads the French army to victory. At the beginning of the play, she defeats the Dauphin in single combat, but the French courtiers punctuate the encounter with lewd comments, and even the words with which Joan accepts the Dauphin's challenge, "while I live, I'll ne'er fly from a man"(I.ii.103), invite sexual interpretation—an interpretation confirmed at the end of the play when she claims to be pregnant with a bastard child, having engaged in illicit sex with the Dauphin and a number of his courtiers as well.

The same associations between heteroerotic passion and loss of gender identity appear in *2 Henry VI*, where the only erotic moment is the anguished leave-taking between Margaret and her adulterous lover Suffolk, a scene charged with erotic power. "If I depart from thee," Suffolk declares, "I cannot live":

> And in thy sight to die, what were it else
> But like a pleasant slumber in thy lap?
> Here could I breathe my soul into the air,
> As mild and gentle as the cradle-babe
> Dying with mother's dug between its lips.

> (III.ii.388–93)

Suffolk's passion for Margaret deprives him of his manhood, reducing him to the condition of a gentle, genderless infant; and Margaret, like Joan, is not only dangerously sexual but also dangerously masculine, depicted, in fact, as the epitome of all those masculine qualities "unbeseeming" her "sex." Like Joan, Margaret usurps the masculine prerogative of warfare; like Joan she appears shockingly, on stage, in masculine battledress. In *3 Henry VI* the Duke of York elaborates the many ways in which Margaret is no true woman. "Women are soft, mild, pitiful, and flexible," he complains, "Thou stern, obdurate, flinty, rough, remorseless." Denouncing

Margaret as an "Amazonian trull," he links the masculinity of the female warrior with the sexual promiscuity of the harlot (I.iv.111–42).[10]

Shakespeare was not the only playwright to associate masculine behavior in women with heteroerotic promiscuity. In Jonson's *Epicoene*, there is a group of mannish women who live apart from their husbands and call themselves "collegiates." Before any of them appears on stage, we learn that they "cry down or up what they like or dislike ... with most masculine or rather hermaphroditical authority."(I.i.74–76) Nonetheless, their masculinity is expressed, not in passion for each other, but in aggressive courtship of the play's male hero.

In life as on the stage, masculine women were regarded as whores.[11] In *The Description of England*, published in 1587, William Harrison complained about the female habit of wearing masculine clothing: "I have met some of these trulls in London so disguised that it hath passed my skill to discern whether they were men or women." The misogynist pamphlet *Hic Mulier or The Man-Woman*, published in 1620, described the woman in masculine dress as wearing a "loose, lascivious ... French doublet, being all unbuttoned to entice ... and extreme short waisted to give a most easy way to every luxurious action."[12] All of these authors were male, but, as Gwynne Kennedy has pointed out, when one of the few female writers of the period, Lady Mary Wroth, wished to condemn female characters in her *Urania* for overaggressive courtship of men, she made the same associations, comparing the lustful women to boys playing women's parts on stage.[13] Driven by lustful desire for men, these women lose their femininity.

[10]The same linkage appears in Shakespeare's representation of Tamora in *Titus Andronicus* and also in Renaissance descriptions of Amazons. See Ania Loomba, *Gender, Race, Renaissance Drama* (New York: St. Martin's Press, 1989), 47; and Simon Shepherd, *Amazons and Warrior Women: Varieties of Feminism in Seventeenth-Century Drama* (Brighton: Harvester, 1981).

[11]For numerous examples of this association during the period, see Susan C. Shapiro, "Amazons, Hermaphrodites, and Plain Monsters: The 'Masculine' Woman in English Satire and Social Criticism from 1580–1640," *Atlantis* 13 (1987):65–76. Carroll Smith-Rosenberg informs me that European medical discourse continued this argument through the nineteenth century, lesbianism being believed to be particularly commonplace among prostitutes, and that Lombroso, in particular, saw them as twinned atavistic phenomena.

[12]William Harrison, *The Description of England*, ed. Georges Edelen (Ithaca: Cornell University Press, 1968), 147; *Hic Mulier; or, The Man-Woman*, in *Half Humankind: Contexts and Texts of the Controversy about Women in England, 1540–1640*, ed. Katherine Usher Henderson and Barbara F. McManus (Urbana: University of Illinois Press, 1985), 267.

[13]In a valuable unpublished paper entitled "Boy Actors and Unfeminine Women," Kennedy quotes three comparisons between female characters and boy actors taken from Wroth's *The Countesse of Mountgomeries Urania*. In two of the examples, the female character is lecherously courting a man; in the third, she is behaving madly. I am grateful to Kennedy for giving me permission to cite this work.

The point of all these examples is to suggest that historical differences make it difficult for us to understand the representations of gender and sexuality in Shakespeare's plays and that we should not be too quick to assume we understand their implications. Consider, for instance, the evasions of scholarly editors confronted by the variously directed erotic passion of the speaker in Shakespeare's sonnets, the difficulties encountered when twentieth-century productions of Shakespearean plays have attempted to use all-male casts, or the perplexities and debates of recent critics as they try to decide whether the erotic desire evoked by Shakespeare's cross-dressed heroines should be characterized as "homosexual" or "heterosexual" or both.[14]

The examples I have cited and the critical perplexities they provoke suggest important points of difference between current assumptions about gender and sexuality and those implicit in Shakespeare's texts. The problem with all these examples is not that they are inexplicable: numerous, and conflicting, explanations have been advanced. The problem is that the associations they imply are counterintuitive to modern consciousness. They demand and resist explanation because they imply an ideology of sex and gender that is radically different from our own. In the case of the boy heroines, for instance, although most educated people know that transvestism is by no means inconsistent with what we call "heterosexual" desire and activity, our knowledge of that fact is insufficient to resist the pressure of a gender ideology that constructs cross-dressing as a mark of what we call "homosexuality." Grounded on sexual desire, our assumptions about gender are based on models of sexual *orientation*. Contemporary gender ideology constructs a kind of metaphysics of desire that assumes, first, that it is the norm to desire *either* men or women (not both) and, second, that the gender of the object of sexual desire determines the desiring person's psychic and gender identity. According to our culture's prevailing norms, a person—either male or female—who desires women is defined as "masculine," and a person—either female or male—who desires men is defined as "feminine." A person who desires both men and women, we call "bisexual." In the latter

[14]On the sonnets, see David Buchbinder, "Some Engendered Meaning: Reading Shakespeare's Sonnets," *Works and Days* 14 (1989):7–28; and Gregory W. Bredbeck, *Sodomy and Interpretation: From Marlowe to Milton* (Ithaca: Cornell University Press, 1991), 167–85. On the boy heroines, see Lisa Jardine, *Still Harping on Daughters: Women and Drama in the Age of Shakespeare* (Totowa, N. J.: Barnes and Noble, 1983), 9–36; Stephen Orgel, "Nobody's Perfect: Or Why Did the English Stage Take Boys for Women?," *South Atlantic Quarterly* 88 (1989):7–30; and Phyllis Rackin, "Androgyny, Mimesis, and the Marriage of the Boy Heroine on the English Renaissance Stage," *PMLA* 102 (1987):29–41.

case, the desiring subject is conceived as divided (*bisexual*) in order to maintain the ideologically motivated gender categories as inviolate.[15]

At this point, you are probably saying, "Not me, that is not what *I* think." And I am saying that too. The kind of large, schematic oppositions I am suggesting ignore the variety, the complexity, and the contradictions of current discourse on gender, not to mention that of a remote—and finally inaccessible—past.[16] Discourse is polyphonic, expressing the myriad distinctions of class, geography, and gender that determine the cultural locations and interests of various speakers. Moreover, the dominant features of a culture coexist with residual "elements of the past" as well as "emergent" elements that are in process of "being created."[17] Even in Shakespeare's texts, anticipations of the biologically grounded ideology of compulsory heterosexuality that authorizes the nuclear family can be found in plays that focus on the life of the proto-bourgeoisie. In *The Taming of the Shrew*, for instance, Kate's final speech rationalizes the submission of wives to husbands not only on the traditional analogy between husband and king ("Such duty as the subject owes the prince, / Even such a woman oweth to her husband"), but also on the physical differences between male and female bodies ("Why are our bodies soft, and weak, and smooth, / … But that our soft conditions and our hearts / Should well agree with our external parts?"). Renaissance texts contain anticipations of modern constructions of gender and sexuality as well as vestiges of medieval ones, and vestiges of earlier formulations persist in our own discourse. Nonetheless, I think it is important to mark the places where Renaissance gender ideology differed from our

[15]For a brilliant analysis of these issues, which anticipates mine at a number of points, see Valerie Traub, "Desire and the Difference It Makes," in *The Matter of Difference: Materialist Feminist Criticism of Shakespeare*, ed. Valerie Wayne (Ithaca: Cornell University Press, 1991), 81–114.

[16]Because heat was regarded as superior to cold, men were regarded as naturally "hotter" than women, but women were also regarded as more lustful than men. Men were considered more spiritual, but the ladies celebrated in Renaissance sonnets were often depicted as inspirations to spiritual transcendence. Silence was considered naturally proper to women, but women were typically condemned for the tendency of their sex to loquaciousness. Renaissance gender ideology, like our own, was fraught with conflict and contradiction.

[17]Raymond Williams, *Marxism and Literature* (New York: Oxford University Press, 1977), 121–127. I am also indebted here to Carroll Smith-Rosenberg's adaptation of Bakhtinian theory. See her *Disorderly Conduct: Visions of Gender in Victorian America* (New York: Alfred A. Knopf, 1985). On the contradictions between divergent views of homoeroticism during this period, see Bredbeck, *Sodomy and Interpretation*, especially 149–60, where he discusses the hostile reception of Richard Barnfield's celebration of homoerotic love in *The Affectionate Shepheard* (1594) and Barnfield's disclaimer in his next book, *Cynthia*, of any personal stake in the poetic speaker's passion.

own because the differences are what tend to be occluded in much of what we write about the constructions of gender and sexuality in Shakespeare's time.

One place where those differences are clearly visible is in the way we dress our children. In early modern England, sumptuary laws contained elaborate regulations of male attire to ensure that men's clothing would express their exact place in the social hierarchy, but from 1510 to 1574 women's clothing was exempted from regulation.[18] Moreover, throughout the period, male and female children were dressed in the same attire—in skirts—until they reached the age of seven.[19] The physical difference that separated boys from girls was insignificant: what mattered was the difference in social rank that separated one man from another. In our own culture, by contrast, clothing is gendered from birth, but it is rarely a reliable indicator of status and rank. The President of the United States appears on television dressed in blue jeans, and teenagers from working-class families wear full formal regalia to their high-school proms. Our children, however, are wrapped in pink or blue blankets even in hospital nurseries, insisting on the innate, biological difference between male and female while eliding the distinctions of status and privilege that the egalitarian ideology of modern American democracy denies.

Less clearly visible—at least in current scholarly discourse—is the fact that in the Renaissance sexual passion had not yet achieved the privileged position it now holds, especially for men.[20] Excessive passion in either sex was condemned, but it was especially dangerous to men because it made them effeminate. Women were believed to be more lustful than men (in contrast to the still-prevalent Victorian assumption

[18]Wilfred Hooper, "The Tudor Sumptuary Laws," *English Historical Review* 30 (1915): 433–49. Hooper points out that despite previous regulation of women's dress, "the act of 1510 excluded all women, without distinction" (433) and that this exclusion persisted in every subsequent enactment until 1574. (444) Cf. Ruth Kelso, *Doctrine for the Lady of the Renaissance* (Urbana: University of Illinois Press, 1956), 33–36, on the relative lack of attention paid by Renaissance writers to social distinctions among women and the contingency of women's status on that of their husbands.

[19]For a provocative discussion of the implications of this practice, see Orgel, "Nobody's Perfect," 14–16. Equally revealing is the use of "it" rather than a gendered pronoun to refer to children. Barbara Traister informs me that medical casebooks in the period referred to children of both sexes as "it" until they reached the age of puberty.

[20]Thomas Greene makes this point in "Anti-hermeneutics: The Case of Shakespeare's Sonnet 129," in *Poetic Traditions of the English Renaissance*, ed. Maynard Mack and George deForest Lord (New Haven: Yale University Press, 1982), 148. The sonnet describes "lust in action" as "th' expense of spirit in a waste of shame"; but as Greene points out, "the sexual act is ... impoverishing only if one holds the medieval and Renaissance belief that it shortens a man's life ... in place of the restorative, therapeutic release our post-Freudian society

that it is men who have those strong-animal-drives-which-cannot-be-denied). Female images of angels on contemporary American Christmas cards express popular notions that asexual purity is feminine. In sharp contrast, the sculptured images of the deadly sins that adorned medieval cathedrals depicted lust as a woman.[21] Valuing sexual passion, the popular wisdom of contemporary culture associates it with the more valued gender, assuming that men feel it more often and more strongly. Despising lust as a mark of weakness and degradation, Renaissance thought gendered it feminine, attributed more of it to women, and regarded excessive lust in men as a mark of effeminacy. Reduced to its simplest terms, it is the difference between seeing heterosexual sex as the place where manhood is proved and affirmed in a conquest of the female and seeing it as the place where it is contaminated and lost in congress with her. The danger was that husband and wife would become, quite literally, one flesh, a fantasy that was expressed in fables and images of passionate lovers transformed into monstrous hermaphrodites.[22]

In modern terms, that danger might be understood as a loss of identity, the fictions of individual identity being highly prized and identity being incomprehensible to us without gender. According to Rosi Braidotti, in fact, "the privilege granted to the discourse of sexuality and reproduction as the site of production of truth about the subject is the trademark of modernity."[23] It is not at all certain that either of those assumptions obtained at the time Shakespeare wrote. It seems more likely to me that such a union was seen as dangerous not simply or even primar-

---

perceives." Cf. Michel Foucault's argument in *The Use of Pleasure*, vol. 2 of *The History of Sexuality*, trans. Robert Hurley (New York: Vintage Books, 1990), 82–86, that for the Greeks the "dividing line between a virile man and an effeminate man did not coincide with our opposition between hetero- and homosexuality" but instead distinguished a man who yielded to his appetites from one who exercised control over them. Rebecca W. Bushnell demonstrates the persistence of this idea in Renaissance representations of tyrants in *Tragedies of Tyrants: Political Thought and Theater in the English Renaissance* (Ithaca: Cornell University Press, 1990).

[21]Bonnie S. Anderson and Judith P. Zinsser, *A History of Their Own: Women in Europe from Prehistory to the Present*, I (New York: Harper and Row, 1989), 255. See also 435, where they describe the continuing belief in the Renaissance that women were insatiably lustful.

[22] This fear is vividly figured in the words of the seventeenth-century French preacher Paul Beurrier, who warned, "Our bodies resemble glasses that break when they touch one another." See Jean Delumeau, *Sin and Fear: The Emergence of a Western Guilt Culture, 13th-18th Centuries*, trans. Eric Nicholson (New York: St. Martin's, 1990), 445. For a variety of examples from medieval and Renaissance texts that construct the Ovidian figure of the hermaphrodite as a symbol of heterosexual lust, see Carla Freccero, "The Other and the Same: The Image of the Hermaphrodite in Rabelais," in *Rewriting the Renaissance: The Discourses of Sexual Difference in Early Modern Europe*, ed. Margaret W. Ferguson, Maureen Quilligan, and Nancy J. Vickers (Chicago: University of Chicago Press, 1986), 149–51.

[23]"Organs without Bodies," *Differences* 1 (Winter, 1989):147.

ily because it was a union but because it was a union of *flesh*. Spiritual union, even the union of male and female, was highly prized. The image of the hermaphrodite as a medical monstrosity or social misfit had its positive counterpart in the idealized image of the androgyne, represented in Neoplatonic, alchemical, and biblical tradition as a symbol of prelapsarian or mystical perfection.[24] If sensual lovers risked degeneracy into the beast with two backs, spiritual lovers could transcend the limitations of fallen physical life in the perfection of androgynous union. One has only to think of the lovers in Donne's "Valediction: Forbidding Mourning" or Shakespeare's "Phoenix and Turtle": "Single nature's double name / Neither two nor one was called."

Modern valorization of the body has produced a nostalgic conception of the Renaissance as a period when, as Francis Barker has argued, "the body [had] a central and irreducible place ['fully and unashamedly involved'] in the social order."[25] But fear and loathing of the body was a still living legacy in the Renaissance, rationalized in medieval Christian contempt for the flesh, grounded and verified in a present material reality of stinking bodies, desperately vulnerable to disfiguring disease and early death.[26] In medieval thought, the body itself, male as well as female, tended to fall on the wrong side of the binary opposition that divided masculine from feminine gender. A woman, said St. Jerome, is "different from man as body is from soul."[27] These associations did not disappear with the Reformation.[28] To Martin Luther, "we are the woman because of the flesh, that is, we are carnal, and we are the man because of

---

[24] The term "hermaphrodite" was also used in a positive sense. See, e.g., the comparison of heterosexual lovers locked in passionate embrace to the figure of the hermaphrodite in Spenser's *Faerie Queene* III.xii.45. See also Rackin, "Androgyny," and "Shakespeare's Boy Cleopatra, the Decorum of Nature, and the Golden World of Poetry," *PMLA* 87 (1972):201–212. For a variety of positive images of the hermaphrodite and androgyne, see Edgar Wind, *Pagan Mysteries in the Renaissance* (London: Faber and Faber, 1960), 211–14. For extensive studies of the ambivalence of the figure of the hermaphrodite, see Nancy Hayles, "The Ambivalent Ideal: The Concept of Androgyny in English Renaissance Literature," Ph.D. Diss. University of Rochester, 1976, and Jones and Stallybrass, "Fetishizing Gender."

[25] *The Tremulous Private Body: Essays on Subjection* (London: Methuen, 1984), 23.

[26] See Delumeau, *Sin and Fear*, esp. chap. 16, "The Ascetic Model." For a well-known Shakespearean example, see Sonnet 146 ("Poor soul, the centre of my sinful earth"), which draws on the same tradition of ascetic dualism as the newly crowned Henry V's admonition to Falstaff, "Make less thy body (hence) and more thy grace, / ... know the grave doth gape / For thee thrice wider than for other men." (2 *Henry IV*, V.v.52–54)

[27] Quoted in Anderson and Zinsser, 83.

[28] See Rosalie Osmond, *Mutual Accusation: Seventeenth-Century Body and Soul Dialogues in Their Literary and Theological Context* (Toronto: University of Toronto Press, 1990); and Marilyn R. Farwell, "Eve, the Separation Scene, and the Renaissance Idea of Androgyny," *Milton Studies* XVI (1982):3–20.

the spirit ... we are at the same time both dead and set free." This same distinction between masculine spirit and feminine flesh can be seen as late as the middle of the seventeenth century when Gerrard Winstanley condemned sinners who had "been led by the powers of the curse in flesh, which is the *Feminine* part; not by the power of the righteous Spirit which is Christ, the *Masculine* power."[29]

The gendered opposition between masculine spirit and female flesh, although rationalized in Christian theology, was not confined to theological discourse. It played an important part, in fact, even in medicine, the discourse of the body. Medical accounts of procreation, despite the influence of Galenic theory, frequently echoed the Aristotelean explanation that the male parent contributed form and soul to the fetus, while the mother provided only its physical matter. According to Aristotle,

> the female always provides the material, the male that which fashions it, for this is the power we say they each possess, and *this is what it is for them to be male and female....*While the body is from the female, it is the soul that is from the male.[30]

The same distinction between male form, equated with soul, and female matter is repeated in *The Problemes of Aristotle*, a popular Elizabethan medical guide:

> the seede of the man doth dispose and prepare the seed of the woman to receive the forme, perfection, or soule, the which being done, it is converted into humiditie, and is fumed and breathed out by the pores of the matrix, which is manifest, bicause onely the flowers [i.e. the menses] of the woman are the materiall cause of the young one.[31]

This congruence between medical and theological discourse suggests a conception of gender difference just as coherent as our own, although

---

[29]*The New Law of Righteousness*, in *The Works of Gerrard Winstanley*, ed. George H. Sabine (Ithaca: Cornell University Press, 1941), 157, quoted in Allison P. Coudert, "The Myth of the Improved Status of Protestant Women: The Case of the Witchcraze," in *The Politics of Gender in Early Modern Europe*, ed. Jean R. Brink, Allison P. Coudert, and Maryanne C. Horowitz, *Sixteenth Century Essays & Studies*, XII (1989), 81.

[30]*Generation of Animals* 2.4.738b20–23, quoted in Laqueur, *Making Sex*, 30. [Italics mine]

[31]*The Problemes of Aristotle, with other Philosophers and Phisitions* (London: Arnold Hatfield, 1597), sigs E3–E4, quoted by Louis Adrian Montrose in "Shaping Fantasies," 43. As Montrose explains, this text conflates Galenic and Aristotelean theories of procreation. For opposed views of the relative importance of Galenic and Aristotelean influence on early modern medical theory, see Laqueur, *Making Sex*, which emphasizes the Galenic influence, and "Destiny is Anatomy," a review of Laqueur's book by Katharine Park and Robert A. Nye in *The New Republic* (February 18, 1991):53–57.

significantly different from it. Modern gender ideology, like modern racism, constructs its binary oppositions on the basis of physical difference.[32] Grounded in a mystified body, it finds a prehistorical basis for masculine privilege in male physical strength, an ahistorical explanation for psychic difference in one small idealized part of the male body. Mystified as phallic power, its presence or absence becomes the defining characteristic of an always already gendered subjectivity.[33] In the Renaissance, by contrast, masculine superiority tended to be mystified in the spirit, feminine oppression justified by the subordinate status of the body.[34] As is well known, the body served as a map, not of gender difference, but of social and political hierarchy. The system of analogies that rationalized the social hierarchy included the subordination of women to men, but its essential axis of difference was social and political status rather than embodied sex.[35] The relation of the head to the lower parts formed the basis for the ideological representation of the state as the body politic—the king as its head, the lower orders as its subordinate members. The same analogy also rationalized the subordination of women: like common people of both sexes, women were regarded as appetitive creatures, easily enslaved by bodily lusts and irrational passions. Incapable of rational self-government, they were associated with the lower parts of the body. Male authority resided in the higher regions. The king was the head of the state; the husband was the head of the household. Their domi-

[32]Here again, anticipations of contemporary attitudes can be found in Renaissance texts. In *The Merchant of Venice*, for instance, although Venetian anti-Semitism is rationalized in terms of religion, Jessica's "Jewishness" does not disappear with her conversion, and Morocco's dark complexion is foregrounded as the mark of racial difference and inferiority. "Mislike me not for my complexion" is the burden of his opening speech (II.ii.1–12). "Let all of his complexion choose me so" (II.vii.78–79) is Portia's delighted response to his failure to choose the casket that would entitle him to claim her in marriage.

[33]On the difficulty of separating "phallus" from "penis," see Jane Gallop, *The Daughter's Seduction: Feminism and Psychoanalysis* (Ithaca: Cornell University Press, 1982), 95–100.

[34]The body, in fact, was a site of radical instability. Classical myths of metamorphosis, popular in the Renaissance, make a similar point—the transformation of physical form by the pursuit, avoidance, or fulfillment of sexual desire. The transformation of ravished maidens reflects the sociological facts of a culture that defined women by their sexual status—as maidens, whores, wives, or widows; but the fact that male figures, including Jove himself, are often transformed in these stories implies that sexuality itself was held to compromise bodily identity.

[35]Queen Elizabeth, for instance, habitually referred to herself as a "prince," even in statements in which she designated Mary, the deposed Queen of Scots, as a "princess." See Leah S. Marcus, *Puzzling Shakespeare: Local Reading and its Discontents* (Berkeley: University of California Press, 1988), 56. Compare Alan Bray's argument in "Homosexuality and the Signs of Male Friendship in Elizabethan England," *History Workshop* 29 (1990):3, that sodomy (designated by Edward Coke as a *crimen laesae majestatis*) was defined in political terms.

nance, however, was justified by fictions of superior rationality embodied in the head rather than by fictions of phallic power embodied in the penis.

Looking for Renaissance conceptions of gender difference, scholars turn to Renaissance anatomy books, only to discover that biological science itself was still subordinate to the authority of classical texts. Renaissance anatomists, unlike the ancients, performed dissections and illustrated their texts with pictures of what they saw. But, as Thomas Laqueur has brilliantly demonstrated, what they saw was framed and limited by their study of ancient models. In Renaissance drawings, he shows, the anatomical parts were often literally framed by classical models: the internal organs of the human body displayed within cavities excavated in the torsos of classical statues.[36] Conceptually framed by Galen's models of genital structures, the observable differences between male and female anatomy were reduced to terms of simple inversion. Empirical observation had resulted in the medical rediscovery of the clitoris, but the vagina was still conceived as an inverted penis. Male and female sexual organs were perfectly homologous, the women's simply remaining inside the body because they were less "perfect" than those of men; in many cases, in fact, women could turn into men. In the best-known of these cases, widely quoted in recent scholarship, a fifteen-year-old girl, chasing her swine in a field, and leaping a ditch in hot pursuit, suddenly felt her genitalia extruded outward, impelled by the heat of the chase. Henceforth, she was recognized as a man. The reason, as reported by the famous sixteenth-century surgeon, Ambroise Paré, was that

> Women have as much hidden within the body as men have exposed outside; leaving aside, only, that women don't have so much heat, nor the ability to push out what by the coldness of their temperament is held bound to the interior. Wherefore if with time, the humidity of childhood which prevented the warmth from doing its full duty being exhaled for the most part, the warmth is rendered more robust, vehement, and active, then it is not an unbelievable thing if the latter, chiefly aided by some violent movement, should be able to push out what was hidden within.[37]

---

[36]Laquer, *Making Sex*, 78, 79, 83.

[37]Quoted in Thomas Laqueur, "Orgasm, Generation and the Politics of Reproductive Biology," *Representations* 14 (Spring, 1986):13. For other cases in which masculine behavior produced the physical marks of male sex in people who had formerly been known as women, see Greenblatt, "Fiction and Friction," 66, 73–86, 175–78; and Laqueur, *Making Sex*, 126–28.

In Paré's account, masculine behavior transforms the body to produce the physical signs of male sex, thus inverting the modern assumption that embodied sex is the solid ground that regulates gendered behavior. This does not mean, however, that gender differences were irrelevant or that early modern Europe was a feminist Utopia where real women could assume masculine identity and privilege by the simple expedient of running quickly and leaping across ditches—only that Renaissance gender ideology worked on principles radically different from our own.

II

The first wave of twentieth-century feminist Shakespeare criticism focused on the comedies, especially the ones with cross-dressed heroines, to theorize a theater in which female spectators could find liberating images of powerful, attractive women who violated gender restrictions and were rewarded for those violations with admiration, love, and marriage—a Utopian moment when gender identity was as changeable as the theatrical costumes that transformed boy actors into female characters. The romantic comedies were doubly satisfying to modern feminists, for at the same time that they empowered their female characters, they also celebrated the love between men and women that culminates in marriage. Shakespeare's transvestite comedies satisfied the desires of feminist readers for personal liberation without disturbing the dominant gender ideology of our own time; for they also celebrated the heterosexual passion that provides the basis for the ideal nuclear family, held together by the love between husband and wife, the avenue for personal self-fulfillment and the foundation for the good order of society.

Shakespeare's history plays, however, tell a very different, much less optimistic story. In a recent survey of feminist Shakespeare criticism, Ann Thompson remarks that feminist critics have tended to neglect the English history plays.[38] Given the roles of women in those plays, this omission is not surprising. Female characters and heteroerotic passion, both central to the comedies, are marginalized or vilified in the histories. The hierarchy of dramatic genres was also a hierarchy of social status: the subjects of history were kings and the great noblemen who opposed them; women and commoners occupied only marginal places in historical narratives.

To move from comedy and history is to move up the generic hierarchy, into the exclusions of the dominant discourse, which was also the

---

[38]"'The Warrant of Womanhood': Shakespeare and Feminist Criticism," in *The Shakespeare Myth*, ed. Graham Holderness (Manchester University Press, 1988), 85.

discourse of patriarchal dominance. If theology was the master discourse of the middle ages and biology and psychology those of our own, the discourse that authorized the social hierarchy in Shakespeare's time was that of history. Tudor historians produced fables of ancient descent to authenticate a new dynasty's claim to the English throne. Tudor subjects provided a thriving business for the heralds who constructed the genealogies by which they attempted to secure their places in an unstable social hierarchy. The patrilineal genealogy that organized the structure of Tudor history and Tudor society alike required the repression of women and of heteroerotic passion as well because the invisible, putative connection between fathers and sons that formed the basis of patriarchal authority was—as Shakespeare's cuckold jokes endlessly insist—always dubious, always vulnerable to subversion by an adulterous wife. In the case of a king, however, cuckoldry was no laughing matter: not only a source of personal anxiety, it was also a threat to royal succession and therefore the worst possible crime against the state.[39]

In the few cases where heteroerotic passion appears in the histories, it is represented as a dangerous, destructive force, even when it leads to marriage. The comedies look forward to the emergent bourgeois ideal of the loving nuclear family, but the histories look backward to an older conception of marriage as a political and economic union between feudal families—a model that did in fact last longer at the higher levels of the social hierarchy and one that persists to this day among royalty. Shakespeare's Henry VI and Edward IV both reject prudent dynastic marriages in order to marry on the basis of personal passion; both marriages are represented as disastrous mistakes that weaken the men's authority as kings and destabilize the political order of their realms. The desirable marriage between Richmond and Elizabeth, by contrast, the foundation of the Tudor dynasty, is totally uncontaminated by any hint of romantic love— or even by any appearance on stage of the bride-to-be.

Even in their own time, the history plays were understood as a specifically masculine, hegemonic genre. Both the gendered opposition between history and comedy and the ideological uses of the history play can be seen in sixteenth-century debates about the theater. Thomas Nashe, for instance, based his defense of theatrical performance on the masculinity of the English Chronicle play. The "subject" of plays, he claimed, is "(for the most part) borrowed out of our English Chronicles, wherein our forefathers valiant acts ... are revived ... than which, what

---

[39]For a fuller development of this point, see chap. 4, "Patriarchal History and Female Subversion," in my book, *Stages of History: Shakespeare's English Chronicles* (Ithaca: Cornell University Press, 1990).

can be a sharper reproofe to these degenerate, effeminate dayes of ours." Conflating Englishness with masculinity and both with a lost, heroic past, Nashe opposed the masculine domain of English history to the degenerate, effeminate world of present English experience in order to defend theatrical performance as an inspiration to civic virtue and heroic patriotism. He also invoked the masculine purity of English acting companies. "*Our* Players," he boasted, "are not as the players beyond Sea, a sort of squirting baudie Comedians, that have whores and common Curtizens to playe womens partes."[40]

It is important to remember, however, that Nashe's argument that the plays would inspire their audiences to patriotism and manly valor represents only one side of a hotly contested debate. Nashe appropriated the authority of English history on behalf of theatrical performance, but in the eyes of its opponents, the theater was associated with the same destabilizing and effeminating forces of social change that the English chronicles were designed to oppose. Antitheatrical invective focused obsessively on the sexually corrupting allurements of bawdy comedies, the immorality of boys in female costume, and the contaminating presence of women in the theater audiences. As Stephen Orgel reminds us, "the English stage was a male preserve, but the theater was not. The theater was a place of unusual freedom for women in the period; foreign visitors comment on the fact that English women go to the theater unescorted and unmasked, and a large proportion of the audience consisted of women."[41]

The opposition between the authoritative masculine discourse of history and the disreputable feminized world of the playhouse is clearly marked in Shakespeare's history plays. Aliens in the masculine domain of English historiography, the women in those plays are often quite literally alien. Beginning with *1 Henry VI*, where all the female characters are French, the women are typically inhabitants of foreign worlds, and foreign worlds are typically characterized as feminine. Moreover, both the women and their worlds are repeatedly characterized as comic and theat-

---

[40]*Pierce Penilesse his Supplication to the Diuell* (1592) in E. K. Chambers, *The Elizabethan Stage* (Oxford: Clarendon Press, 1951), 4:238–39.

[41]"Nobody's Perfect," 8. See also Ann Jennalie Cook, "'Bargaines of Incontinencie': Bawdy Behavior in the Playhouses," *Shakespeare Studies* 10 (1977):271–90. On the role of gender in antitheatrical anxieties see Jean Howard, "Crossdressing, the Theatre, and Gender Struggle in Early Modern England," *Shakespeare Quarterly* 39 (1988):439–40, and Laura Levine, "Men in Women's Clothing: Anti-theatricality and Effeminization from 1579 to 1642," *Criticism* 28 (Spring, 1986):131–37. On the presence of women in the commercial playhouses, see Andrew Gurr, *Playgoing in Shakespeare's London* (New York: Cambridge University Press, 1988), 59–64 and appendices I and II; and Richard Levin, "Women in the Renaissance Theatre Audience," *Shakespeare Quarterly* 40 (1989):165–74.

rical. The marginal status of women in Shakespeare's historical sources is reproduced in his history plays by a process of geographical and generic containment, which also marks the boundaries between the idealized masculine England of historical narrative and the feminized scene of present theatrical performance. In *Henry IV*, for instance, women are completely excluded from the English historical action, but they play dominant roles in two places—the unhistorical, lowlife world of Eastcheap and the foreign world of Wales. Both Eastcheap and Wales are separated from the central scenes of English historical representation, and both are associated with the illicit powers of female sexuality and theatrical performance. This geographical marking also replicates the situation in the theaters of Shakespeare's time; for although English women never appeared on stage, French and Italian companies, which included women, did occasionally perform in England.[42]

The Boar's Head Tavern in Eastcheap is a plebeian, comic, theatrical, anachronistically modern world that mirrors the disorderly push and shove of the playhouse itself (the Boar's Head, in fact, was the name of at least six real taverns in Shakespeare's London, one of them used for a theater).[43] Shakespeare represents his Boar's Head as a kind of theater as well. Frequented, like the playhouse, by a disorderly, socially heterogeneous crowd, it is also the scene of play-acting. Falstaff pretends to be Hal, Hal pretends to be Falstaff, and both degrade the dignity of royalty by playing the part of the reigning king. The pleasures of the Boar's Head are illicit, and they are also dangerous. The disreputable crowd the tavern attracts is given to every sort of transgression, from drunkenness and brawling to thieving and prostitution. Here, as in the antitheatrical tracts, the dangers of the playing house are most prominently represented by women and sexuality. Like the prostitutes who looked for customers in the theater audiences, Doll Tearsheet infects her customers with venereal disease; and at the end of *2 Henry IV*, when Doll and the Hostess are arrested, we learn that "there hath been a man or two lately killed about her." (V.iv.5–7) Whether "her" means Doll or the Hostess and whether "about" means "concerning" or "near," clearly the women are a source of danger. A. R. Humphreys, the editor of the Arden edition, glosses this line

---

[42]See Orgel, 9 and 28 n. 2. I am also indebted here to an unpublished paper by Frances K. Barasch, "The Lady's Not for Spurning: An Investigation of Italian Actresses and Their Roles in Commedia dell'Arte as Shakespeare's Inspiration." Barasch makes the intriguing suggestion that Shakespeare's witty, independent female characters may have been inspired in part by the performances of Italian actresses, who, because they worked from scenarios rather than from scripts, were in some measure the authors of their own theatrical selves.

[43]See Samuel Burdett Hemingway, ed., *A New Variorum Edition of Henry the Fourth Part I* (Philadelphia: Lippincott, 1936), 124–25, and Chambers, 2:443–45.

with a quotation from Dekker's *Honest Whore*: "O how many thus ... have let out / Their soules in Brothell houses ... and dyed / Iust at their Harlots foot." (III.iii.77–80)

It is significant that the proprietor of the Boar's Head is a Hostess, not a Host, and that she speaks in malapropisms, disrupting the King's English just as the fictional scenes in her tavern disrupt—as they interrupt, retard, and parody—the historical action. The Hostess's economic power, as Jean Howard has observed, recalls the economic power of the women who were paying customers in the playhouse. Her linguistic deformities bespeak her exclusion from the dominant official discourse. Just as the fictional scenes in Eastcheap have no basis in history and no place in the historical action, neither do the women they contain.

It is also significant that although the tavern is clearly marked as a feminized, theatrical space, the character who dominates that space is not the Hostess, or any other woman, but Falstaff. Physically a man and a womanizer, Falstaff is plainly gendered masculine in terms of the binary logic of modern thought. The analogical patterns of Shakespeare's discourse, by contrast, place Falstaff in a feminine structural position. His incompetence on the battlefield, his contempt for honor and military valor, his inconstancy, his lies, his gross corpulence, and his womanizing all imply effeminacy within the system of analogies that separated aristocrat from plebeian, man from woman, and spirit from body. Contemplating what he thinks is Falstaff's corpse at the end of the battle of Shrewsbury, Hal asks, "What, old acquaintance! could not all this flesh keep in a little life?" (V.iv.102–3) Falstaff himself, in a usage that would have been clearly intelligible to Shakespeare's audience, refers to his fat belly as a "womb" (*2 Henry IV*, IV.iii.22: "My womb, my womb, my womb undoes me"); and he compares himself to a "sow that hath overwhelm'd all her litter but one." (I.ii.12) Moreover, *1 Henry IV* ends with the spectacle of Falstaff mutilating Hotspur's corpse. (V.iv.128) Wounding the dead hero's thigh, he reenacts the female threat to manhood and military honor symbolized in the opening scene by the report of the Welsh women's mutilation of the corpses of English soldiers. (I.i.43–46)[44]

The parallel between the two veiled references to castration suggests an analogical relationship between the world of Eastcheap and that of Wales, both associated with the loss of masculine honor. Analogy, however, is not identity. Although both settings are clearly marked as comic and theatrical and thus as opposed to history, the low comic scenes in the Boar's Head Tavern recall the disorderly scene of present theatrical per-

---

[44]On Falstaff's female characteristics, see Valerie Traub, "Prince Hal's Falstaff: Positioning Psychoanalysis and the Female Reproductive Body," *Shakespeare Quarterly* 40 (1989): 456–74.

formance, while the scene in Wales, with its emphasis on magic and romantic love and its exotic setting, recalls the Shakespearean genre of romantic comedy. The women in the tavern are too familiar to enter history, too much like the disorderly women in the theater audience. The woman in Wales, by contrast, is marked as an exotic creature from another world, like the French and Italian actresses who occasionally appeared on the English stage, or the heroine of a narrative romance or romantic comedy.

Or, perhaps, like Queen Elizabeth herself. In this connection, the epilogue to 2 *Henry IV* is revealing. Despite the absence of women in the preceding scene, the representation of the great historical moment when the wild Prince Hal of popular legend takes his historical place as Henry V, the epilogue contains two references to female presence. One recalls the world of Eastcheap as it acknowledges the presence of women—and of sexual transactions between men and women—in the theater audience: "All the Gentlewomen here have forgiven me," he says, and "if the gentlemen will not, then the gentlemen do not agree with the gentlewomen, which was never seen in such an assembly." The other acknowledges the presence of a woman on the English throne, kneeling "to pray for the Queen."

The matter of Wales, like the presence of a woman on the English throne, haunts the borders of the historical world that Shakespeare constructed in his Lancastrian histories. Both evoked powerful, and related, anxieties for the genealogically obsessed patriarchal culture ruled by Queen Elizabeth—a female monarch who traced her patriarchal right to a Welsh grandfather who had turned to the dim mists of Welsh antiquity to buttress his tenuous genealogical authority, incorporating the red dragon of Cadwallader in the royal arms and giving his eldest son the name of Arthur. Located at England's geographical border, Wales represents a constant military threat, but it also represents the unspeakable realities of female power and authority that threatened the idealized England of masculine longing constructed by Shakespeare's historical myths.[45]

At the beginning of 1 *Henry IV*, the Earl of Westmerland comes to the English court with bad news from a Welsh battlefield: Mortimer's army

[Handwritten margin note: Wales is feminine]

[45]The double association of Wales with savagery and with female power has a precedent as ancient as Geoffrey of Monmouth's *Historia Regum Britanniae*, which records that the name Welsh derives "either from their leader Gualo, or from their Queen Galaes, or else from their being so barbarous." (xii. 19) See *The History of the Kings of Britain*, trans. Lewis Thorpe (Harmondsworth, Middlesex: Penguin Books, 1966), 284. The country of the Others, a world of witchcraft and magic, of mysterious music, and also of unspeakable atrocity that horrifies the English imagination, Wales is defined in terms very much like those that define the woman. For an extended discussion of this point, see Rackin, *Stages of History*, chap. 4. A similar construction of Wales appears in *Cymbeline*, a play based on Holinshed and taking the name of its heroine from Innogen, the wife of the legendary Trojan founder of the British

has been defeated in battle, Mortimer captured by Owen Glendower, a thousand of his soldiers killed. Westmerland also reports that after the battle, the Welshwomen committed some "beastly shameless transformation" upon the bodies of the dead English soldiers—an act, he says, "as may not be without much shame retold or spoken of." (I.i.44–46) Refusing to describe the act, Shakespeare follows Holinshed, who anxiously reported, "The shamefull villanie used by the Welshwomen towards the dead carcasses, was such, as honest eares would be ashamed to heare, and continent toongs to speake thereof." In Shakespeare's historical source as in his play, Wales is identified as the scene of emasculation and female power—and also as the site of a repression in the English historical narrative.[46]

---

royal line. A land of miracles and music and also of mortal danger, the Wales in *Cymbeline* is also the place where the true heirs to the British throne (disguised with the historically resonant names of Polydore and Cadwal) are sequestered. For the mythic-historical associations of the Welsh material in *Cymbeline*, see Frances Yates, *Majesty and Magic in Shakespeare's Last Plays* (Boulder, Colorado: Shambhala, 1975), 39–62, and Emrys Jones, "Stuart Cymbeline," *Essays in Criticism* 11 (1961), 84–99.

[46]Holinshed, *Chronicles of England, Scotland and Ireland* (1587; rpt. London: J. Johnson et al., 1808), 20. The threefold association of female power, foreignness, and atrocity appears to be a persistent feature of early modern European discourse. Ralegh's *Discoverie of Guiana* (1596), 28, quoted by Montrose, 46, reports that Amazons "are said to be very cruel and bloodthirsty." Even more suggestive is a late-sixteenth-century travel narrative quoted by Stephen Greenblatt in *Renaissance Self-Fashioning: From More to Shakespeare* (Chicago: University of Chicago Press, 1980), 181, which reports that "near the mountains of the moon there is a queen, an empress of all these Amazons, a witch and a cannibal who daily feeds on the flesh of boys. She ever remains unmarried, but she has intercourse with a great number of men by whom she begets offspring. The kingdom, however, remains hereditary to the daughters, not to the sons." What is especially interesting for my argument is that this account, like Fleming's interpolation of the female atrocities in Wales, comes to its readers doubly mediated. It is recorded in the diary of Richard Madox, an English traveler in Sierra Leone, but Madox claims that he heard the story from a Portuguese trader. Still another account of female savagery, most closely resembling Fleming's, appeared in *The Columbian Magazine and Monthly Miscellany* I (Philadelphia, 1787), 549. This account is also represented as doubly mediated (told to the writer by an unnamed "gentleman" met "near Alexandria, in Virginia, in 1782"). In this report, a surveyor named Colonel Crawford, captured by Indians, "was delivered over to *the women*, and being fastened to a stake, in the centre of a circle, formed by the savages and their allies, the female furies, after the preamble of a war song, began by tearing out the nails of his toes and fingers, then proceeded, at considerable intervals, to cut off his nose and ears; after which they stuck his lacerated body full of pitch pines, large pieces of which they inserted (horrid to relate!) into his private parts; to all of which they set fire, and which continued burning, amidst the inconceivable tortures of the unhappy man, for a considerable time. After thus glutting their revenge, by arts of barbarity, the success of which was repeatedly applauded by the surrounding demons, they cut off his genitals, and rushing in upon him, finished his misery with their tomahawks, and hacked his body limb from limb." I am indebted to Carroll Smith-Rosenberg for the material from *The Columbian Magazine*.

The shame that narrative represses is clearly intelligible to modern readers—the threat of castration, the founding event in Freudian myths of gender differentiation, but a symbol that proliferates in Shakespeare's play in ways that cannot be contained within the binary logic of modern gender ideology.[47] Veiled references to castration reappear not only in Falstaff's desecration of Hotspur's corpse but also in Kate's playful threat to break Hotspur's "little finger" (II.iii.87)[48] and, for playgoers well-acquainted with Holinshed, in the description of Douglas's capture after the battle of Shrewsbury. Shakespeare follows Holinshed in reporting that the Douglas was captured in flight after the battle because "falling from a hill, he was so bruis'd / That the pursuers took him" (V.v.21–22); but Holinshed specifies the nature of the bruise: "falling from the crag of an hie mounteine, [he] brake one of his cullions, and was taken."[49] In neither case, however, does the wound appear to be a cause for shame; in fact, both Shakespeare and Holinshed immediately add that the Douglas was, because of his great valor, at once set free. Because of his "valiantnesse" (Holinshed), "valors" and "high deeds" (Shakespeare), the Douglas is honored as a noble man, a status unaffected by the genital wound.

Moreover, although Westmerland's veiled reference to female savages who intrude on the masculine space of the battlefield to deprive the English soldiers of their manhood and honor characterizes the Welshwomen in terms that signal "masculine woman" to us, that characterization appears to be completely reversed in Act III, when Shakespeare moves beyond the boundary of English historical narration to stage a scene in Wales. Mortimer is happily married to Glendower's daughter, and the castrating savages of Westmerland's report are nowhere to be seen. The only Welshwoman we see is perfectly feminine—Glendower's weeping daughter, who is so devoted to her husband that she cannot bear the thought of his impending departure. The lady cannot speak English, but her father translates. She also expresses her love in tears, in kisses,

---

[47]As Stephen Greenblatt points out, images in Renaissance texts that seem "to invite, even to demand, a psychoanalytic approach" often turn out "to baffle or elude that approach." The "mingled invitation and denial," Greenblatt proposes, can be understood historically by considering that "psychoanalysis is at once the fulfillment and effacement of specifically Renaissance insights: psychoanalysis is, in more than one sense, the end of the Renaissance." See "Psychoanalysis and Renaissance Culture" in *Learning to Curse: Essays in Early Modern Culture* (New York: Routledge, 1990), 131.

[48]Cf. Coppélia Kahn, "Whores and Wives in Jacobean Drama," in *In Another Country: Feminist Perspectives on Renaissance Drama*, ed. Dorothea Kehler and Susan Baker [Metuchen, N.J.: Scarecrow Press, 1991], 255. Kahn gives a suggestive analysis of the incident in *The Changeling* when De Flores gives Beatrice-Joanna Alonzo's severed finger to prove his murder as "insinuat[ing] that the sexually active woman is a castrating woman."

[49]*Chronicles*, III:26.

and in singing "the song that pleases" Mortimer. Music, as Shakespeare's Orsino tells us, was considered the "food of love." Philip Stubbes, well known for his warnings against the dangerous consequences of theatre-going, also warned that music could corrupt "good minds, [making] them womanish and inclined to all kinds of whoredom and mischief." In fact the spectacle of a woman singing was widely regarded in Shakespeare's time as an incitement to lust.[50]

Suffused with luxurious sensuality, the scene in Glendower's castle replaces the horrified report of Welsh barbarism with the glamour of Glendower's poetry and his daughter's singing, the castrating savages of the battlefield with the seductive allure of the lady in the castle. What makes this replacement baffling to modern consciousness is that Glendower's daughter is *associated* with the castrating women of the battle-field. Unwilling to part with her amorous companion, she resolves that "she'll be a soldier too, she'll to the wars." Moreover, Mortimer's passion for his wife does indeed seem to emasculate him. Although Shakespeare emphasizes Mortimer's lineal claim to the English throne, Mortimer himself prefers what he calls the "feeling disputation" of kisses with his wife to military battle in pursuit of that claim. "As slow as hot Lord Percy is on fire to go" to join the battle that will decide the future of the English kingdom, Mortimer has lost his manhood to female enchantment.[51] Hotspur's male "heat," by contrast, makes him eager to leave his wife for battle.[52]

Shakespeare's Welsh interlude replaces the unspeakable horror of castration with the theatrical performance of seduction. A similar displacement seems to characterize Shakespeare's relation at this point to his

---

[50]Linda Austern, "'Sing Againe Syren': Female Musicians and Sexual Enchantment in Elizabethan Life and Literature," *Renaissance Quarterly* 42 (1989):397–419. Stubbes, *Anatomie of Abuses* (1583, sig. D4, qtd. Austern, 424). See also 2 *Henry IV*, II.iv.11–12, where it is the prostitute, Doll Tearsheet, who "would fain hear some music." Poetry was also considered effeminating, as Mary Ellen Lamb demonstrates in a fine unpublished paper, "Apologizing for Pleasure in Sidney's *Apology for Poetry.*"

[51]Matthew Wikander, *The Play of Truth and State: Historical Drama from Shakespeare to Brecht* (Baltimore: The Johns Hopkins University Press, 1986), 14–25.

[52]Both Goldberg and Sinfield recognize Hotspur's misogyny as an expression of anxiety, but while Goldberg argues that the object of that anxiety is in the "taint" that "lies in playing the woman's part with another man" (168), Sinfield associates it with the early modern assumption, grounded in Renaissance biological theory as well as gendered codes of behavior, that men could be rendered "effeminate" by "[t]oo much devotion to women." (131) Cf. Hotspur's earlier declaration of independence from Kate: "when I am a' horseback I will swear I love thee infinitely," II.iii.102. The sexual symbolism is clearly intelligible in modern terms, but here, as in the case of Falstaff's "uncolting" in II.ii.1–39, the older commonplace analogy between rational control of the passions and a rider's control of his horse is at least as relevant.

historical source. The love scene has no historical precedent, but its structural position in Act III of the play is similar to that of a passage inserted by Abraham Fleming in the 1587 edition of Holinshed's *Chronicles* (the edition Shakespeare used). Fleming interrupts the account of a later battle to insert a detailed account of the act Holinshed had refused to describe:

> The dead bodies of the Englishmen being above a thousand lieng upon the ground imbrued in their owne bloud ... did the women of Wales cut off their privities, and put one part thereof into the mouthes of everie dead man, in such sort that the cullions hoong downe to their chins; and not so contented, they did cut off their noses and thrust them into their tailes as they laie on the ground mangled and defaced.[53]

(handwritten marginal note: wow!)

Fleming seems delighted with the grisly story, introducing it with numerous references to gory atrocities committed by women against men in classical times, but he also feels constrained to defend his decision to write the problematic material into the English historical record. He notes the precise location in Thomas Walsingham's Latin chronicle where he found it, and he explains,

> though it make the reader to read it, and the hearer to heare it, ashamed yet bicause it was a thing doone in open sight, and left testified in historie; I see little reason whie it should not be imparted in our mother toong to the knowledge of our owne countrimen, as well as unto strangers in a language unknowne.[54]

Fleming's belated account of the atrocities performed by the Welshwomen seems to lie behind Shakespeare's deferred Welsh scene, but Shakespeare transvalues the terms of Fleming's gruesome description. Fleming's account of bloody corpses lying on the ground, their organs of bottom and top horribly transposed, becomes the lady's seductive invitation to Mortimer to lie down upon the "wanton rushes," his head luxuriously resting in her lap, while she sings "to charm his blood with pleasing heaviness," a delicious languor like the state "twixt wake and sleep." The strange tongue from which Fleming translated his gruesome story becomes the sweet babble of the lady's Welsh, a sound that Mortimer calls "ravishing," and compares to a song "sung by a fair queen in a summer's bow'r" and that Shakespeare represents by repeated stage directions, "*The lady speaks in Welsh.*"

[53]*Chronicles*, III:20, 34
[54]Ibid.

Like the historical record of the Welshwomen's barbarism, and like the French that Katherine speaks in *Henry V*, Glendower's daughter speaks in a language that requires translation. Departing from theatrical convention to write the women's lines in foreign tongues, Shakespeare excludes them from the linguistic community that includes all of the male characters—French and Welsh as well as English—along with his English-speaking audience.[55] The difference, however, is that while Katherine learns English in order to communicate with Henry, Mortimer proposes to learn Welsh. Bewitched and enthralled in Wales, he proposes to abandon the King's English, the discourse of patriarchal authority, in order to enter the alien discourse of a world that lies beyond the bounds of English historical narration.[56]

Shakespeare's representation of Mortimer in Wales interrupts the progress of the English historical plot to depict the dangerous allure of a world that is feminine and effeminating, and also theatrical. It enacts Renaissance beliefs that excessive sensuality would make a man effeminate, and it recalls the antitheatrical arguments that the theater encouraged idleness and lechery. It also reveals the difficulty of writing sexuality into history. Geographically and dramatically isolated, the Welsh scene of sexual seduction anticipates modern conceptions of love and war as alternative activities, linked in gendered antithesis: the romantic interludes that interrupt the military action in modern war movies; the poignant jux-

[55]With its insistent physicality and bawdry, the scene of Katherine's language lesson reiterates the foreign/female/illicit sexuality association that appears in the representation of Glendower's daughter. For a brilliant exposition of those associations in contemporary language texts, see Juliet Fleming, "*The French Garden*: An Introduction to Women's French," *ELH* (1989): 19–51. For suggestive glosses on the women's exclusion from language and their association with body, see D. J. Gordon's observation in *The Renaissance Imagination*, ed. Stephen Orgel (Berkeley: University of California Press, 1975), 80, that in masques the visual aspect was called the body and the words the soul, and Hélène Cixous's argument in "Castration or Decapitation," trans. Annette Kuhn, in *Signs: Journal of Women in Culture and Society*, 7 (1981):43, 49, that "the backlash, the return, on women of [masculine] castration anxiety is its displacement as decapitation" or the reduction to "complete silence." Women, Cixous argues, may "overflow with sound: but they don't actually *speak....* They always inhabit the place of silence, or at most make it echo with their singing.... They remain outside knowledge."

[56]Steven Mullaney, *The Place of the Stage: License, Play and Power in Renaissance England* (Chicago: The University of Chicago Press, 1988), 77, 162, points out that although Henry VIII had outlawed Welsh in 1535, the alien language ("nothing like, nor consonant to the natural Mother Tongue within this realm") consistently defied English efforts "to control or outlaw it." Resisting repeated "pressures of assimilation and suppression ... Welsh remained a strange tongue, a discomfiting reminder that Wales continued to be a foreign and hostile colony, ruled and to an extent subjected but never quite controlled by Tudor power."

taposition of idealized love and dirty war in novels like Hemingway's *Farewell to Arms*; and the famous rallying cry of the 1960s, "make love, not war."[57] But it is difficult to find modern counterparts for Shakespeare's conflation of heteroerotic desire with the loss of sexual identity. The closest modern analog I can think of is boys in a schoolyard, afraid to play with the girls because having a girlfriend will make a boy a sissy. But the analogy shouldn't be pushed too far. By the time those boys are eighteen, they'll boast about "scoring" to prove their manhood. It really *was* different. On Shakespeare's stage, the Welsh lady herself was a boy. Unwritten, the incomprehensible language that masks the lady's meaning changes with every performance. All we have is her father's translation.

[57]For an analysis of this coupling in a historically and culturally diverse series of examples, see Nancy Huston, "The Matrix of War: Mothers and Heroes" in *The Female Body in Western Culture: Contemporary Perspectives*, ed. Susan Rubin Suleiman (Cambridge: Harvard University Press, 1985), 119–136.

I am indebted to helpful suggestions and criticisms in response to earlier versions of this paper presented at the CUNY Graduate Center, the Riverside-Berkeley Shakespeare Conference, the Glasgow conference "European Renaissance: National Traditions," the Center for Twentieth-Century Studies at the University of Wisconsin-Milwaukee, the seminar on the Diversity of Language and the Structures of Power at the University of Pennsylvania, and the University of Wisconsin at Madison. I especially wish to thank David Lorenzo Boyd, Gregory W. Bredbeck, Margreta de Grazia, Heather Dubrow, Mary Hazard, Jean Howard, Ann Rosalind Jones, Constance Jordan, Gwynne Kennedy, Mary Ellen Lamb, Donald Rackin, Carroll Smith-Rosenberg, and Peter Stallybrass.

The Globe, Shakespeare's Theatre

FOUR

The Taming-School:
The Taming of the Shrew
as Lesson in Renaissance
Humanism

Margaret Downs-Gamble

> *Ay, mistress, and Petruchio is the master,*
> *That teacheth tricks eleven and twenty long,*
> *To Tame a shrew and charm her chattering tongue.*
> 4.2.56–58

> *knowledge of the oppressor*
> *this is the oppressor's language*
>
> *Yet I need it to talk to you*
> Adrienne Rich,
"The Burning of Paper Instead of Children"

A Pleasant Conceited Historie, called The Taming of a Shrew (1594), like the more familiar Shakespearean *The Taming of the Shrew* (1623), relates a battle between the sexes. In both plays, a father burdened with unmarried daughters will not allow the numerous suitors to woo the younger and milder daughter until the older and forward Katherine (Kate/Katherina) has been suitably wed. The suitors to the younger are relieved to find Ferando/Petruchio capable of taming the shrewish Kate, who eventually displays her submission in an argument for "natural" order which demands a woman's hand be placed beneath her husband's foot.

More striking than the plays' similarities, however, are their disparities, most apparent at those points when their plots correspond. Reading *The Shrew* alongside *A Shrew* reveals the extent to which the "taming" techniques in Shakespeare's play parallel the educational programs advocated by Renaissance humanists. Ferando's coercion of his willful wife Kate in *A Shrew* contrasts sharply with Petruchio's "education" of Kate in *The Shrew*. While both husbands tame their wives, Petruchio, *rhetor* and orator in *The Shrew*, "educates" Katherine, simultaneously refiguring unruly woman, humanist pupil, and uncontrolled language. The other suitors in *The Shrew* disguise themselves as masters of various liberal arts to gain proximity to Bianca but, proving their ineptitude as humanist scholars, determine their subsequent failure as lords, while Petruchio, orator-extraordinaire, teaches Kate, in a series of violent lessons, the value of a humanist education. Desiring control over her own words, Kate rails against Petruchio's education: "I will be free, / Even to the uttermost, as I please, in words." (IV.iii.77–80)[1] To be "free ... *in* words," quite distinct from free *as* words, was, in a very real sense, the promise of Renaissance humanism. But because a substantive philosophical transformation supposedly accompanies rhetorical mastery, Katherine is trapped within a gendered paradox. Kate can only be free "in words" if she is educated, but to be educated is to be tamed.

Cicero's focus on the transformation of the pupil into *vir eloquentissimus*, literally "most eloquent man" but normally translated as "orator," shaped the educational schemes of Rudolph Agricola and Desiderius Erasmus, who subsequently influenced the pedagogy and ideology of English educators such as Roger Ascham and Thomas Elyot. Eloquence, oratorical skill, was regarded as the single most important attribute for a civil servant: "Alas you will be ungentle gentlemen, if you be no scholars: you will do your prince but simple service, you will stand your country but in slender stead, you will bring yourselves but small preferment, if you be no scholars."[2]

Though Thomas Elyot, in *The Govenour* (1531), emphasizes the importance of educating the boy for his place in public life, Roger Ascham, in *The Schoolmaster* (1570), includes women among his pupils.[3] Since Ascham uses the noble figures of Lady Jane Grey and Elizabeth I as examples of female students, he may not have meant to include generic Woman. However, the classical model that descended through Erasmus to English educators implicitly connected eloquence and moral superi-

---

[1]References to scene, act, and line numbers from *The Shrew* are taken from *The Riverside Shakespeare*, ed. G. Blakemore Evans (Boston: Houghton Mifflin Company, 1974). Internal textual notations which refer to page numbers are taken from *A Pleasant Conceited Historie, called The Taming of a Shrew* (1594).

[2]G. Pettie, *The civile Conversation of S. Guazzo*, 1586, Av.

[3]See Thomas Elyot, *Defense of Good Women*, ed. Edwin Johnston Howard (Oxford, Ohio: Anchor Press, 1940), esp. the characterization of Zenobia, who is domesticated "by [her] studye in moral philosophy." (55) For interpretations of Elyot's *Defense*, see Linda Woodbridge, *Women and the English Renaissance, Literature and the Nature of Womankind, 1540–1620* (Urbana: University of Illinois Press, 1986), and Carole Levin and Jeanie Watson, eds., *Ambiguous Realities, Women in the Middle Ages and Renaissance* (Detroit: Wayne State University Press, 1987).

ority. As moral inferiors, women were targeted by numerous pedagogists for refiguration under humanism.

But the union of eloquence, specifically public eloquence, with Pauline Christianity complicated the position of female pupils at yet another ideological level. Though women were not entirely excluded from humanist education, at least the rationale of Erasmus in promoting study for women focuses on the power of education to control "the whole soul," to impress rules, and to dispatch idleness :

> The distaff and spindle are in truth the tools of all women and suitable for avoiding idleness.... Even people of wealth and birth train their daughters to weave tapestries or silken cloths.... It would be better if they taught them to study, for study busies the whole soul.... It is not only a weapon against idleness but also a means of impressing the best precepts upon a girl's mind and of leading her to virtue.[4]

Erasmus wants to turn women from textile to textual study, from the spinning of wool to the spinning of words—a metaphorical conflation to deflect "idleness." But the control of the female "soul", and the "impression" of "virtue" upon the traditionally uncontrollable female are themselves metaphors for the capacities of rhetorical training; the master orator controlled and impressed passionate language with "virtue." The conflation of Woman and language embedded in the masculine rhetorical tradition of Renaissance humanism imposed upon female scholars a nonnegotiable position as subject, object, and medium of study.

The literary model, *The Taming of the Shrew,* is a Renaissance artifact that promotes humanism as a device for taming the woman-language dyad; but as uncontrolled language and passionate woman, Kate exposes the paradox of *vir eloquentissimus.* As humanist pupil, Katherine's inability to re-gender herself, however she may refigure herself, determines her eventual submission to masculine authority, Petruchio, the orator-philosopher. No such rhetorical justification for female suppression exists in the earlier play, but its absence in *A Shrew* elucidates its presence in *The Shrew.*

In the opening scene, we listen as Lucentio explains to his servant Tranio the reason for their journey to Padua. He has come to the "nursery of arts." (I.i.2)

---

[4]As translated in Anthony Grafton and Lisa Jardine, *From Humanism to the Humanities, Education and the Liberal Arts in Fifteenth- and Sixteenth-Century Europe* (London: Gerald Duckworth & Co. Ltd., 1986), 32, n. 10.

Here let us breathe, and haply institute
A course of learning and ingenious studies

. . . .

And therefore, Tranio, for the time I study,
Virtue and that part of philosophy
Will I apply that treats of happiness
By virtue specially to be achiev'd.

(I.i.8–9, 17–20)

According to the humanist tradition, an arduous training in grammar was followed by instruction in formal rhetoric. As Lisa Jardine and Anthony Grafton have pointed out, "in theory this was a rounded education in philosophy as well as expression."[5] Lucentio has completed his grammatical instruction, and even the initial instruction in rhetoric, but he clearly seeks the training classically supplied by the *rhetor*.

Tranio's answer to Lucentio firmly unites the methodology of humanism with the appearance of his master, while urging him toward lighter entertainment:

Mi perdonato, gentle master mine;
I am, in all affected as yourself,
Glad that you thus continue your resolve
To suck the sweets of sweet *philosophy*.
Only, good master, while we do admire
This *virtue* and this *moral discipline*,
Lets be no *Stoics* nor no stocks, I pray,
Or so devote to *Aristotle's checks*
As *Ovid* be an outcast quite abjur'd.
Balk *logic* with acquaintance that you have,
And practice *rhetoric* in your common talk,
Music and *poesy* use to quicken you,
The *mathematics*, and the metaphysics,
Fall to them as you find your stomach serves you:
No profit grows where is no pleasure ta'en.
In brief, sir *study what you most affect*.

(I.i.25–40, emphasis added)

Though the Riverside editors gloss "study what you most affect" as meaning study that is "most pleasing" (114, n. 40), I would argue that what Lucentio most "affects" *is* his study, the outward manifestation of a humanist male. Lucentio is a living example of the success of his education, but that education is incomplete. This becomes increasingly important as the play progresses. Lucentio's education, because of its incompleteness, denies him moral wisdom and causes lapses in his judgment. Lucentio's, and surprisingly also Tranio's, goodly speech is only the external appearance of a lord, not as is the case with Petruchio, the state itself.

Lucentio's failure to instruct his own pupil, Bianca, is the final indication that Lucentio is still a student rather than a master of moral philosophy. Bianca's failure to attend to her husband when he calls her at the end of the play displays her own incorrect understanding of her place, but also emphasizes his inadequate preparation to instruct her in her duties. Both Gremio—"she's too rough for me" (I.i.55)—and Hortensio—"No mates for you / Unless you were of gentler, milder mould" (I.i.59–60)—acknowledge themselves inadequate to the task of instructing Katherine. But Lucentio, the product of humanism, should recognize that Kate is in fact the superior pupil. His failure to do so reflects, in part, his incomplete education, also amply displayed as he shifts so quickly from philosopher to lover at the sight of Bianca. Tranio questions the too rapid transition: "I pray, sir, tell me, is it possible / That love should of a sudden take such hold?" (I.i.146–47) In case the audience misses the reason for Lucentio's sudden change, Shakespeare notes it twice: "while *idly* I stood looking on / I found the effect of love in *idleness*." (I. i.150–51, emphasis mine) Ascham, Elyot, and as noted above, Erasmus, consider idleness a danger to the state. In idleness Lucentio is drawn from philosophy to carnal desire, from, it might appear, matters of state to the domestic sphere. Idleness also manifests itself in lapses in judgment. Lucentio makes the mistake, again warned of by both Ascham and Elyot in reference to the Italianate scholars who go abroad accompanied only by their servants, of asking his man Tranio for advice: "Counsel me, Tranio, for I know thou canst / Assist me, Tranio, for I know thou wilt." (I.i.157–58) In Italy, in the company of an inferior person, Lucentio is doomed to marry the shrew instead of the sheep, having mistaken sheep for shrew.[6]

The corresponding scene in *A Shrew* runs quite differently. While conversing with Polidor, Aurelius (Lucentio) sees three daughters walking with their father; the master/servant exchange is replaced by an exchange between "two yoong Gentlemen." (6) The individual object of desire (Bianca) is replaced by Aurelius' collective "delight in these faire dames," and only made specific by Polidor's information that the oldest daughter (Kate) is a shrew, and the youngest, Emelia (a third sister, corre-

[6]The *O.E.D.* notes that women were categorized in the sixteenth and seventeenth centuries by attributes that aligned them squarely as sheep or shrews.

sponding to the widow in *The Shrew*), has promised herself to Polidor. (7) By default, rather than by allure, Aurelius chooses to woo Philema (var. Phylema). The women are passively chosen rather than actively seductive in *A Shrew*; though the men are the source of activity in both plays, here the women are not responsible for male action, nor are they blamed for distracting men from the more important matters of their education and service to the state.

In *The Shrew*, Lucentio's and Tranio's "inventions meet and jump in one." (I.i.190) Lucentio "will be schoolmaster / And undertake the teaching of the maid." (I.i.192–93) For Lucentio to refigure himself as "schoolmaster," Tranio must play Lucentio, and he disguises himself as a lord. This is but one of an evolving series of pretenses in which outward appearance is transformed. The Renaissance conflict between "being and seeming" is central to the pedagogical writings of Ascham and Elyot, as it is to the practical expression of this conflict within *The Shrew*. Even education and eloquence, especially when turned away from their rightful duty to the state and used instead to gain the object of carnal desire, are not in themselves assurance that a scholar has achieved a position of moral superiority.[7]

While Lucentio operates in concert with his inferiors, Petruchio and Grumio are polarized characters. There is no mistaking master and servant in this instance. Both verbal and intellectual disparities highlight their first appearance on the stage. Petruchio's rhetorical abilities are clear even before Grumio praises his master for his "rope-tricks":

> She may perhaps call him half a score knaves or so. Why, that's nothing; and he begin once, he'll rail in his *rope-tricks*. I'll tell you what, sir, and she stand him but a little, he will throw a *figure* in her face, and *so disfigure her with it*, that she shall have no more eyes to see withal than a cat. You know him not, sir.
>
> (I.ii.110–16, emphasis added)

---

[7]Hired by Gremio as tutor to Bianca, Lucentio promises:

What e'er I read to her, I'll plead for you
As for my patron, stand you so assur'd,
As firmly as yourself were still in place,
Yea, and perhaps with more successful word
Than you— unless you were a scholar, sir.

(I.ii.154–58)

And Gremio responds, "O this learning, what a thing it is." (I.ii.159) The apparent superior is instead the fool, but so, eventually, is the would-be schoolmaster.

Petruchio's rhetorical skill, at least from the viewpoint of a servant, is something very like magic, with the power to "dis-figure" language. Though surely Petruchio's skill will confound and transform "Katherine the curst" from shrewish woman to sheepish wife, from witty, aggressive pupil to scholar, when he "disfigure[s]" the "face" of language with a rhetorical "figure," Katherine is the feminized language whose features will be disfigured.

Hortensio, who might be listening and learning about Petruchio's powers, is instead concerned with his own disguise as "a schoolmaster / Well seen in music, to instruct Bianca." (I.ii.133–134) Among an ever-escalating number of suitors disguised as instructors and servants disguised as lords, Petruchio stands alone as the only adept philosopher. When the schoolmasters are presented to Baptista for his daughters, Petruchio alone, and without need of disguise, successfully manipulates circumstances to his will. Accused of being "blunt" and "[dis]-orderly" (II.i.45), Petruchio nevertheless proceeds to gift Baptista with the disguised Hortensio, to praise his host's daughter, Katherine, and to identify his geographical and familial associations before anyone has the opportunity to intervene. In this scene, only one suitor has the skill to actually instruct. Once alone, Petruchio considers Katherine's potential responses to prepare himself for his pupil, understanding that the student will determine his approach to her instruction:

> Say that she rail, why then I'll tell her *plain*
> She sings sweetly as a *nightengale*;
> Say that she frown, I'll say she looks as clear
> As morning roses newly washed with dew;
> Say she be mute, and will not speak a word,
> Then I'll commend her volubility,
> And say she uttereth *piercing eloquence*
>
> (II.i.170–176)

As master *rhetor*, Petruchio considers the various approaches and figures which he might employ to persuade the pupil, silence the woman, and control female language. Petruchio's "plain" speech controls chaotic feminine language, and Katherine's railing, by transforming her words into the sweet song of Philomela.[8] He will ignore her own expression, reconstructing it as traditional female *topos*, "morning roses newly washed with

---

[8]Raped by her brother-in-law Tereus, who then cuts out her tongue, Philomela is changed into a nightingale. The nightingale, traditionally associated with lyric poetry, descends to us in a tradition that violates and silences women. The inarticulate "song" of the nightingale as masculine construct is an example of the appropriation of the female body and tongue for the translation of male art.

dew." But most pointedly here, he will translate female silence into "piercing eloquence"— his own. There is, significantly, no corresponding scene for this one in *A Shrew*, no overt plotting to manipulate pupil, woman, and words.

But Petruchio, the master, also teaches us as he teaches Kate the internal construction of what it is to be a lord, by teaching "eloquence" through an understanding that he must first commend her eloquence. Petruchio, or rather Shakespeare, has learned from pedagogists like Thomas Elyot— "I wode nat haue them inforced by violence to lerne ... [but] to be swetely allured therto with praises and suche praty gyftes as children delite in"[9]— and Roger Ascham— "there is no such whetstone to sharpen a good wit and encourage a will to learning as praise."[10] Both Ascham and Elyot use Quintilian's instructions to the potential tutor, Ascham paraphrasing Quintilian: "[Bad Schoolmasters], when they meet with a hard-witted scholar, they rather break him than bow him, rather mar him than mend him."[11] Kate, though refigured by her instruction, is not broken.

The subsequent, introductory battle between Katherine and Petruchio/Ferando differs considerably from one version to another. In *A Shrew* Ferando tells her in the space of the sixteen-line scene little more than "I know thou lou'st me well." Kate's questions, "Was euer seene so grosse an asse as this?" and "Why father what do you meane to do with me / To give me thus vnto this brainsick man," though humorous, do not rely on the pretended misunderstandings and punning found in *The Shrew*.

Though told that she was "rough," Petruchio finds Kate "pleasant, gamesome, passing courteous / But slow in speech," and then asks, "Why does the world report that Kate doth limp?" (II.i.243, 245–6, 252) In the middle of his false critique of her eloquence, this is no shift in subject, but a continuation of it: "O let me see thee walk. Thou dost not halt." (II.i.256) Slower in speech than he, perhaps, Kate's "gait" is yet declared "princely" (II.i.259):

> Did ever Dian so become a grove
> As Kate this chamber with her princely gait?
> O, be thou Dian, and let her be Kate,
> And then let Kate be chaste, and Dian sportful.

(II.i.258–61)

---

[9] Thomas Elyot, *The Boke Named The Govenour*, 2 vols., ed. Henry Herbert Stephen Croft (London: Kegan Paul, Trench, & Co., 1883), I:32.

[10] Ascham, 15.

[11] Ibid., 20.

Katherine's chastity is a matter of some concern to Petruchio. Her verbal skill implies wantonness. Petruchio's pun on Katherine's being both chaste and chased demands at once her closure to the world and her openness to him. The end of this first exchange includes an important moment of revelation for the student, both Kate and the audience:

> Kate: Where did you study all this goodly speech?
> Pet: It is extempore, from my mother-wit.
>
> (II.i.262–63)

Petruchio's mastery of "extempore," and the Renaissance assumption that extempore was possible if "mother-wit" had been adequately ingrained through *imitatio*, displays itself in the course of *The Shrew*.[12] But *imitatio* was not the goal, only a means toward achieving the goal of a humanist education.

As Petruchio teaches Katherine moral philosophy and eloquence, he denies her food, drink, and sleep, specifically identified by Elyot as potential excesses that hinder scholarship.[13]Though pretending to offer Katherine elegant apparel, Petruchio never intends that she shall "deck [her] body with ... ruffling treasure." (IV.iii.60) When he denies her the external trappings of new clothes, both her feminine and verbal ornaments, Petruchio's lesson is philosophical:

> Well, come, my Kate, we will unto your father's
> Even in these honest mean habiliaments;
> Our purses shall be proud, our garments poor,
> For 'tis the mind that makes the body rich;
> And as the sun breaks through the darkest clouds,
> So honor peereth in the meanest habit.
>
> (IV.iii.169–74)

This lesson in substance versus appearance, combined with his test of her skill at *imitatio*, forces Katherine to rely upon a masculine understanding of her place as woman and language, as well as upon Petruchio's tutelage.

The corresponding scene in *A Shrew* offers no similar instruction, being little more, as Kate seems to understand, than the means "to make a foole of [her]" (34):

> Come Kate we now will go see thy fathers house
> Euen in these honest meane abilliments,
> Our purses shall be rich our garments plaine,
> To shrowd our bodies from the winter rage,
> And thats inough, what should we care for more.
>
> (35)

---

[12]Ibid., 87; Elyot, 76.
[13]Elyot, 97.

Though at times startlingly similar, these corresponding moments in *The Shrew* and *A Shrew* serve very different purposes. Clothes that "shrowd … bodies from the winter rage" are a form of protection; but "honor peereth" as the sun appears through an opening in the clouds, when the protective covering of ornamentation is removed.

At a time when property could increasingly be used to inscribe an individual with a more glorious past, elevating the individual thereby, pedagogues like Thomas Elyot and Roger Ascham urged the fathers of the aristocracy to educate their children, most often sons but also their daughters, to an understanding of their positions in the state, most specifically in service to their prince. This understanding, it was believed, could only be gained through the stripping away of excess and the application of discipline. Petruchio combines the various lessons of moral philosophy, as do Elyot and Ascham, for his advancing scholar. Katherine increasingly understands her attachment to and dependence upon Petruchio, which simultaneously gives her a position in the masculine, humanist tradition. This masculinized *locus* allows Katherine to extend mere *imitatio* to include *declamatio*.

Kate certainly learns by direct imitation, changing not merely her words, but the sense of things, to conform to the wishes of Petruchio; however, Petruchio's control of his pupil / wife's words simultaneously elevates the power of feminine language to name masculine objects:

> Pet.... Good Lord, how bright and goodly shines the moon.
> Kath. The moon! the sun—it is not moonlight now.
> Pet. I *say* it is the moon that shines so bright.
> Kath. I know it is the sun that shines so bright.
> Pet. Now by my mother's son, and that's myself,
> It shall *be* moon, or star, or what I list,
> Or ere I journey to your father's house....
> Kath....And *be* it moon, or sun, or what you please;
> And if you please to call it rush-candle,
> Henceforth I *vow* it shall *be* so for me.
> Pet. I *say* it is the moon.
> Kath. I *know* it is the moon.
> Pet. Nay *then you lie*; it *is* the blessed sun.
> Kath. Then God be blest, it ...[14] the blessed sun,

[14]The *Riverside* editors supply "is" at this point in the text. I reject their emendation because it would appear that the omission of "is" in that particular line of the text is not accidental. At each point in this scene Katherine's carefully constructed counterargument transforms Petruchio's language without direct refutation—except in the case of the emended "is."

But sun it *is not*, when you *say* it is not;
And the moon changes even as your mind.
What you will have it *nam'd*, even that *it is*,
And so it shall be for Katherine.

(IV.v.2–22)

This interchange must not be mistaken for instruction in *pracecepta* only. While arguing his superior method of double translation from Latin model to English and back to Latin, Ascham explains, citing Caesar and Cicero that, for training the young scholar, *praecepta* are not condemned: "[W]e gladly teach rules, and teach them more plainly, sensibly and orderly than they be commonly taught in common schools."[15] While the lessons taught in Petruchio's school are hardly "orderly," Katherine excels Petruchio in eloquence as she follows his lead in distinguishing "moon, or sun, or what you please." As pupil, she does not stop with mastery of rules, or even imitation—impossible in Petruchio's shifting lesson—but transmutes the models of sun and moon to moon and Petruchio's lunatic mind. By aligning Petruchio's mind with the changeable moon, Kate stops the rhetorical double translation.

At this moment in *The Shrew*, the conflation of action and essence—Katherine's act of naming serving to determine the object named—most clearly presents Kate as simultaneously pupil and language. As pupil, she must follow Petruchio's lead. As language, Katherine has the capacity to determine the object that she names. But she must understand, not merely imitate, her instructor. Petruchio "says" that sun is moon; Kate in superior understanding "knows" it to be otherwise. Petruchio appears to believe that if Kate will imitate him in calling the sun "moon," it will "be" the object named. In frustration, Kate "vows" that it "be so." Trying her, Petruchio then "says" moon, but Kate "knows" moon. Her imperfect translation from declaration to knowledge causes Petruchio to correct her: "you lie; it is the blessed sun." Petruchio recognizes that Kate has misunderstood his lesson.

The verb usage in this scene equates name and essence. Petruchio does not demand belief that the sun is the moon; he desires Kate's verbal imitation. But Kate must understand what she is imitating, and when Kate makes the correction to "it," indicating "the blessed sun / But sun it *is not*, when you *say* it is not. / What you will have it *nam'd*, even that *it is*," seems not merely acquiescence on the part of the pupil. Kate does not repeat her mistake to declare again that "it [*is*] the blessed sun," except via the Riverside editors. What has long been considered an omission in the text is instead, I believe, a very carefully structured choice that displays Katherine's mastery of the lesson, declaring it only "not" the sun

[15]Ascham, 16–17.

when Petruchio *says* it is not. The name determines essence, and though the instructor may have triumphed over the pupil here, language seems to have won the day. Kate, as pupil/imitator, succumbs to Petruchio's instruction by accepting his verbal model. As language, Kate's naming supplies essential understanding in the masculine game. Kate's action, her naming, is the hermeneutic translation of the thing. Not so the corresponding scene in *A Shrew*.[16]

Whereas *imitatio* appears to extend into *declamatio* in *The Shrew*, Ferando in *A Shrew* does not seek "free composition," but only rote memorization from Kate. For Kate to become a humanist scholar, she must transform the models of her instructor, not merely imitate them. Though the rules are not always clear, either to Katherina or the reader-audience, as we are being instructed in *imitatio*, the lesson of *declamatio* is in fact learned.

Katherine's final speech in both versions is addressed to the wives who did not come when called by their husbands; but in *The Shrew*, it is also her first lesson to wayward *female* pupils, Bianca and the widow, and the display of her rhetorical skill. Katherine's instruction simultaneously displays her mastery of feminine language (as orator), her position as female in the Renaissance hierarchy (as wife/subject), and her subjugation of all feminized things to masculine mastery (as "masculine" humanist scholar). It is impossible not to recall Samuel Johnson's "Sir, a woman preaching is like a dog's walking on his hind legs. It is not done well; but you are surprised to find it done at all." The only model she transmutes is the model of *masculine* scholar.

Katherina's lesson is an eloquent rendition of the place of the humanist in Renaissance society. She does not rely on cues from her tutor, and her dependent status is not quantitatively different from the status of any Renaissance citizen, except that her authority is lower than her lord's. Katherina's caveat that female obedience depends upon her

[16]Feran. Come Kate the Moone shines cleare to night
Methinkes.
Kate. The moone? why husband you are deceiued
It is the sun.
Feran. Yet againe come backe againe it shall be
The moone ere we come at your fathers.
Kate. Why Ile say as you say it is the moone.
Feran. Iesus saue the glorious moone.
Kate. Iesus saue the glorious moone.
Feran. I am glad Kate your stomack is come down,
I know it well thou knowest it is the sun,
But I did trie to see if thou wouldst speake,
And crosse me now as thou hast donne before,
And trust me Kate hadst thou not named the moone,
We had gon back againe as sure as death. (39)

lord's "honest will" is the same specified by Renaissance humanists concerning masculine obedience to the prince. As unattractive as is the role Katherine espouses, it is no less attractive than that prescribed by Renaissance humanism to its male adherents. But Katherine is not male. She turns her superior "reason," the superiority of which isolates her from her sisters, her now "disfigure[d]" mother-wit, against them and herself. As a master of language within this public forum, Kate in *The Shrew* gains status as orator at the expense of all things feminine; but as she cannot, in actuality, be regendered, her action is essential silencing and self-destruction. In *A Shrew*, however, Kate's final soliloquy moves her sister to suggest the superiority of feminine excess:

> Eme. How now Polidor in a dump, what sayst thou man?
> Pol. I say thou art a shrew.
> Eme. Thats better than a sheepe.
> Pol. Well since tis don let it go, come lets in.
>
> (50)

Polidor does not contest Emelia's assertion that a shrewish wife is superior to a sheepish one; neither his estate nor the state is undermined by what appears to be little more than Emelia's, or Philema's, or even Kate's shifting moods. But as Leah Marcus notes in her examination of the divergent ideologies of these *Shrew* plays,

> Kate's rationale for obedience in *The Shrew* is given a political base: ... The machinery of state lying behind th[e] appeal for submission [in *The Shrew*] is rather more awesome and immediate than the diffuse and generalized appeal for order in *A Shrew*.[17]

Kate's education, the source of her public power in *The Shrew*, is the means of her domestic oppression.

Because the humanist tradition conflates female and language, it is almost impossible in a discussion of *The Shrew* to speak of one in isolation from the other. But the problem which is elucidated by *The Shrew* exists at the level of all discourse, with Woman, not merely Kate, the *tabula rasa* for masculine impression. Her display of eloquence and *masculine* moral superiority in *The Shrew* silences her sisters, and their inept tutors as well, who, unlike her own *rhetor*, have been more concerned with their appearance as instructors than with the act of instruction. Because *fatti maschii, parole femine* ("women are words, men deeds") the inferior tutors indict themselves in the effeminacy of inaction. Kate's education does not make

---

[17]Leah Marcus, "The Shakespearean Editor as Shrew Tamer," *MS*, 4, forthcoming, *English Literary Renaissance*.

her subservient to the lesser scholars, Lucentio and Hortensio, who fail in the instruction of their pupils and in their responsibilities as "govenour and lord." Their limitations are reflected in the failure of their "pupils," Bianca and the widow, to follow Kate' s example and place their own hands beneath their lords' feet. However, Kate's act, her oratory, promotes essential masculine superiority through an infinite series of descending masters and *female* pupils. In this final, tragic pretense of *The Shrew*, Kate acts in the guise of *vir eloquentissimus*—with female language shackled by misogynist education, female hand ground beneath male boot, and female mouth infibulated with the threads of humanist rhetoric.

For the many and worthwhile discussions that contributed to the formulation of this paper, I wish to thank Leah Marcus and Rita Copeland.

GOOD FREND FOR IESVS SAKE FORBEARE,
TO DIGC THE DVST ENCLOASED HEARE:
BLESE BE Y MAN Y SPARES THES STONES,
AND CVRST BE HE Y MOVES MY BONES.

Inscription on Shakespeare's Tomb in Stratford Church

A scene from Coriolanus by L. du Guernier (1677–1716) in
William Shakespeare, *Works*, ed. N. Rowe. London, 1714.

FIVE

An Intertextual Study of Volumnia: From Legend to Character in Shakespeare's *Coriolanus*

Catherine La Courreye Blecki

The most persistent element in the legends of Volumnia and Coriolanus is their confrontation before Rome that concludes with her successful intercession on behalf of Rome. Although her success in saving Rome made her a hero to Greek and Roman writers, she posed a problem to male writers in the middle ages and Renaissance who retold her story and included her as a model of civic virtue in their historical and literary collections of stories about illustrious women. Volumnia's eloquence and political success over her son threatened male sovereignty in a period that extolled chaste, silent, and obedient women who did not interfere in the public affairs of men, especially if it meant opposing male members of their own house. Sir Walter Ralegh's ironic aside in his account of Coriolanus in the *History of the World* (1614) reflects what many writers implied, but few stated, as he mused that Coriolanus' mother and wife showed themselves "better Subjects to their Countrie, than friends to their sonne and husband."[1]

Volumnia's reputation in the twentieth century arouses more negative than positive critical commentary. According to Alexander Leggatt and Lois Norem, who have compiled the most recent (1989) annotated bibliography on Shakespeare's *Coriolanus*, most critics see her as a "she-

---

[1] Sir Walter Ralegh, *The History of the World* (London, 1614), 294. Ralegh's source for this anecdote is probably Livy's history of Rome since, like Livy, he calls Coriolanus' mother Veturia.

wolf who has brutalized her son and [who] ends by killing him."[2] To examine Shakespeare's Volumnia from the vantage point of classical sources, however, enables us to understand the historical and artistic patterns Shakespeare was drawing upon when he created her character. This approach gives us a fresh perspective on Shakespeare's formidable maternal figure.

Shakespeare had access to two complete accounts of the classical story of Volumnia and Coriolanus, the older account written by Livy (59 B.C.–A.D. 17), who began writing *On the Foundation of the City* around 27–25 B.C.. Plutarch (A.D. 46–c.126), who wrote the *Parallel Lives* about A.D. 104–115, however, was Shakespeare's main source.[3] In these histories Volumnia became the exemplum of civic virtue because she was the intercessor who persuaded her son to spare Rome. As Sarah Pomeroy points out, "[intercession] was the only traditionally commendable, active political role for women in Rome."[4] A third source, Plutarch's *Gunaikon aretai,* or *Mulierum virtutes* ["The Bravery of Women"] may also have influenced Shakespeare indirectly through Philemon Holland's 1603 translation of Plutarch's *Moralia,* of which it is a part. Written in the last decade of his life (A.D. 116–126) and dedicated to Clea, a priestess at Delphi, *Gunaikon aretai* followed "the same principle of using historical examples to discover moral truth [that] underlies many of the essays in the Moralia" as well as many of the "anecdotes in the *Lives.*"[5] In the introductory summary to his 1603 translation, Philemon Holland raises some questions about women's valor that will offer a useful perspective as we trace the legend of Volumnia from its classical sources to its Renaissance version.

In *Of the Foundation of the City,* Livy only includes one scene with Volumnia: her confrontation with Coriolanus before the gates of Rome. In

---

[2]Alexander Leggatt and Lois Norem, "Introduction," in *Coriolanus: An Annotated Bibliography,* Garland Shakespeare Bibliogrphies 17 (New York: Garland, 1989), xvii. For examples of this portrayal of Volumnia, see Janet Adelman, "'Anger's my meat': Feeding, Dependency, and Aggression in *Coriolanus,*" in *Shakespeare: Pattern of Excelling Nature,* ed. Jay L. Halio and David Bevington (Newark: University of Delaware Press, 1978), 108–124; Coppelia Kahn, "The Milking Babe and the Bloody Man in *Coriolanus* and *Macbeth,*" in *Man's Estate: Masculine Identity in Shakespeare* (Los Angeles: University of California Press, 1981), 151–173; Madelon Sprengnether, "Annihilating Intimacy in *Coriolanus,*" in *Women in the Middle Ages and the Renaissance,* ed. Mary Beth Rose (Syracuse: Syracuse University Press, 1986), 89–111.

[3]Alan D. Lehman, "The Coriolanus Story in Antiquity," *Classical Journal* 47 (1952):330, 333.

[4]Sarah B. Pomeroy, *Goddesses, Whores, and Slaves: Women in Classical Antiquity* (New York: Schoken, 1975), 186.

[5]Philip Stadter, *Plutarch's Historical Methods: An Analysis of the "Mulierum Virtutes"* (Cambridge: Harvard University Press, 1965), 2–3, 11.

his account, Veturia, his name for Coriolanus' mother, is an intercessor, but he also adds another dimension to her character by conveying her outraged motherhood in her oration to her son. As she confronts Coriolanus, Veturia is direct and impassioned: "Let me know (quoth she) before I suffer thee to embrace me, whether I am come to an enemie or to a sonne, whether I be in thy campe as a captive prisoner, or as a naturall mother." She equates country and family when she challenges him with the questions: "Couldst thou finde in thine heart to waste and spoyle that countrey which bred thee, which fostered thee, and brought thee up? ... And being come within the sight of Rome, arose not this in thy mind & thought, Within those wals yonder is my house, there are my house goods, my mother, my wife, my children?" Veturia even blames her motherhood: "Why then, belike if I had never been a mother, and borne a child, Rome had not been assaulted." Furthermore, if she had not had such a son, she could have died "well ynough in my native countrey, whiles it remained free."[6]

In addition to charging him with ingratitude to country, family, and mother, Veturia is angry with Coriolanus for threatening the freedom of Rome. In this, she reflects a significant theme in Livy's history: the growing personal and social freedom that is now a part of Rome's rule of law. In the beginning of Book 2 where Livy recounts Coriolanus' story, he sets out his theme, which is to tell the story of "the acts both of war and peace of the people of Rome, a free state now from this time forward." Although to act and endure valiantly is still praised as the Roman way, it is not the final arbiter of good; now there is "the authoritie and rule of laws, more powerfull and mightie than that of men" that will "bring forth and beare the good and wholsome fruits of libertie."[7] The stories that follow are to be read as they furthered or hindered this ideal of liberty under the law. As a result "what really matters to Livy in the Coriolanus story is ... that thanks to the intervention of the women, Rome herself escaped destruction and even acquired a fine new temple dedicated to Fortuna Muliebris."[8] In his commentary on Livy's history, R. M. Ogilvie, however, describes the tragic character of the speech by citing its many tragic echoes from Greek and Roman literature.[9] Both the political and tragic implications of the story probably drew Shakespeare's attention.

---

[6]Titus Livius, *The Romane Historie*, trans. Philemon Holland (London, 1600), 70. All subsequent references to Livy's history are to this volume.

[7]Ibid., 44.

[8]Anne Barton, "Livy, Machiavelli, and Shakespeare's *Coriolanus*," *Shakespeare Survey* 38 (1985): 116, 118.

[9]For a very complete discussion of Livy's treatment of the Coriolanus story, see R. M. Ogilvie, *A Commentary on Livy: Books 1–5* (Oxford: Clarendon, 1965), 334.

Plutarch's *Lives* makes the relationship between Coriolanus and his widowed mother central to Coriolanus' biography. The only significant modification that Shakespeare makes in their relationship as set forth in Plutarch is that his Volumnia encourages, rather than passively allows, Marcius' military training, even though this means her son must leave her to pursue it. In both Plutarch's narrative and in Shakespeare's play, Marcius is a model of Roman *pietas* to his mother, though Shakespeare seems to place some limits on Coriolanus' devotion in terms of their domestic arrangement. In Plutarch, Marcius "did not only content himself to rejoice and honour her [Volumnia], but at her desire tooke a wife also, by whom he had two children, and yet never left his mother's house."[10] But as M. W. MacCallum notes, in Shakespeare's play "there is no word of Marcius' marrying at his mother's desire, and though she apparently lives with him, it is in his, not in her house."[11]

Shakespeare's most significant departure from Plutarch, however, is the omission of the scene in which Valeria petitions Volumnia and Virgilia to ask Coriolanus for mercy. In this passage, we get a better understanding of Volumnia's divided heart and the reasons that finally persuade her to confront Coriolanus. Valeria, speaking for the women of Rome, places her argument within the tradition of Roman history by linking the action that she hopes Volumnia and Virgilia will take with Roman precedents like "the daughters of the Sabynes [who] ... procured loving peace, in stead of hatefull war, between their fathers and their husbands." Volumnia's reply gives us an insight into her feelings:

> My good ladies, we are partakers with you of the common miserie and calamite of our countrie, and yet our griefe exceedeth yours the more, by reason of our particular misfortune: to feele the losse of my sonne Martius former valiancie and glorie, and to see his persone environed now with our enemies in armes, rather to see him forth comming & safe kept, then of any love to defend his person. But yet the greatest griefe of our heaped mishaps is, to see our poore country brought to such extremitie that all the hope of the safetie and preservation thereof, is now unfortunately cast upon us simple women: because we know not what account he will make of us, since he hath cast from him all care of his naturall countrie and common weale, which heretofore he hath holden more deere and precious, than either his mother, wife or

---

[10]Plutarch, *Lives of the Noble Grecians and Romanes,* trans. Thomas North (London, 1579), 239.

[11]M. W. MacCallum, *Shakespeare's Roman Plays and Their Background* (1910; London: Macmillan, 1935), 496.

children. Notwithstanding, if ye thinke we can do good, we will willingly do what you will have us: ... For if we cannot prevaile, we maye yet dye at his feete, as humble suters for the safetie of our countrie.[12]

Volumnia movingly expresses her feelings of loss for her son's reputation, "his valiancie and glorie," and his physical presence. While she is not defending him, she is puzzled over his change of loyalties—troubled that he has cast off "all care of his naturall countrie" which he held more "deere and precious, then either his mother, wife or children." North adds the word "naturall" here which his French source, Amyot, who is following the original more closely, does not use.[13] Volumnia's motivation for confronting Coriolanus is that his rejection of the natural piety that he owes his family now threatens his "naturall countrie." In Plutarch's narrative, she confronts Coriolanus as the spokesperson for the women of Rome.

Why does Shakespeare omit such a useful and powerful scene? By placing the women's decision making offstage, Shakespeare gives the impact of Coriolanus' attack on Rome greater speed and force. We only hear about the women's decision indirectly through Cominius. After his mission to plead with Coriolanus fails, he decides to go "haste them [the women] on." (V.ii.70–75)[14] Thus, Volumnia has a more profound role in the play because she becomes the spokesperson for all those who would save Rome, men and women, patrician and plebeian.

In both classical sources, Volumnia's scene with her son before the gates of Rome is the climactic moment of the story. As many critics before me have noted, Shakespeare took more from Plutarch's version of Volumnia's oration than he did of anything else in the source.[15] What may not be so well known is that North altered a good deal of the material that he found in his own source, Jacques Amyot's translation. As Hermann Heuer demonstrated in his excellent study, Shakespeare is indebted to North for the most significant pattern of imagery and rhetorical appeal in the scene, the repetition of "natural" as opposed to "unnatural" and the appeal to Nature.[16] Since Shakespeare's account is dramatic rather than

[12]Plutarch, *Lives*, 255–56.

[13]Plutarque, *Les Vies des Hommes Illustres*, trans. Jacques Amyot, Bibliothèque de la Pléiade 43 (Tours: Gallimard, 1951), 510.

[14]William Shakespeare, *Coriolanus*, ed. Philip Brockbank, 7th ed. (London: Routledge, 1988), V.iii.141. All subsequent references are to this text.

[15]MacCallum, 484.

[16]Hermann Heuer, "From Plutarch to Shakespeare: A Study of *Coriolanus*," *Shakespeare Survey* 10 (1957):50–59.

narrative, however, he adds another symbolic dimension to the character of Volumnia and the suppliants, which I will turn to shortly.

The third classical source, Plutarch's *Mulierum virtutes* (wr. A.D. 116–125), offers a significant insight into both classical and Renaissance attitudes toward women's valor, and thus a useful perspective on Volumnia's actions at the gates of Rome. In *Mulierum virtutes*, Plutarch declares that the virtues of men and women are equal, but as Constance Jordan has shown, he fails to uphold his thesis when he illustrates it with examples: "His typically virtuous woman assists and inspires men; if necessary, she sacrifices herself for their welfare or that of the state."[17]

What is implicit in Plutarch is explicit in Holland's summary before his translation of "The Bravery of Women." Holland begins with the conventional wisdom that women's virtue "proceedeth from feeble instruments"; yet he agrees with Plutarch that "it were meere injurie and too much iniquitie, either to forget or to despise those women who for their valour have deserved, that their name and example should continue." As he commends women's valor, however, it is clear that their bravery is related to the Renaissance stereotype of the good woman as chaste, silent, and obedient. Holland notes that their courage includes "divers graces and commendable parts, but especially an extreame hatred of tyrannie and servitude, an ardent love and affection toward their countrey, a singular affection to their husbands, rare honestie, pudicitie, chastitie joined with a generous nature, which hath caused them, both to enterprise and also to execute heroique acts."[18]

So as we move from the classical sources to the Renaissance collections of stories praising illustrious women, it is good to remember that although Veturia/Volumnia was celebrated as a hero for her successful intercession with her son on behalf of Rome, the story of the complex nature of her choice had yet to be told. In the Renaissance, her courage was now evaluated by a different set of cultural assumptions. Her rhetorical ability and the political nature of her victory put her in the category of "masculine woman," yet she had none of the negative traits associated with the stereotype, such as sexual promiscuity, prophecy, or witchcraft.[19] As a result, male writers frequently raised questions about the effect of her victory on male supremacy, or they hinted that her eloquence had a

[17]Constance Jordan, *Renaissance Feminism: Literary Texts and Political Models* (Ithaca: Cornell University Press, 1990), 37, n. 43. Jordan discusses the history of Aretaphilia as an example.

[18]Philemon Holland, "The Vertuous Deeds oe [sic] Women," in Plutarch's *Morals*, trans. Holland (London, 1603), 482.

[19]Marilyn L. Williamson, "'When Men Are Rul'd by Women': Shakespeare's First Tetralogy," *Shakespeare Studies* 19 (1987):41.

devious quality to it. My discussion of this tradition will be limited to works that include Coriolanus' mother as an example and that were published before 1609/10 when *Coriolanus* was performed.[20]

It is interesting to note that writers before Shakespeare refer to Coriolanus' mother by the name Livy gave her, Veturia. This probably indicates that they were using Livy as a source or another writer, such as Boccaccio, who based his portrait on Livy. Boccaccio's *De Claris Mulieribus* (wr. and rev. 1355–59; pub. 1539, Berne) is the transitional work between the classical and renaissance stories of Coriolanus' mother.[21] In her study of the historical and literary collections of illustrious women, Linda Woolbridge claims that Boccaccio "is the most important single source of classical *exempla* used in the formal controversy [over women] between 1520 and 1620."[22] Modern commentators on Boccaccio have pointed out that he is not unbiased in his representation of women. Guarino, his translator, writes that "as always, Boccaccio moves forward instinctively towards a new era, but his progress is hindered by the *impedimenta* of traditions and prejudices of a former age.... [His] comments and digressions give a picture of the world as he saw it, and as he would have preferred it to be."[23] For Boccaccio, Constance Jordan notes, "woman's fame or *claritas*, is a form of notoriety."[24] It is not surprising that Boccaccio's portrait of Veturia is an ambivalent one.

In Boccaccio's expanded version of Livy, Veturia is an outraged mother as well as a patriot. Here is the way Boccaccio introduces Veturia's oration: "With Coriolanus' wife on one side and his children on the other, Veturia cast aside motherly love and became angry as soon as she saw her son. She had left Rome as a suppliant to go to the enemy's camp, but she now became the castigator, and gathering strength in her feeble body said to him: 'Stand still, wild youth. Before I embrace you, I wish to know whether you have come to receive me as your mother or as a captive

[20]I am therefore omitting the portrait of Volumnia in Thomas Heywood's *Gunaikeion: or Nine Bookes of Various History* (1624). Since William Bercher's *The Nobility of Women* (1599) was not published until 1904, I am also excluding his brief references to Volumnia and Veturia.

[21]Guido A. Guarino, "Introduction," in Giovanni Boccaccio, *Concerning Famous Women*, trans. Guarino (New Brunswick, New Jersey: Rutgers University Press, 1963), xxxi.

[22]Linda Woolbridge, *Women and the English Renaissance: Literature and the Nature of Womankind, 1540–1620* (Urbana: University of Illinois Press, 1984), 15. Jordan also notes that Boccaccio's model was Plutarch's *Mulierum virtutes* (*Renaissance Feminism*, 37, n. 43).

[23]Guarino, "Introduction," xxvii.

[24]Constance Jordan, "Boccaccio's In-Famous Women: Gender and Civic Virtue in *De mulierbus claris*," in *Ambiguous Realities: Women in the Middle Ages and Renaissance*, ed. Carole Levin and Jeanie Watson (Detroit: Wayne State University Press, 1987), 27.

enemy.'"[25] Boccaccio's interpretive introduction makes explicit that Veturia's anger meant that she "cast aside motherly love," a point which shows that the writer's sympathies are closer to the vengeful son.

Boccaccio's most extensive addition to Livy is a moralizing commentary attached to the portrait that trivializes Veturia's victory. In his account, the women not only received recognition by the dedication of a temple in their honor, but men were also required to "rise and give way to women," and worse, women received permission to wear "purple finery," which caused men to become "poor, losing the inheritance of their ancestors.... But what can I say? The world belongs to women, and men are womanish."[26] For Boccaccio, the fact that Rome is saved is a minor matter compared with the social and domestic damage of Veturia's victory on male dignity and wealth.

Edward Gosynhyill, in *The Praise of all women called Mulieru[m] Paen* (c. 1542), brought Boccaccio's version of Livy's story to England and rewrote the narrative in rhyme royal. In praising women, he was paying back what he owed them for composing the misogynist *The Schole house of women* (c. 1541), but in his portrayal of Veturia, he retains Boccaccio's bias. He describes the confrontation between Coriolanus and Veturia in this way:

> Large were the teres that from her eyes ran
> Her brestes before hym when she dysplayde
> Beholde she sayde thou unkynde man
> Thy natural mother thus wretchely arayde
> Nature shulde move the[e], thou wyll denayde
> To warre with other than thy natyfe countre
> Peace sayde he mother so shall it be.[27]

It is probably coincidental that Gosynhyill anticipates North's treatment of Volumnia's appeal to "nature" in her oration by his many references to "nature," "natural," and "native." The last stanza, however, breaks this sympathetic line of argument and dwells, like Boccaccio, on what men lost by the women's victory. A law was passed that from that day forward "to the femynyne / Eche man shulde bowe," and it was also granted that a woman might use any type of "broche ... or rynge / Velvet purple or any other thyng."[28]

---

[25]Boccaccio, 119.
[26]Ibid., 120–1.
[27]Edward Gosynhyill, *The Praise of all women called Mulieru[m] Paen* (London, n.d.), Eiir.
[28]Ibid.

After Gosynhyill, Renaissance humanists in England turned to other continental sources. The tone of David Clapham's translation of Agrippa's *De nobilitate et praecellentia Foemenei sexus* or *A Treatise of the Nobilitie and exellencie of woman kynde* (1542) takes a more serious view of women who are models of civic virtue. Jordan notes that Clapham's translation is "the most explicitly feminist text to be published in England in the first half of the century."[29] Clapham is sincere in his tribute to women like Veturia, who "by their wonderfulle power and pollycie, in moste extremytie, and whan there was no hope of helpe loked for, recovered theyre country."[30] But when he writes specifically about Veturia, he does not explain the nature of her power and policy. His account is very general: "Whanne Coriolanus with the Volscians, had besieged Rome, & soo sharpely assayled it, that the Romaynes were not able to defende them selves agaynste hym: an auncient woman Veturia his mother, soo handled the mattier, that she overcame his rage and furye, and reconcyled hym ageyn to the Romaynes."[31] How did Veturia handle the matter? Clapham leaves it to our imagination. The happy ending is Clapham's addition to the story, but this ending removes the tragic ramifications of Veturia's decision and Coriolanus' submission.

Antony Gibson's *A Womans Woorth, defended against all the men in the world* (1599) addresses the issue of Veturia's eloquence by suggesting that her rhetoric was so persuasive because it included an element of guile: her "using so manie great maximes of and for the state, to her sonne being then the citties enemie: as all the *Xenophons, Tacitusses, Machiavels,* yea, whatsoever Councellors to the Princes of Europe may justly learne example by those noble resolutions, and admit them amongst the very cheefest dessignes."[32] By adding Machiavelli, Gibson qualifies his praise, suggesting there is something devious about Veturia's rhetoric, but, like Clapham, he does not say enough to be convincing.

The last writer before Shakespeare who refers to Coriolanus' mother as an example of civic virtue is Lodovick Lloyd in *The Choyce of Jewels* (1607). Like Clapham, Lloyd is sincere in his praise, but his reference to Veturia is so brief that he does not add anything to the content of the story. Both Gibson and Lloyd, however, add a new pattern and thus a new issue to the tradition. Both writers follow the example of Veturia with one from *Mulierum virtutes* about another woman who saved Rome: the vestal virgin Cloelia who escaped from King Porsena's captivity by

[29]Jordan, *Renaissance Feminism*, 122.
[30]David Clapham, *A Treatise of the Nobilitie ... of woman kynde* (London, 1542), f1r.
[31]Ibid., f2r.
[32]Anthony Gibson, *A Womans Woorth* (London, 1599), 6.

riding a horse "over the River Tiber, and opening the secrets of *Porsenna* to the Roman Senators."[33] The sequence of stories suggests that neither writer distinguished between the moral courage of Veturia and the physical courage of Cloelia.

Although Shakespeare probably did not take anything directly from these collections of stories, they constituted a tradition upon which he could draw. In contrast with Livy and Plutarch, Renaissance writers generally view the mother of Coriolanus with qualified praise. She may have saved Rome, but her victory cost men their supremacy and her eloquence is tinged with guile. Writers like Clapham and Lloyd, who saw her in a positive light, failed to develop her as a memorable character. In comparison with his classical sources, Shakespeare gives a much greater role to Volumnia and to Virgilia as her foil. Valeria's role is diminished in comparison with Plutarch's history, but she retains a symbolic role as the virgin, the sister of Publicola, and the third member of the group of women. In contrast with Plutarch, who only brings in Volumnia at the beginning of the narrative and, with the other women, in the penultimate scene, Shakespeare gives them dramatic prominence throughout the play in seven scenes. Their appearance singly or collectively, as a dyad or triad, is a significant part of the emblematic juxtaposition and grouping of women characters in the play. In their pivotal scene of supplication before Rome, the group of women implicit in Plutarch's story is made explicit by Shakespeare; they are a triad, representing a united feminine power—mother, wife, virgin, widow—who agree that the city must be saved, not just for patricians, but for all its citizens. Although they do not state this directly, their united presence indicates that for them the survival of family and community is more important than personal happiness or personal vengeance or class divisions. The women and young Marcius present a visual icon of the suppliant family and city.

In Plutarch's narrative and Shakespeare's play, both groups of suppliants are on their knees. This gesture reverses the natural piety of mother and son and summarizes, in one iconic moment, the position of the suppliants. Ironically, this nonverbal gesture is probably Volumnia's most telling argument.[34] In Shakespeare's hands, the scene is intensified by antithetical emotional appeals as she rejects all familial ties with Coriolanus, just when she has so painstakingly reestablished them, and then,

---

[33]Lodowick Lloyd, *The Choyce of Jewells* (London, 1607), D1r.

[34]The commentaries on the significance of gesture in this scene have been especially eloquent: Paul Gaudet, "Gesture in *Coriolanus*: Textual Cues for Actor and Audience," *The Upstart Crow* 8 (1988):77–92; Bevington 90–91; Howard 85–87; Dyke 145; Helen Gardner, "Tragic Mysteries," in *Shakespeare's Pattern of Excelling Nature*, ed. David Bevington and Jay L. Halio (Newark: University of Delaware Press; London: Assoc. UP, 1976), 89–90.

in another reversal, refuses to desert her son by giving him the responsibility to dismiss them: "Yet give us our dispatch." (V.iii.180) Instead, "[Coriolanus] holds her by the hand, silent." (183)

Coriolanus' gesture silences Volumnia, and his next statement ironically defines her victory: "You have won a happy victory to Rome; / But for your son, believe it, O, believe it / Most dangerously you have prevail'd, / If not most mortal to him." (186–89) The irony of this scene is striking when it is compared with the discourse of Plutarch's women in the scene omitted by Shakespeare. In Plutarch's story, the women hope to procure "loving peace, in stead of hatefull war." In Shakespeare's play, the women are silent as Coriolanus assumes the role of "peacemaker" and significantly alters their perception of war and peace: "though I cannot make true wars, / I'll frame convenient peace." (190–1)

With its series of antithetical emotional appeals, the powerful impact of the circle of suppliants, the juxtaposition of eloquent sounds and silent gestures, Shakespeare has taken the legendary confrontation between mother and son to its ultimate theatrical dimension. While he seems to keep what mattered most to his Roman sources, the story of the woman who was "the patroness, the life of Rome" (V.v.1), Shakespeare undermines the clear-cut victory that Livy and Plutarch gave to the women by including Coriolanus' commentary, which implies that in spite of his submission, he prefers the heroic life of "true wars" over the civilian life of "convenient peace." The Renaissance sources of the legend may have contributed to the sense that the women's victory came at men's expense. Philemon Holland defines women's valor as "an ardent love and affection toward their countrey," *and* "a singular affection to their husbands" (and by extension, their sons). As Ralegh put it so memorably, Volumnia and Virgilia showed themselves better patriots than mothers and wives.

Shakespeare's vision is even more deeply ironic than Ralegh's because he seems to ask: was there a victory for the women? He leaves our understanding of Volumnia's feelings, her interior life, to our imaginations at the end of the play. When we see the women (V. v), they pass over the stage, silent, while the citizens and senators rejoice around them. In contrast with the elaborate stage directions and internal cues for gestures in V.iii, Shakespeare uses no words or gestures to give a clue to their feelings. It is in keeping with the ironic tone of this tragedy that our final vision of Volumnia, a woman legendary for her eloquence, is a silent one, leaving the audience puzzling.

Portrait of Shakespeare
From title page of edition of 1625

SIX

Domesticating the Dark Lady

Jean R. Brink

Theoretical models are frames through which we examine the particular events and specific individuals inscribed in documentary and literary texts. At their best, frames, like genres and literary conventions, suggest questions to be addressed; at their worst they obscure our vision, relegating to the periphery or concealing entirely anything that does not square with our assumptions. Since frames must select and focus, they render more abstract the complex texture of the material we examine.

Surely this selectivity explains at least in part the phenomenon of diametrically opposed theoretical conclusions about whether Shakespeare supported or subverted patriarchy.[1] In examining Shakespearean criticism on gender, we are repeatedly confronted by oppositions that are very difficult to resolve. In a recent collection of essays on Shakespeare's personality, for example, Carol Neely traces in his works a disturbing masculinist ideology that women are dangerous, while Shirley Garner finds Shakespeare maintaining the view that women are divinely forgiving.[2]

Descriptions of the culture offstage are also far from transparent.[3] The same kinds of contradictions are encountered when we look at historical

---

[1] For useful summaries and discussions of these contradictions, see Lisa Jardine, "Cultural Confusion and Shakespeare's Learned Heroines: 'These are old paradoxes,'" *Shakespeare Quarterly* 38 (1987):1–18; Peter Erickson, "Rewriting the Renaissance, Rewriting Ourselves," *Shakespeare Quarterly* 38 (1987):327–37; and Walter Cohen, "Political Criticism of Shakespeare," *Shakespeare Reproduced: The Text in History and Ideology*, ed. Jean E. Howard and Marion F. O. O'Connor (New York and London: Routledge, 1987), esp. 26.

[2] *Shakespeare's Personality*, ed. Norman N. Holland, Sidney Homan, and Bernard J. Paris (Berkeley: University of California Press, 1989).

[3] Jonathan Goldberg, "Shakespearean Inscriptions: The Voicing of Power," in *Shakespeare and the Question of Theory*, ed. Patricia Parker and Geoffrey Hartman (New York and London: Methuen) provocatively asks: "Perhaps—just perhaps—the reason we cannot find Shakespeare reflecting his culture's supposed patriarchalism and sexism is that the culture represented on the stage *is* the culture offstage." (135) Alison Wall, "Elizabethan Precept and Feminine Practice: The Thynne Family of Longleat," *History* 75 (1990):23–38, admirably addresses the problems of reconstructing the past.

responses to the question of whether women did in fact have a Renaissance. While it is true that some literary scholars have uncritically inferred the social context from a formalist analysis of Shakespeare's texts, we need to be aware that "historical contexts" are themselves constructed.[4] In order to address the question of whether women had a Renaissance in early modern England, scholars have had to develop from surviving records a set of assumptions about what life was like in medieval English society and then to juxtapose this construct with an equally hypothetical set of postulates about the position of women in early modern England. At its most fruitful, the dialogue that has emerged has increased our awareness of the complexities of the intersection of political, legal, economic, and cultural status. When we encounter the scene between Hotspur and Kate in Shakespeare's *Henry IV, Part One*, we not only see a domestic interchange that puts Hotspur's character in a more attractive light (and that serves as foil for the tavern parody in which Falstaff and Prince Hal construct Hotspur's domestic personality), but we also recognize that we are not dealing with a *single* culture, either on or off stage. From Hotspur's teasing ridicule of Kate, we learn that social class complicated linguistic codes. Hotspur teases his wife Kate for saying "in good sooth" (III.i.244), telling her to "swear me, Kate, like a lady as thou art, / A good mouth-filling oath, and leave 'in sooth,' / And such protest of pepper-gingerbread, / To velvet-guards and Sunday-citizens." (III.i.251–54)[5] He ridicules the linguistic delicacy of a "comfit-maker's wife," leaving no doubt that considerations of social class affected codes of conduct for women.

Although we live in a poststructuralist theoretical environment in which scholarly discourse about sexuality has become fashionable, the surprised reaction of students to Shakespeare's bawdy puns should remind us that ours is also a post-Victorian society. Our linguistic codes of what is acceptable to say in "polite company," i.e., groups including women, are probably more "gendered" than were those of the Elizabethans.[6] The conduct manuals, whether Elizabethan or Victorian, do not reflect a value-free culture in which women and men are perceived as individuals unencumbered by mores of class and gender. Even though Elizabethan conduct books advocated that a virtuous woman be "chaste,

---

[4] Jardine (n.1, above) points out that it is a mistake to assume that there "exists a reliable body of social and cultural historical 'fact', to be tested against the 'fiction' of literary representation." (4)

[5] References to Shakespeare's plays will be cited parenthetically from *The Complete Pelican Shakespeare*, ed. Alfred Harbage (London: The Penguin Press, 1969).

[6] For a related discussion of anachronistic conceptions of gender and sexual difference, see the analysis by Phyllis Rackin in this volume.

silent, and obedient," we have no way of knowing how effective this advocacy was.

For this reason, I want to limit my analysis to a few selected women who were—or are—threatening to patriarchy, to an established social order in which male dominance and female subservience are assumed. I propose to use the literary archetype of a female figure who is promiscuous, assertive, and unruly—the Dark Lady of the *Sonnets*—to interrogate the patriarchal structure of two of Shakespeare's Roman plays, *Titus Andronicus* and *Antony and Cleopatra*. My purpose is not to offer formal analyses of these plays or even character studies of the women themselves, but to examine how they fare in the intensely patriarchal world of Shakespeare's Roman plays. Then, I will look at secondary scholarship on *Coriolanus*, principally as a means of suggesting how the unexamined gender stereotypes of critics influence perceptions of patriarchy. Post-Victorian criticism, I will argue, sets out to "contain" powerful women, because it habitually sentimentalizes the feminine. This literary and cultural analysis will shed light on why critics have reached such contradictory conclusions regarding Shakespeare's strategies for representing women.

One of Shakespeare's most troubling but perennially fascinating literary archetypes is the Dark Lady of his *Sonnets*. The Dark Lady has so intrigued his readers that speculation regarding her historical identity has generated shelves of books devoted to literary detection.[7] An archetype, as I shall use the term in this paper, invites, but rejects being flattened into a conventional bad woman—whore or shrew. It is precisely this resistance to placement that characterizes and generates the power of the Dark Lady. Shakespeare's sonnet mistress, moreover, is but one of several Dark Ladies who resist domestication in their respective literary contexts: to describe their fortunes in his plays is hardly to chart the history of sixteenth-century women, but analysis of their representation can assist us in understanding and confronting the interpretive politics that prompts the investigation.[8] It is too simplistic to suggest, as Constance Jordan has, that "the image itself—of a woman who is the virtuous equal of the man—is always an image of the culturally alien. The figures of Hippolyta, Semiramis, Dido, Camilla, and Artemisia, among others, are united not

---

[7]For a survey of this material, see Samuel Schoenbaum, *Shakespeare's Lives* (New York: Oxford University Press, 1970).

[8]For a cogent argument that psychologized authorship of the *Sonnets* has been used to explain ambiguities of gender and desire, see Margreta de Grazia, "The Motive for Interiority: Shakespeare's *Sonnets* and *Hamlet*," *Style* 23 (1989):430–44.

only by their virility but also by their barbarism."[9] In fact, the critical reception of Shakespeare's Dark Ladies affords us a particularly illuminating record of how interpretive politics operates. Changing political ideologies and gender stereotypes can reconstruct heroines as monsters or aliens as romantic figures.

Although not an entirely coherent group, Shakespeare's sonnets numbered 127–152 depict a woman "colored ill" (144, 4) whose dark hair and eyes reflect an inner darkness that Shakespeare describes "as black as hell, as dark as night" (147, 14).[10] The sonneteer is both attracted to and repelled by this woman whom he characterizes as leading him to expend his spirit in "a waste of shame" (129, 1).[11] If the narrative of these sonnets is construed literally, an intriguing story emerges in which the sonneteer's dark-haired mistress has seduced a young man "right fair" (144, 3), whose patronage and affection are important to the sonneteer. In one of many types of attempts to "domesticate" the Dark Lady, readers of Shakespeare have persisted in identifying her with actual women such as Mary Fitton or the Italian musician Emilia Lanier.[12]

Shakespeare's Dark Lady, unlike Daniel's Delia, an anagram for Ideal, or Drayton's Idea, is highly sensual. She is untrustworthy and promiscuous, but her very promiscuity renders her powerful. Not only can she reject the poet, she can betray and humiliate him. The Dark Lady of the *Sonnets* dominates men, controlling her relationship with both the poet and the young man. She is "the bad angel," who will "fire ... out" (144, 14) the "man right fair" (144, 3). In her relationship with the sonneteer, she exercises mastery, acting as a sovereign. When the poet begs her to "Use power with power, and slay me not by art" (139, 4), he hopes that she will use her sexual power with authority, that she will not tease him into submission and then deny him.

---

[9]Constance Jordan, *Renaissance Feminism: Literary Texts and Political Models* (Ithaca: Cornell University Press, 1990), 79. See also p. 35. "Because women did not (and were not supposed to) do anything to earn them public notice, a famous woman was almost a contradiction in terms, either actually infamous or simply fantastic."

[10]Since I am approaching the Dark Lady as a literary archetype, a conscious creation of Shakespeare's, I do not make any claims concerning Shakespeare's unconscious or appeals to his biography. For an analysis of the women in Shakespeare's family, see Carol Thomas Neely, "Female Sexuality in the Renaissance," *Feminism and Psychoanalysis*, ed. Richard Feldstein and Judith Roof (Ithaca and London: Cornell University Press), 214–16.

[11]For a recent discussion of the Dark Lady as the product of a Protestant consciousness, see Hugh Richmond, "The Dark Lady as Reformation Mistress," *The Kenyon Review* 8, 2 (1986):91–105.

[12]Although the most notable example is A. L. Rouse, ed., *The Poems of Shakespeare's Dark Lady* (New York: Clarkson N. Potter, 1979), see also Hugh Calvert, *Shakespeare's Sonnets and the Problems of Autobiography* (Chippenham: Antony Rowe, 1987).

Sonnet 143 offers the most revealing example of the male sonneteer's helplessness when faced with female potency. In this sonnet, the Dark Lady is imagined to be a "careful housewife." (143, 1) The term "housewife" could be used for a prostitute and had connotations retained in our word "hussy." The housewife is a mother who puts her child down in order to pursue "one of her feathered creatures." (2) The sonneteer describes himself as "I, thy babe" (10) and imagines his mother/mistress catching the creature that she pursues and then returning to him. He invites her to "play the mother's part, kiss me, be kind." (12)

Freud has taught us to be very sensitive to the potentially sexual overtones to the relationship between mother and son, but cultural mores, possibly more resonant in early modern England than in our own day, further problematize this relationship. In a patriarchal system, a mother's honor insures that her son will be "legitimate," recognized as a lawful participant in the patriarchal state. To call into question the chastity of a man's mother remains to this day a value-laden insult in our slang. Further, as more than one critic has pointed out, in a patriarchal system, when a woman marries, her honor, like her property, passes into her husband's keeping.[13] We have only to reflect upon the profound suffering of Othello when he believes that Desdemona has betrayed him to recognize the emasculating and humiliating threat of female promiscuity.

The taboo against female promiscuity seems also to have extended to sexual relationships occurring outside marriage. Claudio in *Much Ado about Nothing* has not yet married Hero, but he responds to the threat of her infidelity as though he had indeed been betrayed and cuckolded. In the archetype of the Dark Lady, Shakespeare forges powerful psychic links between mother and mistress, between the female as a source of nurture and sexual gratification and the female as a powerful "other," capable of subverting male honor and threatening patriarchal order.

The Dark Lady of the *Sonnets* demonstrates a remarkable affinity with the villainous Tamora of *Titus Andronicus* and Cleopatra, the dark temptress, whose wiles enslave Antony in *Antony and Cleopatra*. Analysis of these parallels enables us to probe the gender politics of these fictional constructs. *Titus Andronicus*, written early in Shakespeare's career, portrays Tamora as a Dark Lady, not only alienated from, but in opposition to the dominant patriarchal culture. Few plays illustrate so vividly the way

---

[13]For further discussion of male and female psychology in a patriarchal system, see Coppelia Kahn, "The Absent Mother in *King Lear*," 33–49, and Peter Stallybrass, "Patriarchal Territories: The Body Enclosed," 123–42, esp. 137, in *Rewriting the Renaissance: The Discourses of Sexual Difference in Early Modern Europe*, ed. Margaret W. Ferguson, Maureen Quilligan, and Nancy J. Vickers (Chicago and London: The University of Chicago Press, 1986).

in which patriarchy and patriotism can combine to crush the Dark Lady and so to eradicate any threat posed by female power.[14]

As a brief summary of the events in the opening scene suggests, Tamora, the barbarian queen, is represented sympathetically by Shakespeare at the outset of the play. Titus, who has conquered the Goths, is introduced as the spokesman for patriotic values. He hails Rome as "victorious in thy mourning weeds" (I.i.73) because his victory over the Goths has been won at the price of his sons' lives. His piety has led him to carry their bodies back for burial in Rome. At the burial site of his brothers, Titus' son Lucius urges the sacrifice of the highest ranked among the captured Goths. Since Titus has captured Tamora and her three sons, leading them as captives to Rome, the eldest of her sons has the highest rank among the prisoners. When Tamora's son is selected to be dismembered and sacrificed to appease the shades of the slain Romans, among them Titus' sons, she appeals to Titus as a father to respect her maternity. She asks him to pity "[a] mother's tears in passion for her son." (I.i.109) Imploring Titus to value familial bonds over political allegiance, she cries out:

> O, if to fight for king and commonweal
> Were piety in thine, it is in these.

(I.i.117–18)

Within the framework of the play, Tamora is allowed this one moment of humanity in the opening scene before she comes to epitomize inhuman cruelty. Titus, however, brushes aside Tamora's appeal to maternal and paternal values and authorizes the religious rites in which her son will have his limbs "lopped" (I.i.146) and entrails fed to the "sacrificing fire." (143–45)

In revenge Tamora sets out to destroy Titus and his family. Her position as a barbarian queen, her lust for the black Aaron, her politic deceptions, and her gleeful savagery intensify our awareness of the threat she poses to the patriarchal structure. In *Titus Andronicus* patriarchy is linked to the patriotic issue of Rome's future government. The city is in the pro-

---

[14]For an analysis suggesting that it is "largely through and on the female characters that Titus is constructed and his tragedy inscribed," see Douglas E. Green, "Interpreting 'her martyr'd signs': Gender and Tragedy in *Titus Andronicus*," *Shakespeare Quarterly* 40 (1989):317–26. I disagree with his comment that "just as Elizabeth's gender was submerged, in interludes and entertainments, 'in the complex iconography of her paradigmatic virtue,' always in accord with patriarchal notions of her power as prince, so Shakespeare's notable and notorious female characters are here made to serve the construction of Titus—patriarch, tragic hero, and from our vantage point, central consciousness." (319) Precisely because she retains her agency, Tamora is a threat to patriarchy.

cess of choosing a new emperor, and Titus, who is offered the throne, becomes an arbitrator. Owing to Titus' belief in the hallowed patriarchal tenet of primogeniture, Saturnius is elected the emperor and offers to make Titus' daughter Lavinia his empress. No sooner has Saturnius committed himself to the fair, "lily-like" Lavinia, than he expresses his preference for Tamora: "A goodly lady, trust me, of the hue / That I would choose, were I to choose anew." (I.i.264–65) Tamora's "hue" or complexion is never explicitly identified as dark, and a surviving contemporary illustration depicts her as white, but Saturnius' preference for her "hue" over that of the pale Lavinia allows us to infer that her character, like that of the Dark Lady of the *Sonnets*, may be "colored ill." Her erotic involvement with the black Moor Aaron, who holds her "fett'red in amorous chains" (II.i.15), further associates her with dark passions. Like the Dark Lady, she dissembles, pleading with Saturnius to pardon Titus while she plots to massacre his family and faction. After the opening scene, the maternal values, which Tamora so poignantly expressed when she begged for her son's life, are overshadowed by her fierce pride in her rank as queen and unremitting lust for revenge against

> The cruel father, and his traitorous sons,
> To whom I sued for my dear son's life;
> And make them know what 'tis to let a queen
> Kneel in the streets and beg for grace in vain.
>
> (I.i.455–58)

When Lavinia, faced with rape, appeals to Tamora for pity and asks her to sympathize as a woman and mother, Tamora disclaims any knowledge of tenderness.

The contrast established between the alien and promiscuous Tamora and the fair-haired Lavinia illustrates the pervasive authority of patriarchy and its power to marginalize women. In the first scene, Tamora pleads for motherhood as an important human bond, calling into question the patriarchal and patriotic values which Titus espouses. Within the paternal structure of this play, her challenge to these values seems to require that she be discredited and denigrated. By the end of the play, she is portrayed as a "ravenous tiger" (V.iii.195), consumed by her ambitious pride and lascivious, adulterous passion. Tamora ceases to be a woman, even to be human: she metamorphoses into something akin to the bloodthirsty allegorical Revenge of *The Spanish Tragedy*.[15]

---

[15]For a study of Shakespeare's use of Ovidian material and perceptive comments on its affinities with *The Spanish Tragedy*, see Maurice Hunt, "Compelling Art in *Titus Andronicus*," *Studies in English Literature* 28 (1988):197–218.

If Tamora comes to embody Revenge, Lavinia figures as the quintessential female victim. Lavinia exists only as a cipher for the male honor of her brothers and father.[16] When Titus insists that Lavinia be restored to the emperor, her brother Lucius says, "Dead, if you will." (I.i.300) Later, she dies by her father's hand because she "should not survive her shame" and by her "presence still renew his sorrows." (V.iii.41–42) Before killing his daughter, Titus asks if it were "well done of rash Virginius / To slay his daughter with his own right hand, / Because she was enforced, stained, and deflowerd?" (V.iii.36–38) In the best-known Elizabethan versions of the story, Virginius kills his daughter to prevent her rape, but Titus kills Lavinia because her loss of honor, however involuntary, shames him. Raped and mutilated, Lavinia is sentenced to death by the emperor and then killed by her father. Her death sentence is delivered with no indication that her life matters except insofar as her mutilated body may give pain to the paternal custodian of her honor.[17] In contrast to the victimized Lavinia, whose speechless body alone pleads her case, Tamora openly challenges patriarchal justice. For challenging the system, Tamora is condemned to lose her humanity; her life is "beastly" and, as Lucius adds, "devoid of pity." (V.iii.199) Although Tamora is excluded physically from the play's conclusion, and indeed from the human community, the last scene of the play in which Lucius sentences her to be eaten by birds remains troubling.

How seriously are we to take the patriarchal justice administered? Are we expected to view Tamora's end as a kind of poetic justice, in which she gets what she deserves for failing to accept her son's death? The new ruler of Rome will be Titus' son, Lucius, and it is the very same Lucius who first proposed that the noblest of the Goths be sacrificed upon the altar of Roman dead. Lucius savors how he will "hew his limbs and on a pile / *Ad manes fratrum* sacrifice his flesh." (I.i.100–01) After announcing that "Alarbus' limbs are lopped," he triumphantly exclaims that the smoke consuming his flesh "like incense doth perfume the sky." (I.i.148) Lucius lauds human sacrifice at the beginning of the play; at the end he has been acclaimed emperor. He delivers the last speech, which sums up the justice to be dispensed to those responsible for the tragedy.

We should note that his justice is far from blind to gender. Saturnius, the dead Roman emperor who actually killed Titus Andronicus, is for-

---

[16]See Heather B. Kerr, "*Titus Andronicus:* Models of Textuality and Authorship," *Cahiers Elisabethains* 41 (1992):17–32. Gillian Murray Kendall elaborates this point in "'Lend me thy hand': Metaphor and Mayhem in *Titus Andronicus,*" *Shakespeare Quarterly* 40 (1989):299–316.

[17]For a compatible, but more political reading of this episode, see Leonard Tennenhouse, *Power on Display: The Politics of Shakespeare's Genres* (New York and London: Methuen, 1986), 106–22.

given for his role in bringing to pass the tragic events and will be given "burial in his father's grave." (V.iii.192) The male figure of authority is allowed honorable burial because he was deceived and dishonored by the Dark Lady. No funeral rites are allowed to Tamora. Queen of the Goths and erstwhile Empress of Rome, Tamora will be "thrown forth to beasts and birds to prey." (V.iii.198) Lavinia is sacrificed to patriarchal justice while Tamora is betrayed by that same justice and then excluded from the patriarchal rituals that she has dared to challenge. To privilege gender in a reading of *Titus Andronicus* is to valorize patriarchy.

In turning to *Antony and Cleopatra*, a later and more complicated study of the Dark Lady in conflict with a Roman world, we find the same endorsement of patriarchal values in the action of the play. Nevertheless, the complex function of gender in *Antony and Cleopatra* has been repeatedly sentimentalized in secondary criticism in order to explain away the patriarchal politics of the play. In early psychoanalytic studies of Shakespeare's works, critics elaborated a scheme in which issues of gender were resolved in the tragedies in order to prepare for the late romances where they were understood to be fully transcended. In his study of *Antony and Cleopatra*, Murray M. Schwartz, for example, claims that the dialectic between male and female, Rome and Egypt, duty and pleasure, reason and passion is transcended.[18] Antony, he argues, is no less a man for breaking out of the mold of the Roman soldier into Cleopatra's realm. Those are certainly not the views of either Enobarbus or Octavius.

Even in studies focusing on Shakespeare's women, Cleopatra has been treated as a happy blend of lover and political person, and her relationship with Antony has been described as one which "mutuality nourishes" their development.[19] Shakespeare's characterization of Cleopatra, however, supports the view that female power and sexuality cannot be reconciled with patriarchy and patriotism. Only by committing suicide in "the high Roman fashion" (IV.xv.90) does Cleopatra win from Octavius a tribute to her royal status:

> Bravest at the last,
> She levelled at our purposes, and being royal,
> Took her own way.
>
> (V.ii.333–35)

---

[18]Murray M. Schwartz, "Shakespeare through Contemporary Psychoanalysis," in *Representing Shakespeare: New Psychoanalytic Essays*, ed. Murray M. Schwartz and Coppelia Kahn (Baltimore and London: The Johns Hopkins University Press, 1980), 21–32.

[19]A convenient bibliographical summary of divergent views of Cleopatra is available in *A New Variorum Edition of Shakespeare, Antony and Cleopatra*, ed. Martin Spevack (New York: Modern Language Association, 1990), 687–99.

Octavius does far more than conquer Cleopatra; he judges her. To him, she seems beautiful even in death, "like sleep, / As she would catch another Antony / In her strong toil of grace." (V.ii.344–46) Although Octavius orders that she be buried with Antony in a "solemn show" (364), he observes that she has not in fact died in "the high Roman fashion." Cleopatra, Octavius notes, has "pursued conclusions infinite / Of easy ways to die." (353–54) Her choice of death by an asp, "[her] baby at [her] breast" (309), preserves her beauty; her crown and robes serve as the costume that she will wear during the "solemn show" of her funeral. She will be buried in one grave with Antony, a grave which will "clip in it" (299) a famous pair. The use of the word "clip," meaning embrace, has sexual connotations that remind us of Cleopatra's dark and emasculating passions even while paying her tribute.

Cleopatra, like the Dark Lady and Tamora, violates the behavioral norms specifying that virtuous women should be chaste, silent, and obedient, but she never exhibits power except through her sexuality and never achieves recognition as a political figure. Her complexion is dark: she is "with Phoebus' amorous pinches black / And wrinkled deep in time" (I.v.28–29). Charmian counsels Cleopatra to please Antony, to give way to his whims and moods, but Cleopatra rejects that accommodating role, commenting that Charmian "teaches like a fool." (I.iii.10) She challenges and provokes, rejecting the traditional wisdom that female influence can best be secured by subordination and acquiescence.

In Act III, Cleopatra does assume the mantle of authority, informing Enobarbus that she will participate in the battle as "the president of [her] kingdom" and "appear there for a man." (III.vii.17–18) In this instance in which she might have been depicted as exhibiting judgment or courage, she is portrayed only as insuring Antony's defeat. Cleopatra's influence over Antony and his enslavement to passion result in the flawed decision to fight on sea rather than on land. Enobarbus comments that "his whole action grows / Not in the power on't" (III.vii.68–69); their leader Antony is being led, and they have been made into "women's men." (70) Antony, who blames Cleopatra's "magic" (III.x.19) for his defeat, obligingly follows her from the sea battle "like a doting mallard." (20) She is described even by Antony as having "full supremacy" (III.xi.59) over his spirit and as his "conqueror." (66) Enobarbus, queried as to who was to blame for the defeat, assures Cleopatra that it was Antony. Antony, he tells her, ought not to have let his will conquer his reason nor to have allowed "the itch of his affection" to nick "his captainship." (III.xiii.7–8) Cleopatra does not achieve heroic stature by acting as "the president of [her] kingdom" and appearing at the battle as a "man" (III.vii.17–1 8), but she succeeds in turning Antony into a woman. In terms of sexual politics, it is the final touch of irony for her to be portrayed as accepting Enobarbus' easy assurance that the defeat is Antony's fault because as a man—naturally superior in responsibility—he should have known better than to let himself be overruled by a woman.

Octavius says that "[w]omen are not / In their best fortunes strong" and that "want will perjure / The ne'er-touched vestal" (III. xii.30–31), a misogynist observation that Cleopatra's behavior in this play largely justifies. She immediately concedes to Octavius' messenger that her honor was never "yielded" to Antony (III.xiii.61), agreeing that she was "conquered." (62) She sensually flirts with Caesar's messenger, flaunting her sexual promiscuity with erotic allusions to her affair with Julius Caesar. When Antony suspects her of treason with Octavius, she feigns death. Too craven to leave her monument to bid farewell to Antony, she insists that her dying lover be drawn up to her on a pulley.

After she resolves to die in the "high Roman fashion," she conceals a large portion of her fortune from Caesar. It is when she becomes convinced that she will be led captive to Rome and mocked on the stage that she reconciles herself to dying by her own hand. Significantly, she describes her decision to preserve her royal honor as banishing the woman from her:

> My resolution's placed, and I have nothing
> Of woman in me; now from head to foot
> I am marble-constant; now the fleeting moon
> No planet is of mine.
>
> (V.ii.238–41)

For Cleopatra, to be resolute, "marble-constant," is to banish the "women in [her]."[20] To be female is as weak and fickle a state to Cleopatra as it is to Octavius. Earlier, when Octavius comments on Antony's Egyptian debauchery, he describes him as "not more manlike / Than Cleopatra," adding that the "queen of Ptolemy" is not "[m]ore womanly than he." (I.iv.6–7) Octavius sneeringly insinuates that Cleopatra has emasculated Antony, and the action of the play validates his judgment.

In *Titus Andronicus*, Tamora is expelled from the human community, denied even burial. Twentieth-century critics agree that it is death that confers nobility on Cleopatra, but it is a death that she chooses only after she has expunged her gender. When Cleopatra says "I have nothing / Of woman in me," she means that she has the courage to choose death over

---

[20]Neglecting to note that Cleopatra's resolve is achieved by banishing the woman in her, Richard Hillman, in "Antony, Hercules, and Cleopatra: 'the bidding of the gods' and 'the subtlest maze of all'," *Shakespeare Quarterly* 38 (1987):444, comments that "there is no trace either of Juliet's escapist desperation or of her own former impulsiveness. She is 'marble-constant' (l. 239) in making herself 'fire and air' (l. 288)."

dishonor. The power that Cleopatra exhibits is sexual, and she uses it to "tie up [Antony] in a field of feasts" and "prorogue his honor." (I.v.23, 25) Octavius, who judges Cleopatra principally on her sexuality and treats her as a pawn in power politics, describes her as beautiful in death, but does not fail to observe that she chose an easy death. Shakespeare's Tamora and Cleopatra, like his Dark Lady, are powerful "others," whose female sexuality threatens male hierarchy. Even though Shakespeare's Dark Ladies are sensual, promiscuous, deceitful, calculating, untrustworthy, and emasculating, moral retribution alone does not bring on their catastrophes. Death is the price that the Dark Lady pays for challenging or subverting the patriarchal order, and, in the case of Cleopatra, we, like Octavius, regret her loss. The quality of life has been impoverished by the triumph of Octavius and the restoration of patriarchy has been costly.

The world of the Roman play *Coriolanus*, like that of *Titus Andronicus* and *Antony and Cleopatra*, is informed by a strongly patriarchal system, but the action in this highly political play portrays the threatening woman as triumphant. Volumnia, however, differs from the Dark Lady because she is chaste, albeit far from silent and obedient.[21] Her passionate rhetoric led Furnivall in his 1877 Introduction to the Leopold Shakespeare to celebrate her virtue: "from mothers like Volumnia came the men who conquered the known world and have left their mark for ever on the nations of Europe ... no grander, nobler woman was ever created by Shakespeare's art."[22] The Furness *Variorum* of 1928 offers equally strong endorsements of Volumnia. Mrs. Jameson celebrates her "lofty patriotism, her patrician haughtiness, her maternal pride, her eloquence and her towering spirit," adding that "the truth of female nature is beautifully preserved, and the portrait, with all its vigour, is without harshness."[23] In the same *Variorum* collection, Hudson remarks that "Volumnia is a superb figure indeed, yet a genuine woman throughout, though with a high strain of what may be called manliness pervading her womanhood." (690) And, Grace Latham observes that "To this day Volumnias are not by any means uncommon in England, especially in periods of national

[21]For a more detailed study of the complex history of Volumnia, see Catherine La Courreye Blecki's essay in this volume.

[22]*The Leopold Shakespeare*, Introduction by F. J. Furnival (London: Cassell, Petter and Galpin, 1877), lxxxiii. Furnival sees Cleopatra and Volumnia as opposites: "Against the stifling colours of the kaleidoscope of Cleopatra's whims and moods, against the hail and storm of her passions, the lurid glow of her lust, the fierce lightening of her wrath, rises the pure white figure of Volumnia, clad in the dignity of Honour and the Patriotism, the grandest woman in Shakespeare...."(lxxxiii)

[23]The positive discussions of Volumnia which follow are conveniently reprinted in *The Variorum Shakespeare, The Tragedy of Coriolanus*, ed. Horace Howard Furness (Philadelphia and London: J. B. Lippencott, 1928), 688–701.

struggle and danger, combining with great pride of place an intense devotion to their country, to which they will sacrifice not only their pride, but the family ties which are yet dearer to their women's hearts." (691) Latham then describes Virgilia as Volumnia's foil, observing that she "is one of those quiet, gentle, persistent women with whom we often meet, who seem all submission, but who in the long run mostly get their way." (692) Commenting that Coriolanus' wife Virgilia was "an irritating daughter-in-law," she notes that Volumnia is "too large minded to make petty quarrels" and that "she puts [Virgilia] forward to walk first in the procession which goes to implore mercy for Rome." (693) To Latham, Volumnia's silence at the conclusion of the play is fully in keeping with her character: "She has made the greatest of all sacrifices for her country; and just as she would not show her anxiety when her Marcius was at the wars, so now she hides her pain and goes home to weep." (697) Furnivall, Jameson, Hudson, and Latham appropriate Volumnia as their heroine, treating Coriolanus not as the product of an unnatural mother, but as an independent agent responsible for his own unwise choices and final catastrophe.

To understate the shift in perspective, Volumnia's stature as a noble, powerful, and respected female figure has come under attack in the latter part of the twentieth century. Just short of a hundred years after Furnivall, in 1967, G. R. Hibbard in his introduction to the Penguin Shakespeare anatomizes her flaws: "To Volumnia the fulfilling of her ambitions for her son is more important than any principles. The honour she has held up before him proves to be a tainted thing. She advises him to practice lying and dissimulation, to cultivate the art of flattery, which he has always despised, in order to recover the power he is in such danger of losing. There is, in fact, nothing to choose between her and the Tribunes."[24] In contrast, Virgilia is lauded by Hibbard as "'the gracious silence' at the heart of this stormy play" on the grounds that she does "acknowledge her own feelings and is not afraid of them." (29)

Harold Bloom's recent statement that "Volumnia hardly bears discussion, once we have seen that she would be at home wearing armor in *The Iliad*" represents a late-twentieth-century critical consensus.[25] Not surprisingly, Bloom includes in his recent collection of essays offering critical perspectives on *Coriolanus*, a highly influential essay by Janet Adelman, who views Volumnia's nurture as cruel and suggests that Coriolanus channeled his need for nourishment into phallic aggression:

---

[24]*Coriolanus*, ed. G. R. Hibbard (Middlesex and Baltimore: Penguin Books, 1967), 39.
[25]Harold Bloom, Introduction to *Coriolanus* (New York: Chelsea House, 1988), 4.

When Volumnia triumphs over his rigid maleness, there is a hint of restitution in the Roman celebration of her as 'our patroness, the life of Rome' (V.v.1). But like nearly everything else at the end of this play, the promise of restitution is deeply ironic: for Volumnia herself has shown no touch of nature as she willingly sacrifices her son; and the cries of 'welcome, ladies, welcome!' (V.v.6) suggest an acknowledgment of female values at the moment in which the appearance of these values not in Volumnia but in her son can only mean his death.[26]

The crucial point in this summary is reached when Adelman claims that the play is unsatisfactory because it is Coriolanus who exhibits the "female" values assumed to be lacking in the unnatural Volumnia.

Late twentieth-century critical perspectives on Volumnia are thus highly revealing. Volumnia violates the modern codes of femininity and maternity held by female and male critics. Her "nurturing" is most frequently described as "cruel" because her behavior does not accord with sentimental stereotypes of the mother as the natural source of nourishment and nurture.[27] In her final plea to Coriolanus, she describes herself as a "poor hen, fond of no second brood" who has "clucked him to the wars, and safely home / Laden with honour." (V.iii.162–64) Even a critic who is sympathetic to Volumnia has written of this passage:

The bathos of Volumnia's presentation of herself as a 'poor hen, fond of no second brood' (V.iii.162–63), in its absurd incongruity comes close to domestic comedy, but may also suggest her clumsy approach to new feelings.[28]

Like Shylock, representations of Volumnia on the stage vary radically, ranging from the fierce virago to Jewish-American mother. The reviewer of a 1972 Royal Shakespeare Company production describes her as "an

---

[26] Janet Adelman, "'Anger's My Meat': Feeding, Dependency and Aggression in *Coriolanus*," reprinted in Bloom (above); from Shakespeare's Pattern of Excelling Nature, ed. Jay L. Halio and David Bevington (Newark: University of Delaware Press, 1978), 121 (n. 7).

[27] Northrop Frye, in *Fools of Time: Studies in Shakespearean Tragedy* (Toronto: University of Toronto Press, 1967), comments that her "supreme happiness as a mother consists not so much in giving her son life as in exposing him to death." (49) On Volumnia's dissembling, see also Stanley D. McKensie, "'Unshout the noise that banish'd Martius': Structural Paradox and Dissembling in *Coriolanus*," Shakespeare Studies 18 (1986):189–205.

[28] Christina Luckyj, "Volumnia's Silence," *Studies in English Literature* 31 (1991):337. This critic, although aware that she is writing against the prevailing view, remains sympathetic to Volumnia and offers a valuable discussion of stage performances. See also Harriet Hawkins, *The Devil's Party: Critical Counter-Interpretations of Shakespearian Drama* (Oxford: Clarendon Press, 1985), 145.

exultantly bourgeois matriarch seen at her most typical when computing the number of her son's battle wounds as if they were cricket runs."[29] It is enlightening to imagine the reaction of late-nineteenth-century critics who appropriated Volumnia as the noblest of Shakespeare's heroines to these representations of her as a comic and bourgeois mother.

Similarly, the nineteenth-century critic who described Virgilia as an "irritating daughter-in-law" would be surprised to learn that she is now most frequently perceived as the "gracious silence" whose gentle and obedient temperament constitutes an implicit critique of her fierce and unnatural mother-in-law. Is it possible that post-Victorian stereotypes of female behavior coincide more than we recognize with those of the Elizabethan handbooks? For some critics the appropriately female behavior of the chaste, obedient, and, above all, silent Virgilia appears to redeem her from any hint of complicity in the death of Coriolanus. Still, she walks first in the procession to beg Coriolanus to have mercy on Rome and listens to her mother-in-law appeal to the love of Coriolanus for her and her son. When Volumnia says that he will be treading on her womb if he assaults his country, Virgilia echoes her: "Ay, and mine, / That brought you forth this boy to keep your name / Living to time." (V.iii.127–28) But Virgilia is forgiven.

What is especially troubling in many of these recent formulations is the Freudian determinism underlying the assumption that Volumnia can be held responsible for the violent catastrophe that overtakes her son. Over and over again, critics have maintained that it is she who shaped him into a figure who would be slaughtered by the Volscians. Late-twentieth-century defenses of Volumnia do not so much attempt to vindicate her as argue that she is merely the mouthpiece or conduit of Roman patriarchal values.[30] When she delivers her splendid plea for mercy, supported by the presence of the wife and son of Coriolanus, she is asking him to place love of country and family over his personal code of honor and his pride in being "absolute." Her success in moving her son, however, is also held against her. Shakespeare is silent concerning whether Volumnia realizes that she is sending Coriolanus to his death, but late-twentieth-century critics have not been. Northrop Frye calls Volumnia a "white goddess ... whom death it is to love."[31] Volumnia may—or may not—be Robert Graves' white goddess, but she figures as a Dark Lady in late-twentieth-century literary criticism.

[29]Irving Wardle, *Times*, April 12, 1972. Cited in Luckyj, 332.

[30]See, for example, Madelon Sprengnether, "Annihilating Intimacy in *Coriolanus*," in *Women in the Middle Ages and the Renaissance*, ed. Mary Beth Rose (Syracuse: Syracuse University Press, 1986), 106–07.

[31]Frye, 49.

In *Titus Andronicus* and *Antony and Cleopatra*, a patriarchal order is established at the conclusion of each play. In the case of *Titus Andronicus*, Tamora is vilified and denied honorable burial for challenging the patriarchal system. Cleopatra, although hardly relegated to the status of a villainess, succeeds in subverting male hierarchy but remains unsatisfactory as a heroine. Given the flaws in her character, admiring nineteenth-century tributes to her as the quintessential woman are unsettling.[32] Her death ennobles her, but both she and Octavius see her achievement of heroic stature as possible only because she has overcome her gender. In *Coriolanus*, Shakespeare inverts gender expectations by portraying a female figure as the preeminent spokesman for the patriarchal state: Volumnia's private feelings are eclipsed by her civic responsibility. Her son, faced with the dilemma of choosing between affection for family and public honor (his word to the Volscians), chooses the affective bonds even at the price of his life.

Like Tamora and Cleopatra, Shakespeare's Volumnia resists domestication. She may be constructed as a noble patriot, as she was by nineteenth-century critics, or reconstructed as a monstrous inversion of the feminine. In *Coriolanus*, Shakespeare destabilizes gender expectations, calling into question stereotypes frequently voiced in twentieth-century discourse on patriarchy. Aufidius, reflecting upon the character of Coriolanus, says, "So our virtues / lie in th'interpretation of the time." (IV.vii.49-50) His statement holds equally true for the powerful Volumnia, a figure whose nobility, depending upon "th'interpretation of the time," earned her a place in catalogues of female worthies.

---

[32]*Variorum, Antony and Cleopatra*, 687.

SEVEN

Forming the Commonwealth: Including, Excluding, and Criminalizing Women in Heywood's *Edward IV* and Shakespeare's *Henry IV*

Jean E. Howard

Doll Common: "Have yet some care of me, o' your republic."

King Henry V: "We would have all such offenders so cut off."

In *The Sexual Contract* Carol Pateman argues that in the seventeenth century, one conjunction of political theory with patriarchy—political absolutism and classical patriarchalism based on father right—comes to be replaced by another conjunction—social contract theory and modern or fraternal patriarchy based on the brotherhood of man and the exclusion of woman from full rights as civil subjects.[1] In other words, when Locke displaced Filmer, patriarchy did not disappear from political thought; it took a new form. Of course, when a language of fraternity replaced a language of hierarchy, social stratification did not disappear either; it also took new forms. Just as women were not full participants in the social contract, neither were some men. What Patemen's work forcefully emphasizes, however, is that patriarchy and the state were interimplicated with one another, though in varying ways, throughout the seventeenth century, just as they are today.

[1]Carole Pateman, *The Sexual Contract* (Stanford: Stanford University Press, 1988). See in particular chap. 4, "Genesis, Fathers, and the Political Liberty of Sons," 77–116. I am indebted to Bill Deresiewicz for an extremely helpful reading of an earlier version of this essay and for the constructive criticism I received when I presented portions of it at the Department of English at the University of California at Riverside and at the University of Glasgow during the European Renaissance Conference held in summer of 1990.

This essay discusses the role of the English history play in forging and reforging the links between polis and patriarchy in the early modern period. This dramatic genre emerged in the late sixteenth century as part of an ensemble of social developments, including the emergence of the public theater itself, that involved changes in the relationship of woman to man, commoner to aristocrat, subject to monarch and state. As Perry Anderson has demonstrated, Tudor-Stuart absolutism was a relatively short-lived and contradictory phenomenon. Having neither a standing army nor a fully developed apparatus for civil administration, and having quickly squandered most of the revenues obtained from the sale of church properties, Tudor and Stuart monarchs lacked many of the resources that would have given purchase to their claims of absolute power.[2] Incredibly, not until the suppression of the Rising of the Earls in the North in 1569 could Elizabeth feel her control over the great feudal families had to any extent been established and a nation forged out of what had been the parcellized authority of the feudal dispensation. Yet at the same time the monarch was attempting to consolidate power in her hands without undermining the basic hierarchical ordering of society, other social developments were inevitably leading to the dispersion of that power and challenging that hierarchy. Most obvious among these developments were the commercialization of culture and the development of mercantile and agrarian capitalism, a process only imperfectly understood by either Elizabeth or James, but producing an expanding wage labor force and a venture capitalist faction among the traditional aristocracy as well as among "the middling sort."[3]At the same time, realignments in the gender system were occurring, partly as a result of changes in the ideology and practice of marriage among certain groups and partly again because of urbanization and commercialization, both of which put some women in places (public theaters, shops in the Exchange, coaches) where they had not been before and where they engaged in activities which troubled older ideologies of gender.[4]

---

[2]Perry Anderson, *Lineages of the Absolutist State* (London: Verso, 1979), 113–42.

[3]Ibid., 39–42.

[4]The old question about whether women had a Renaissance, that is, whether their economic and legal and cultural status improved in the early modern period, has not and probably cannot be answered in a monolithic way, so different were the circumstances of women in varying religious, class, and geographical positions. That there *were* widespread changes in the gender system during this time does, however, seem indisputable as England became a Protestant, protocapitalist nation with London as its rapidly growing commercial and cultural center. The consequences of these changes for specific categories of women are partly what cultural critics and historians are now attempting to understand. In this paper I will examine two history plays that place several women in the entrepreneurial world of urban

What cultural work the history play did in managing these social changes in late Elizabethan and early Jacobean society is still in many ways an open question. Two Marxist critics, Walter Cohen and Graham Holderness, while producing differing overviews of the genre, both focus on its management of changing class relations.[5] Neither critic pays much attention to gender or to the possibility that renegotiations of social relations between and within classes might also involve a renegotiation of gender relations, or that the figure of woman might be the locus of very particular anxieties about the implications of forging a nation amidst the unstable social conditions of late Elizabethan rule. By contrast, Phyllis Rackin examines the place of "woman" in the history play, particularly the strategies of demonization and marginalization by which women's threats to patriarchal power were managed and contained, though never entirely successfully.[6]

Building on Rackin's work, I here focus on the way several histories use the figure of the whore and the discourse of prostitution to handle cultural anxieties about the leveling implications of social change attendant on the emergence of a "nation" from a factionalized feudal state. I argue that it was not only class privilege, but also male privilege and gender hierarchy, which were at stake in these changes; and that criminalization was one strategy by which female offenders were "cut off" or, through regimes of repentance and punishment, refashioned as reformed and resubordinated subjects.

One of the questions posed by the history plays is: to whom will the commonwealth belong and who will belong to the commonwealth? That is, who will the political body of the state include and on what terms? At the most obvious level, in the Shakespearean history play this concern translates into the question of which family will rule England: the house of Lancaster or of York? But the concern takes other forms as well. What of

---

London. For two analyses of the volatile place of women in this urban milieu see my "Scripts and/versus Playhouses: Ideological Production and the Renaissance Public Stage," *Renaissance Drama* n.s. XX (1989):31–49 and Karen Newman's "City Talk: Women and Consumption in Jonson's *Epicoene*," *ELH* 56 (Fall 1989):503–18.

[5]Cohen, *Drama of a Nation: Public Theater in Renaissance England and Spain* (Ithaca: Cornell University Press, 1985), 218–54, stresses the degree to which the genre reflects an aristocratic hegemony, but also reveals the aristocracy's political adaptation to the centralization of authority in the hands of a strengthened monarchy. Holderness, *Shakespeare's History* (New York: St. Martin's Press, 1985), 40–144, focuses on the implicit bourgeois aspects of Shakespeare's second tetralogy, in particular what he sees as its critique of a feudal culture represented at the moment of its dissolution.

[6] See Phyllis Rackin, *Stages of History: Shakespeare's English Chronicles* (Ithaca: Cornell University Press, 1990), esp. chap. 4, "Patriarchal History and Female Subversion," 146–200.

the commons? What role will they—Jack Cade or Michael Williams—play in the commonwealth? What of France? Is it English by virtue of Edward's conquest or an effeminate and demonized other? And what of Scotland, Wales, and Ireland? Are they in or out and on what terms? And what of women? Mostly erased from the official historical record of the nation, will the history *play* let them in and on what terms? To begin to see how particular history plays address these issues, I am here going to look at William Shakespeare's *Henry IV*, especially at Part II, and at both parts of Thomas Heywood's *Edward IV*. While quite different in what one might call their class politics, these plays uniformly embody anxiety about the leveling consequences of social change, and find common patriarchal ground by in part locating that anxiety in the figure of woman.

From the first act, Heywood's *Edward IV* makes urgent the question of who will be empowered within the commonwealth. London, in the king's absence, is being besieged by a group of commoners, led by the bastard Falconbridge. The play raises the specter of an enraged populace claiming a stake in the wealth and property of England and making them common. Fear of the lower classes seizing the property of their "betters" haunts many sixteenth-century texts. In *The Boke Named the Governour*, Sir Thomas Elyot argues that the use of terms such as *commonweal* and *commonwealth* must be handled very carefully lest they encourage an attack on private property and aristocratic privilege. In the first chapter of his book Elyot distinguishes between a public weal which he defines as "a body living, compacte or made of sondry astates and degrees of men, whiche is disposed by the order of equite and governed by the rule and moderation of reason"[7] and the dangerous notion of a common weal where "every thinge shulde be to all men in commune, without discrepance of any astate or condition."[8] Men who desire such a state "be thereto moved more by sensualite than by any good reason or inclination to humanite,"[9] for "where all thynge is commune there lacketh ordre, and where ordre lacketh there all thynge is odiouse and uncomly."[10] In short, he tries to dispel the absurdity of thinking the common good could be obtained other than by the maintenance of order and degree and private property.

Edward IV shares some ground with Elyot's ideological position. The motley crew marching on London wants to seize the property of the merchants within the walls, and these commoners are unequivocally repre-

[7]Sir Thomas Elyot, *The Boke Named the Governour*, 2 vols., ed. Henry Herbert Stephen Croft (London, 1883; rpt. New York: Burt Franklin, 1967), I:1.

[8]Ibid., 2.

[9]Ibid.

[10]Ibid., 7.

sented as motivated by "sensuality" more than by "reason or inclination to humanity." As he thinks of plundering the shops of Cheapside, the rebel Ned Spicing cries:

> there are the mercers' shops
> Where we will measure velvet by the pikes,
> And silkes and satins by the street's whole bredth:
> We'le take the tankards from the conduit-cocks
> To fill with ipocras and drinke carouse,
> Where chains of gold and plate shall be as plenty
> As wooden dishes in the wild of Kent.[11]

(p. 10)

Also at stake are women. All the rebels are tantalized by the report of the beautiful Jane Shore within the city walls, and Falconbridge vows to sleep with her, in Shore's own house, when those walls have been breached. From the first time she is mentioned, Jane is thus constructed as a spectacle, something to be observed, and then as a prize of war, something to be seized and enjoyed along with other middle-class goods. When the rebels have been repulsed by the sturdy burghers of London, Shore explains to his wife that he fought so desperately

> First to maintain King Edward's royalty;
> Next, to defend the city's liberty;
> But chiefly Jane, to keep thee from the toil
> Of him that to my face did vowe thy spoil.
> Had he prevaild, where then had been our lives?
> Dishonourd our daughters, ravished our fair wives;
> Possessed our goods, and set our servants free;
> Yet all this nothing to the loss of thee.

(pp. 23–24)

Property, degree, and a man's sex right in his wife would all have been undone had the commons succeeded in making free with middle-class possessions. This does not happen. The threat is repulsed early in the first part of this two-part play, and a gruesomely sentimental and patriotic commoner, Hobs the Tanner, is introduced into the dramatic world to embody the qualities the lower orders *should* possess: cheerfulness, industry, deference. The less docile commoners, those who would overturn

---

[11] All quotations from *The First and Second Parts of King Edward the Fourth* are taken from *The Dramatic Works of Thomas Heywood*. 6 vols. (1874; rpt. London: Russell and Russell, 1964), I: 1–187.

degree and make women and property "common," are defeated and their leaders killed.

Crucially, however, though the criminalized lower classes are repulsed and punished, Jane Shore does not escape defilement, and certain other threats to middle-class economic well-being also linger on. For the rest of the text, however, the threats to the sturdy burghers of London come from above, not below. Importantly, characters in the play several times mention that King Edward can grant monopolies and patents that would concentrate in the hands of one subject wealth which should be spread among many. But he is not shown doing so. Instead, Edward seizes Shore's wife, thus acting out a monarchical raid on middle-class property that makes the woman herself "common." Ironically, Jane attracts Edward's attention when serving as hostess at a banquet the Lord Mayor puts on for the King. After this first encounter, the king repeatedly comes to her husband's goldsmith shop, where Jane waits on trade, to induce her to become his concubine. While the play implicitly indicts the king for lacking the will to control his sexual passion (his marriage is also presented as a case of uncontrolled and ill-advised uxoriousness that demeans the king by uniting him with a woman far beneath him in rank), this indictment is obliquely lodged. In the play's second part, Edward goes off to France to fight for England, and all the attention and blame for the adulterous liaison of king and middle-class woman come to rest on Jane. She is made to suffer public humiliation and utter degradation as a result of Edward's intrusive wooing. The figure of Jane Shore thus becomes a highly overdetermined representation through which certain struggles for power within and over the commonwealth are acted out and given imaginary resolution.

Edward IV is a strikingly middle-class text: on the one hand the fantasized rape of Jane by commoners gives voice to middle-class (and aristocratic) fears of the rapacious license of the many-headed monster, the people, who would make free with the property of the privileged; on the other hand, the prerogatives of monarchy are also feared, and they are expressed through Edward's aggressive wooing and appropriation of Shore's wife. The play draws back, however, from the implication that middle-class and monarchical interests are irrevocably at odds by recasting Edward's seizure of Shore's property as Jane's betrayal of her husband's honor. Through this maneuver, the play not only disguises aspects of interclass struggle, it also voices the fear that the middle class man's empowerment within the commonwealth is threatened by his wife's sexuality and autonomy. While this play idealizes, in the union of Shore and his wife, something like what historians have called "companionate marriage," it also makes quite clear that husbands, to *be* husbands, had to have sole proprietary rights in their wives' sexuality.[12] Once Jane becomes Edward's concubine, Shore's very identity, both as husband *and* as citizen, is at risk.

It is, of course, a commonplace that the adulterous wife forfeits any legitimate social place by her actions. Coming upon Jane after she has become Edward's mistress, Shore exclaims:

> Ah Jane, whats he dare say he is thy husband?
> Thou wast a wife, but now thou art not so;
> Thou wast a maid, a maid when thou wast wife;
> Thou wast a wife, even when thou wast a maide;
> So good, so modest, and so chaste thou wast!
> But now thou art divorct whiles yet he lives,
> That was thy husband, while thou wast his wife.
> Thy wifehood staind, by thy dishonour'd life.
> For now thou art nor widow, maide, nor wife.

(p. 84)

Remarkable here is not only the erasure of Jane's legitimate identity, but the suggestion that Shore, too, forfeits his. Once Shore is no longer a husband, the logic of the narrative suggests he is hardly a citizen in the commonwealth, either. After Jane's infidelity, Shore takes ship for foreign shores, becomes a wanderer on the face of the earth, and masks his identity with disguises. He forfeits his name, abode, and occupation. In short, once Shore's chief piece of property, his wife, has been seized and made "common," the nightmare of social indifferentiation descends upon him. He is no one and has no distinctive social place. Ironically, the king is the source of this chaos, and not Ned Spicing or Falconbridge, but it is Jane who bears the blame and must serve as agent of redemption.

The play offers an imaginary resolution to the dilemmas it poses by suggesting that the reformation of women will cure the commonwealth of the ills which beset it. It criminalizes the sexually attractive wife and substitutes for her a woman stripped of dangerous sexuality and autonomy. Conveniently, Jane serves both purposes. Accepting the blame for her "fall," she becomes more saintly, and less sexual, through suffering. Selflessly doing good for others, always trying to help her distressed husband from afar, Jane ultimately undergoes the public punishment of a common whore. As an officer of the King tells her:

---

[12]For a discussion of "companionate marriage" see Lawrence Stone's *Family, Sex, and Marriage in England 1500–1700,* abridged ed. (New York: Harper and Row, 1979). See esp. chap. 8, "The Companionate Marriage," 217–53.

> You must be stript out of your rich attire,
> And in a white sheet go from Temple-barre
> Until you come to Algate, bare footed,
> Your haire about your eares, and in your hand
> A burning taper.

(p. 161)

After this ritual punishment, no one is to give her shelter or food; friends who try to help her are put in danger of whipping and death. Of course, Jane's spiritual virtue is represented as increasing as her physical body dwindles. Jane's beauty and social graces had once made her a magnet for male desire. Yet the play disavows man's responsibility for controlling that desire and blames its object, woman. And this criminalized figure is morally rehabilitated only when she becomes, in effect, a disembodied spirit: an exemplification of total self-abnegation. As such, Jane ceases to be a sexual temptation to other men.

At that point Shore goes to the new king, Richard, reveals his true identity, and claims the right, as Jane's husband, to give her aid. Richard agrees he can if he will again take Jane as his spouse. Shore is spared the humiliation, however, of actually having to cohabit with "a fallen woman" because both he and Jane die of joy and grief when reunited. In this remarkable fantasy resolution, the world is righted when Jane is criminalized, desexualized, and then resubmitted to the authority of her husband. At that point Shore again claims his name and social position, and the threat of all things being held "in common"—the threat displaced onto the figure of the wife turned whore—disappears. Importantly, the work's vision of social order seems to depend as much on desexualizing and resubordinating the middle-class woman as on criminalizing a politicized commons and replacing them with an idealized, deferential populace in the figure of Hobs the Tanner. Patriarchy and polity, gender and class relations, are refashioned together.

In *Henry IV, Part II* we have a different, but nonetheless unmistakably anxious, negotiation of the threat that degree may be endangered in whatever form of polity is emerging from civil strife. Unlike *Edward IV*, however, the Henry plays focus the anxiety about social leveling in the first instance upon the figure of the prince himself. Hal threatens to betray his patriarchal lineage by making the lawless Falstaff his parent and Ned Poins his brother. Falstaff even accuses Poins of giving out that Hal will marry Poins' sister. Shrinking from the court and longing for small beer, the prince for much of the play seems to be out of love with his greatness. The fear of social indifferentiation hangs heavy over the play.[13] In the

---

[13]For an illuminating discussion of this threat and its exorcism see Laurie E. Osborne's "Crisis of Degree in Shakespeare's *Henriad*," *SEL* 25 (1985):337–59.

countryside, Justice Shallow's servant, Davy, overmasters his master; in the city, Falstaff flouts the authority of the Chief Justice and Hal assumes the role of a serving man in an Eastcheap tavern. As has been widely noted, imagery of disease permeates the play, bonding high and low in a gruesome fraternity of illness. The ending of the play can be read as a kind of violent exorcism of this specter of indifferentiation. Hal embraces first his own father and then the Chief Justice, casting off his false father, Falstaff; similarly, the prince casts aside his tavern brothers to embrace his blood brothers in a fellowship founded on their assumed difference from both the English "lower orders" and the French "others." *Henry V* more subtly resecures the same ground, reestablishing Hal's difference from the common man, while mobilizing a rhetoric of fraternity to bond the English, high and low, against the French—though after Agincourt Hal's common brothers are returned, in the roll of the dead, to their nameless, undifferentiated state, while the King uses Fluellen to free himself from the status contamination that would result should he answer directly the challenge of Michael Williams, a commoner.[14] As the final signature of this resecuring of degree, Hal makes a proper dynastic marriage, in one gesture making both woman and France his property and his subordinates.

What I want to linger over, however, is the role of the tavern and the women of the tavern in representing and embodying the threat to a properly, hierarchically ordered commonweal. In part, of course, the tavern in *Henry IV, Part II* comes to embody the threat of female sexuality, free of the control of either father or husband, much more than in *Henry IV, Part I*. A new character, the whore Doll Tearsheet, is introduced into the Eastcheap world. It is tempting, of course, to read the introduction of the prostitute simply as a symbol of how completely all things have been made common in a world where kingly difference is at risk and men made alarmingly "the same." The prostitute challenges degree by recognizing no difference between man and man; Doll Tearsheet also bonds disparate men in disease. As Falstaff says to her: "We catch of you, Doll, we catch of you." (II.iv.45–46)[15] While I want neither to sentimentalize prostitution as "outside" patriarchy, nor to present it as a simple demystification of the economic dimensions of dominant patriarchal gender relations, nonetheless, the prostitute's sexuality is not the exclusive enclosure of any one man, and she uses men's sexual desire for her profit. When

---

[14]Rackin, *Stages of History,* esp. 225–33.

[15]All quotations from Shakespeare's Henriad are taken from *The Riverside Shakespeare,* ed. G. Blakemore Evans, et al. (Boston: Houghton Mifflin Company, 1974).

Doll is carted off at play's end, what is partly being acted out is the violent reimposition of patriarchal control over female sexuality.

In another play of the period, Ben Jonson's *The Alchemist*, men's attempts to circumscribe the sexual behavior of the common whore are more comically rendered in regard to another Doll, Dol Common. In that play, of course, the band of rogues depends in part on the availability of Dol's sexual wares to fleece gulls of their money. Yet, in the first act of the play, when Face praises Dol for reminding him and Subtle of the dangers of the law and the need for cooperation among themselves, he ends by exclaiming, "For which at supper thou shalt sit in triumph, / And not be styled Dol Common, but Dol Proper, / Dol Singular: the longest cut at night / Shall draw thee for his Dol Particular." (I.i.176–79)[16] If only for one night, each man would turn Dol into a *particular* property, interrupt her leveling promiscuity, make her belong to *one* of them.

In *Henry IV, Part II*, it is the state which intervenes at play's end to exert control over the whore's sexuality. But Doll Tearsheet is not the only figure of importance to a feminist analysis of this text. Her addition to the Eastcheap scenes is accompanied by other shifts in the representation of the tavern world and of Mistress Quickly, and these interest me most. In *Part I*, while the tavern world is connected with lawlessness—there the law is eluded after the Gadshill robbery and there the prince participates in mocking the demands of duty and of his father—no pronounced sense of sexual licentiousness hangs over the tavern. Quickly subverts linguistic order with her carnivalesque malapropisms, but drink, not sex, is what she serves, though when Falstaff accuses her of stealing a ring from him, he also accuses her of running a bawdy house (III.iii.98–99) and being a "maid Marian" (III.iii .114) or loose woman. But especially in Act III, scene iii, Quickly is repeatedly said to be "an honest man's wife" (119), to have a husband.

In *Part II*, Quickly seems to lose her husband at the same time she acquires Doll Tearsheet as her friend. Now, as an unmarried woman, Quickly speaks of Falstaff's promise to marry her: "Thou didst swear to me upon a parcel-gilt goblet, sitting in my Dolphin chamber, at the round table by a sea-coal fire, upon Wednesday in Wheeson week, when the prince broke thy head for liking his father to a singing-man of Windsor, thou didst swear to me then, as I was washing thy wound, to marry me and make me my lady thy wife." (II.i.86–92) We have no real evidence as to whether, as the Chief Justice assumes, Falstaff has "made her (Quickly) serve your uses both in purse and in person" (II.i.115–16), but her close

[16]Ben Jonson, *The Alchemist*, ed. Alvin B. Kernan (New Haven: Yale University Press, 1974), 36.

association with Doll Tearsheet colors the audience's perception both of her and of the tavern, now not just a refuge for male criminals and for a wayward Prince, but for female criminality: prostitution and violence against a man. In the last scene Quickly and Doll are accused of having, with Pistol, beaten a man to death, perhaps an unruly male consumer of Doll's sexual wares. In short, it is now women who prey on the commonwealth, endangering its citizens and diverting its wealth from authorized purposes, and not just male highway robbers and throne snatchers. Of course, exactly how sexualized Quickly becomes is an issue made more complicated by her own uncertain control of the English tongue and the double entendres that, consciously or not, dance through her speech. To the Chief Justice she says: "take heed of him. He stabb'd me in mine own house, most beastly, in good faith. 'A cares not what mischief he does, if his weapon be out. He will foin like any devil, he will spare neither man, woman, nor child." (II.i.13–17)

It is significant that even as the tavern becomes increasingly criminalized and increasingly linked with the specific form of criminality called prostitution, it also increasingly figures as a place over which Quickly exerts economic control and through which she has some degree of economic independence. It is she, at the beginning, who calls in the law to make Falstaff pay his debts; she who has the means, if she will, to supply his needs as he sets off for war; she who has plate and painted wall hangings; she who can call for musicians and a whore to entertain her departing friend; she who can serve meat during Lent in her tavern; she who has the set of twelve cushions of which Doll takes one, according to the Beadle, to fake a pregnancy in the play's penultimate scene. The tavern world, now rendered as a sexualized scene of female entrepreneurship, becomes the locus for the play's anxiety about a seemingly anarchic lawlessness. The sexually independent woman and the economically independent woman form a threatening combination: a challenge both to gender hierarchy and to the system of social stratification distinguishing man from man. Predictably, their punishment is severe. At the end of the play Quickly and Tearsheet, unlike Falstaff, are not just banished from the king's presence; they are carted off to be imprisoned and whipped. In *Henry V*, of course, the king continues this project of cutting off "offenders" even as he attempts to construct a renewed sense of national identity and purpose among his followers. Among the old tavern crew, Bardolph and Nym die for plundering, and Pistol endures a mock castration and effeminization. The place of women in the renewed commonwealth is also precarious. While there is a space for Katherine in the dynastic marriage arranged between Hal and the French king, the tavern women fare less well. Criminalized at the end of *Henry IV, Part II*, Quickly interestingly emerges at the beginning of *Henry V* once more a wife—but now not to some unseen "good husband," but to the disreputable Pistol. Her moral stock has fallen. Moreover, at one point she tellingly laments: "we cannot lodge and board a dozen or fourteen gentlewomen that live honestly by the prick of their needles but it will be thought we keep a bawdy house straight" (II.i.32–35), a lament that raises the possibility her entrepreneurial energies are indeed now turned to the keeping of a bawdy house. While her husband is being a horse-leech abroad, from the law's perspective, she may be being one at home. It is therefore not too surprising when the last thing we hear of her in the play is that she died a whore's death—or is it Doll who dies this death? In V.i the humiliated Pistol says:

> News have I that my Doll is dead i' th' spittle
> Of a malady of France;
> And there my rendezvous is quite cut off.
> Old I do wax, and from my weary limbs
> Honor is cudgelled. Well, bawd I'll turn,
> And something lean to cutpurse of quick hand.
> To England will I steal, and there I'll steal;
> And patches will I get onto these cudgell'd scars,
> And swear I got them in the Gallia wars.
>
> (81–89)

Textual editors have a variety of ways of explaining the "curious reference to Doll Tearsheet" which, to quote the Riverside editors, "should properly be to Mistress Quickly, Pistol's wife."[17] But the conflation of the two women, whatever its source, seems to me not only curious, but suggestive. In the world of the Shakespearean history play, there seems to be no place, finally, for the entrepreneurial urban woman other than as a figure of criminality and disease, the common whore. Female economic independence, threatening to man's patriarchal authority, is recoded as sexual transgressiveness and criminalized. The confusion with Doll Tearsheet marks Quickly's disappearance from the play's world. The woman left at center stage is Katherine, who has acceded to the will of a father, learned the conqueror's language, and become a wife in a dynastic transaction.

Despite the pronounced differences between Heywood's and Shakespeare's use of the history genre, each employs the figure of the criminalized woman as part of a complex management of perceived threats to the well-ordered polity. Whether the threats posed by women are represented as economic or sexual, or both, it is clear that the resecuring of gender hierarchy is a key aspect of each play's political economy. But, of course,

---

[17] *The Riverside Shakespeare*, "Note on the Text," 972.

in managing these threats, the drama stages them, puts them in play, so that these representations of history become something more than a record of men's relationship to men on the battlefield and in the council chamber. Nervously gesturing toward a changing sixteenth-century world of commerce and urbanization, and of woman's changing place in both, the plays leave traces of the exclusions upon which their visions of a newly harmonious commonwealth are precariously constructed. Moreover, the Mistress Quicklys and the Ned Spicings of the world are not only present, though criminalized, in these theatrical scripts; they are also endowed with an expressive, carnivalizing speech and a theatrical vitality that make their transgressions a source of theatrical pleasure, problematizing any easy determination of where audience sympathies and allegiances lie.

In conclusion, it is also important to remember that sixteenth-century urban women were present at the theatrical site where these plays were first performed. These female playgoers were themselves often discursively criminalized in the polemic of antitheatricalists like Stephen Gosson who said that by their visibility in such houses of bawdry the good wives of London were putting themselves in the position of the common whore, the position of Jane Shore in the goldsmith shop or Quickly in her tavern.[18] But playwrights such as Shakespeare had to acknowledge, on the fringes of their texts, both the presence and power of these female theatergoers. We see this not only in the epilogues of "love comedies" such as *As You Like It*, but even in the epilogue to *Henry IV, Part II* as well, where the actor, begging the audience's indulgence, says that "All the gentlewomen here have forgiven me; if the gentlemen will not, then the gentlemen do not agree with the gentlewomen, which was never seen in such an assembly." (Epilogue, ll. 22–25) We cannot know how women spectators responded to such a play, but perhaps, unlike Jane Shore, they did not all internalize the rhetoric of criminalization and police themselves in accordance with patriarchal dicta. After all, women kept coming to the theater, despite Gosson. In doing so, they defied the ideologies of gender that attempted to control, enclose, or erase them. They assumed, in short, a public place in the commonwealth, and their struggles to retain and enlarge that place have a history, one we are still writing.

---

[18]For a discussion of Gosson's tract see my "Scripts and/versus Playhouses," esp. 33–36. Significantly, when Shore laments Edward's seduction of his wife, he in part blames himself for putting her on display, as women were said to be on display in the public theater: "Keep we our treasure secret, yet so fond / As yet so rich a beauty as this is / In the wide view of every gazers eye?" (Part I . 68)

A Living Room
Woodcut from Pelerin's De Perspectiva, Toul, 1504.
Reduced

EIGHT

Private and Public: The Boundaries of Women's Lives in Early Stuart England

Retha Warnicke

In the seventeenth century, the Countess of Bridgewater wrote that when a husband was

> fickle and various, not careing much to be with his wife at home, then thus may the wife make her owne happinesse, for then she may give her selfe up in prayer ... and thus, in his absence, she is as much God's as a virgine.[1]

Taking advantage of the opportunity that spiritual devotions offered for solitude had long been a tradition of early-modern English people, for ample evidence indicates that they did value time by themselves. In the account of John Foxe's life, which was written by his son and added posthumously to the *Book of Martyrs*, it was noted, for example, that while Foxe was a fellow at Magdalen College, Oxford, he had taken numerous solitary walks.[2] Despite these and other examples, modern historians have continued to believe and to claim that early-modern people ignored the distinctions between private and public and blended them together in ways that are incomprehensible.[3]

---

[1]Sara H. Mendelson, "Stuart Women's Diaries and Occasional Memoirs," in *Women in English Society*, ed. Mary Prior (New York: Methuen, 1985), 194; see also a discussion of this in Betty Travitsky's forthcoming article in *American Notes and Queries*, a special edition edited by Anne Lake Prescott.

[2] John Foxe, "The Life of Mr. John Fox," *Acts and monuments of matters special and memorable happening in the church* (London: Company of Stationers, 1684), n.p.; John Foxe, *The Acts and Monuments of John Foxe*, ed. George Townsend (8 vols., New York: A.M.S. Press, 1965 repr.), 3–6.

[3]Susan Amussen, *An Ordered Society: Gender and Class in Early Modern England* (Oxford: Basil Blackwell, 1988), 2, for one of many examples.

Since the contemporaries of Bridgewater and Foxe used the words public and private frequently, it is unlikely that they had a blurred understanding of these two concepts.[4] The evidence of prying individuals reporting their neighbors for sexual irregularities or disorderly conduct seems to be largely responsible for fueling modern speculations that no real value was attached to individual or family privacy.[5] Even though it is true that ministers thundered from pulpits against spouses who, like "brute beasts," used the marriage bed for lustful behavior,[6] in practice, as Martin Ingram has pointed out, the church courts, which were relatively efficient during this period, made little effort to regulate marital sexual relations. The activities of the neighborhood spies, who were actually the equivalent of modern private detectives, did not, he also confirmed, "represent normal, spontaneous neighbourly behavior."[7]

Sharp contrasts do, nevertheless, exist between the kinds of acts that resulted in arrest and trial then and now: minor sexual offenders and alleged disorderly wives, called shrews, no longer loom large in court rooms. Changes in the way governments support family integrity mean that local authorities are much more likely to thwart patriarchalism by arresting husbands for beating their wives or parents for abusing their children. Furthermore, modern medical and technological discoveries have neutralized the efforts of the religious establishment to impose or enforce the view that God punished sexual offenders by, as Amelia Lanyer warned her readers, raining "fire and brimstone" on their communities.[8] Usually, only illicit sexual acts committed in public places or for financial gain are now subject to state regulation. Despite the differences in the nature of the cases, it is unclear whether generally family life was any more infringed upon in that period than now. Ingram and others have reminded scholars that advanced technology has given governments the power to intrude into households in a way that those English people would have considered "grossly tyrannical."[9]

---

[4]See Peter Milward, *Religious Controversies of the Jacobean Age: A Survey of Printed Sources* (Lincoln: University of Nebraska Press, 1978), for titles of books that utilized the words public and private.

[5]Amussen, *An Ordered Society,* 2.

[6]William Gouge, *Of domesticall duties: eight treatises* (London: J. Haviland f. W. Bladen, 1622), 197, 416.

[7]Martin Ingram, *Church Courts, Sex and Marriage in England, 1570–1640* (Cambridge: Cambridge University Press, 1987), 7–10, 30–31, 239, 245, 365.

[8]Amelia Lanyer, *Salve deus Rex Judorum* (London: V. Simmes f. R. Bonian, 1611), sig. A3; W. C., *Londons lamentation for her sinnes: a prayer for private families, for the time of this fearefull infection* (London: G. Fagerbeard, 1625).

[9]Ingram, *Church Courts,* 7.

Another social custom that seems to have given rise to the notion that the public intruded into private affairs was the ritual surrounding the dying. Since the rites of passage were controlled by the established monopoly church, parish clergy participated in every step of the pilgrimage of life from birth to marriage to death. Christenings, confirmations, and weddings were expected to take place at Church in a public setting, but the ritual surrounding death, the last rite of passage, usually began at home, rather than in hospitals or in nursing homes as it does now with medical personnel monitoring the dying process.[10]

Since the custom was for the dying to have the support of witnesses, including ministers, kindred, and neighbors, who could testify to how well they had responded to Satan's last temptation and to how well they had prepared for death in the spirit of the *ars moriendi*, the community did penetrate into the private bedchamber, much as guests might enter the modern home.[11] These witnesses were expected and welcomed, and people with diseases such as smallpox who could not have their friends and family present at their deathbed, felt greatly deprived.[12] The community did not otherwise normally intrude into privy chambers, except in the crudely built or very small structures of the lower classes whose poverty prevented them from building the withdrawing chambers present in more expensive homes.[13]

Part of the scholarly confusion about these concepts may well have arisen from the various meanings the words can have. A review of these meanings, which in great part still prevail, although with different emphases, is important to an understanding of early-modern family and community life. Private and public deal with the following issues: 1) relationships, 2) business or trade, 3) spatial dimensions, and 4) secret matters. The family, a term that was used synonymously with household in this period, had a mean size of 4.7 members, as Peter Laslett has determined, and included the nuclear family plus servants.[14] Households

---

[10]Gouge, *Of Domesticall*, 196, 523; Robert Sherrard, *The countryman with his houshold: Being familiar conference, concerning faith and good workes* (London: E. Griffith f. J. Man, 1620), 174.

[11]N. L. Beaty, *The Craft of Dying: A Study in the Literary Tradition of the Ars Moriendi in England* (New Haven: Yale University Press, 1970); Bettie A. Doebler and Retha M. Warnicke, "Magdalen Herbert Danvers and Donne's Vision of Comfort," *George Herbert Journal* 10 (1986–87):5–22.

[12]Stephen Geree, *The ornament of women. Or, a description of the true excellency of women. A sermon at the funerall of Elizabeth Machell* (London: L. Fawne and S. Gellibrand, 1639), 87.

[13]David Flaherty, *Privacy in Colonial New England* (Charlottesville: University of Virginia, 1967), 15, 34.

[14]Peter Lastlett, "Mean Household Size in England since the Sixteenth Century," in *Household and Family in Past Time*, ed. P. Laslett and R. Wall (Cambridge: Cambridge University Press, 1972), 125–59.

varied in size among the social orders, some of the poorest had no servants at all while a few of the wealthiest having one hundred or more; but all, regardless of the numbers, including even the king's court, were viewed as a private family.[15] Then, as now, the domestic unit was far from static: children grew up; parents died; servants left to be married.

Today's greatest difference in terms of family membership is that a live-in servant is now a rare household figure. In contrast, whenever early-modern authors of household books defined family relationships, which they always referred to as "private," they inevitably included a discussion of masters and servants. In 1600, for example, William Vaughan identified three private family relationships: they were the "communion and fellowship of life" between husbands and wives, parents and children, and between masters or mistresses and servants.[16]

Except for a small percentage of elite families, cousins, aunts, uncles, grandparents, and in-laws did not live in the household, and the question of whether strong kinship relations with them even existed beyond the domestic unit has been debated extensively. Scholars agree that among elite families, especially those in which members of the older generation experienced great longevity, remote kinship relationships were kept up. In some villages, as Keith Wrightson and others have argued, community relations may have prevailed over distant private kinship ties, although scholars, such as David Cressy, have recently been challenging this view with some success.[17]

People differentiated sharply between public business that was accomplished on behalf of the community, and private economic enterprise that was undertaken, often in the household, for family gain. In 1630, for example, Richard Brathwait described the vocation of a gentlemen as: "Publike, when employed in affaires or state, either at home or abroad.... Private, when in domesticke businesse he is detained," as in

[15]Marjorie McIntosh, "Servants and the Household Unit in an Elizabethan English Community," *Journal of Family History*, 9 (1984):3–23; for the court, see Robert Horne, *The christian governour, in the commonwealth and private families* (London: T.S. f. F. Burton, 1614), sig. G3. Because the court was the private household of the monarch, his consort and her female attendants could participate in masques.

[16]William Vaughan, *The golden-grove, moralized in three bookes: necessary for all such, as would know how to governe themselves, their houses, or their countrey* (London: S. Strafford, 1600), sig. M7–8.

[17]Keith Wrightson, "Kinship in an English Village: Terling, Essex 1500–1700," in *Land, Kinship and Life-Cycle*, ed. R. M. Smith (Cambridge: Cambridge University Press, 1984), 313–33; David Cressy, "Kinship and Kin Interaction in Early Modern England," *Past and Present*, 113 (1986):38–69; Ralph Houlbrook, *The English Family 1450–1700* (New York: Longman, Inc., 1984), 43–44, 52, 58.

the ordering of his household.[18] This difference had been highlighted even during the early sixteenth century. Erasmus included the following dialogue in his colloquy, "The Poetic Feast." The first speaker inquired:

"Are you a private citizen or do you hold public office?" And the second responded:

I have a public office. Bigger ones were available, but I chose one that would have sufficient dignity to assure respect and be the least troublesome … and what's more, I have means of assisting my friends occasionally.[19]

The holding of public office brought prestige to individuals and was considered praiseworthy. James Cleland, expressed his contemporaries' attitude in 1607 with the words, "a private person is bound to honour those who are publike and in office."[20]

These distinctions still obtain but in slightly different ways. In modern society, references are made to the private business sector but with the difference that most business is now conducted outside the home, for the workshop has been separated from the household. In early Stuart England, private business, which was the family business, was accomplished in the household, which functioned as a unit of production as well as consumption. Rather than performing domestic occupations, many live-in servants were actually apprentices, journeymen, or other employees retained for the family's trade or business.[21] Another variation is that publicly owned corporations now perform business that was formerly conducted in private. Joint-stock companies, primitive institutions that grew into lucrative corporations, such as the East India Company, played a negligible financial and economic role at this time. In their references to public officials, contemporaries explicitly named military, church, and civil office holders, such as magistrates, judges, mayors, soldiers, bishops, and clerics.[22]

---

[18]Richard Brathwait, *The English gentleman: containing sundry excellent rules how to accomodate himselfe in the manage of publike or private affairs* (London: J. Haviland f. R. Bostock, 1630), 136.

[19]*The Colloquies of Erasmus*, trans., C. R. Thompson (Chicago: University of Chicago Press, 1965), 193.

[20]James Cleland, … *or the institution of a young noble man* (Oxford: J. Barnes, 1607), 181; Anthony Fletcher, "Honour, Reputation, and Local Officeholding in Elizabethan and Stuart England," in *Order and Disorder in Early Modern England* (Cambridge: Cambridge University Press, 1985), 93–95.

[21]Peter Laslett, *The World We Have Lost Further Explored* (New York: Charles Scribner's Sons, 1984), 1–21.

[22]Clelland, *Young noble man*, 106; J. Ferne, *The Blazon of Gentrie* (London: J. Windet f. T. Cooke, 1536), 58–59.

The spatial definitions have changed somewhat, for, in the modern period, some public areas, such as church buildings, are overseen by community groups unassociated with the government. In contrast to the public grounds, are the lands and quarters of a private household. Despite many early-seventeenth-century claims that male heads of families operated as "kings" in their public households, scholars have maintained that they and their contemporaries actually placed no great value on privacy, assuming thereby that the space of modern households is more immune to community interference than early-modern ones.[23] Service people of all kinds, nevertheless, have the right to intrude into modern gardens to check a battery of meters, a spatial invasion that hardly existed before the twentieth century. Ralph Houlbrooke has warned against exaggerating "the power of external forces to mould the internal life of the family" in Stuart England.[24]

In discussions of private and public, scholars also seem to have been concluding that formerly no personal or solitary time existed, that everyone acted out her life in the open with witnesses remarking on all that she did or said. A characteristic of early-modern homes that may have led to these assumptions about the lack of solitariness was the way in which chambers were arranged. Even in royal palaces and aristocratic houses rooms emptied one into another; without hallways to separate them, places for sleeping and toiletry were not secreted away as they are today, but screens and draperies did provide some escape from witnesses for those intimate occasions. Private moments, moreover, do not absolutely require being physically out of sight, for people can "internalize a set of barriers."[25] The possession of moments without interruption, even if the individual merely withdraws into a corner of a room, can also be defined as solitariness. In addition, the homes of the elite had small private rooms, called closets because of their diminutive size, which were available for individuals desiring to be alone. In 1581, William Lowthe, for example, translated for publication a work of Bartholomew Battus into English with the title, *The Christian mans closet*.[26] Clearly, at least for religious devotions, some people did seek a few solitary moments.

In admonishing their readers to say prayers every morning and evening, religious authors usually gave advice similar to that of John

---

[23]Vaughan, *Golden-Grove*, sig. Q8, for example.

[24]Houlbrooke, *The English Family*, 23.

[25]Flaherty, *Privacy*, 8, 11.

[26]Bartholomew Battus, *The Christian mans closet*, ed. William Lowth (London: T. Dawson f. G. Seton, 1581).

Brinsley: "The meetest place is, where we may be most secret, and freest from distractions."[27] Lewis Bayley also told his readers:

> And thus having washed thy selfe, and adorned thy body with apparell ...: shut thy chamber-doore, and kneele downe at thy bed-side, or some other convenient place, and in reverent manner lifting up thy heart together with thy hands and eyes, as in the presence of God.... offer ... thy Prayer as a Morning Sacrifice.[28]

A variety of words were used to refer to these secret moments, some people differentiating them from private family prayers by calling them personal or "more private." Emphasizing the common availability of secret times, furthermore, ministers warned their parishioners against being too open about their religious and charitable activities, advising them to perform them privately to avoid public commendations.[29]

People must have regularly withdrawn from the company of others for moments alone, since writers frequently admonished them about their solitary behavior. Although ministers believed that secret times for prayer and meditation were essential for everyone's religious well-being, they suspected that individuals might be tempted to misuse or abuse these moments. In 1614, Robert Horne warned his readers that when they were in their "privatest" rooms such as privy chambers or bed chambers, they were "to do nothing that shall be uncomely" and to refrain from doing "privately that we should be ashamed should it be brought before the face of men." Three-quarters of a century earlier, the excessive number of John Foxe's solitary walks in the dead of night to wrestle with the question of his religious faith aroused the suspicions of the Catholic fellows at Magdalen, and, after inquiring into his beliefs, they expelled him from that college.[30]

Within this early-modern framework, women's lives were expected to be and were much more private than those of their modern counterparts. In sermons and treatises ministers warned women, whether they were puritan or conformist, to remain in the household and to go into public areas only rarely: a housewife was not a "Field-wife" or "Street-wife," and only "gossipy busy bodies" went abroad.[31] That so much

[27] John Brinsley, *The true watch, and rule of life*, 6th edition enlarged (London: E. Griffith f. S. Macham, 1614), 22, 33.

[28] Lewis Bayley, *The Practise of pietie, directing a christian how to walke* (London: f. J. Hodgets, 1613), 319–20.

[29] Horne, *Christian governour*, sig. G3, G7; W. C., *Londons lamentation*, sig. A7.

[30] Horne, *Christian governour*, sig. G8, H1; Brathwait, *Gentleman*, 236; "The Life of John Foxe," n.p.

[31] Matthew Griffith, *Bethel, or a forme for families: all may best serve in their severall places, for usefull pieces in God's building* (London: J. Bloome, 1633), 415.

attention was directed toward preventing them from straying from home probably means that this rule was not always well kept. A few foreigners even claimed that England was a paradise for women. It may have been the bustling activity of the wives and daughters of shopkeepers as well as that of tourists in London that made strangers think these customs prevailed universally.[32] Quantitative analyses are not feasible, but evidence does indicate that some Englishwomen did live by the public and private standards set out for them in sermons and treatises. It will be useful to review that evidence, which mainly describes members of the elite, propertied social orders, and see how these concepts influenced women in their pilgrimages of life from youth to old age.

In a patriarchal society, such as Stuart England, in which family life was viewed as the kingdom writ small, householders expected their wives, children, and servants to obey them as though they were kings. Disorder in the family, it was feared, would give rise to disorders in the kingdom.[33] A softening of this autocratic domestic rule did exist, men being admonished, for example, not to be abusive or to provoke their children to wrath, although daughters, it was thought, would more easily accept the governance of their future husbands if they had learned obedience in their youth. Masters were also to treat their servants with respect and to love their wives, whose private suggestions for improvement, especially in religious matters, should be heeded.[34] Depending on the personality of the family members, room for much give and take existed within this arrangement. As Linda Pollock has said: "Married life was neither perpetual friendship nor constant dissonance, but rather a fluctuating compromise in which relations of power continually presented themselves."[35]

The education of women was directed toward keeping them absorbed in the business of the private household and preventing them from becoming knowledgeable about public matters. Only a few women attended day schools outside the home and none went to the two universities or to the inns of court. Rarely did any of them learn Latin, the language of the scholar and the cleric, primarily because it was of little

---

[32]Lu Emily Pearson, *Elizabethans at Home* (Stanford: Stanford University Press, 1957), 365; Vaughan, *Golden grove*, sig. N8.

[33]William Perkins, *The works of that famous and worthie minister of Christ, in the University of Cambridge* (Cambridge: John Legat, 1603), 912.

[34]Gouge, *Of Domesticall*, 18, 264, 373; Thomas Gataker, *A mariage praier, or succinct meditations: delivered in a sermon* (London: F. Clifton and J. Bowler, 1624), 19, 21; Brathwait, *Gentlemen*, 155; Griffith, *Bethel*, 319.

[35]Linda Pollock, "'An Action Like a Strategem:' Courtships and Marriage from the Middle Ages to the Twentieth Century," *Historical Journal*, 30 (1987):497.

practical value for their employment opportunities, which centered in the household.[36] Reading material for them was supposed to be pious and elegant rather than classical and solid, and some girls who showed an interest in classical languages, as did the goddaughter of Sir Ralph Verney in 1652, were discouraged with the advice:

> Good sweet hart bee not soe covitous; beleeve me a Bible (with the Common prayer) and a good plaine cattichisme in our Mother Tongue being well read and practised is well worth all the rest and much more sutable to your sex.[37]

No young gentlewoman was, moreover, permitted to go on a Grand Tour to the continent, an expensive practice indulged in by most young gentlemen, and in Elizabeth's reign, when a proposal was made to establish an academy for her male wards, no comparable suggestions were put forth to benefit her maids of honor.[38]

The education of girls was the responsibility of their mothers or their governesses. Under the general supervision of their husbands and of the clergy, who warned them against cockering or spoiling their children, women inculcated in the younger generation the negative view of their sex that prevailed in church and society.[39] Men were advised, in fact, to choose virtuous wives so that they could bring their children up in religious education and feminine virtue, which were the passive qualities, as Sara Mendelson has pointed out, of chastity, obedience, piety, and silence; indeed, loquaciousness was considered a particular female vice. They were also to learn housewifery and needlework, since the private household was to frame their world.[40]

Warnings about the need to remain chaste abounded: "Chastity," one mother remarked, "is the beautie of the soule and the puritie of life."[41]

---

[36]Linda Pollock, "'Teach her to live under obedience:' the making of women in the upper ranks of early modern England," *Continuity and Change*, 4(1989):238–44; Retha M. Warnicke, *Women of the English Renaissance and Reformation* (Westport, Ct.: Greenwood Press, 1983), 205–09.

[37]Quoted by Douglas Bush, *English Literature in the Earlier Seventeenth Century, 1600–1660* (Oxford: Clarendon Press, 1962), 22.

[38]Ibid.; Henry Ellis, "Copy of a Plan Proposed to Queen Elizabeth by Sir Humphrey Gilbert, for Instituting a London Academy," *Archaeologia*, XXI (1827):506–20.

[39]John Dod and William Hinde, *Bathshebaes instructions to her sonne Lemuel: Containing a fruitfull exposition of Proverbs* (London: J. Beale f. R. Jackson, 1614), 4; Michelle Z. Rosaldo and Louise Lamphere, eds., "Introduction," in *Women, Culture and Society* (Stanford: Stanford University Press, 1974), 1–15.

[40]Sara H. Mendelson, *The Mental World of Stuart Women: Three Studies* (Amherst: University of Massachusetts Press, 1987), 2.

[41]M. R., *Mothers counsell* (London: J. Wright, 1630?), 1.

Women, and especially young girls in their vulnerable youth, were thought to be susceptible to all kinds of wickedness. When Elizabeth Jocelin, whose grandfather, William Chaderton, Bishop of Chester and Lincoln, had provided her with a classical education, was obsessed by a premonition that she would die in childbirth, she wrote a book of advice as a "Legacy" to her unborn child. Advising against the sin of vanity, she said: "If a daughter, I confesse thy task is harder because thou art weaker, and thy temptation to this vice greater."[42] Girls consequently had extensive supervision and less private time than adults. Juan Luis Vives, whose guide for the instruction of young women was printed as late as 1592, even warned that for the sake of their chastity young girls should never be alone or in a crowd of people but should always be monitored by sober chaperons.[43] Lady Grace Mildmay, who in 1619 wrote the first extant autobiography in English by a woman, recalled the attentiveness of her governess at her childhood home in Wiltshire in the 1560s:

> And when I was not with her she would be sure to be with me at my heels to see where and with whom I was and what I did or spake.[44]

Admitting that she was grateful to her parents for this strict education, Lady Mildmay also remembered that she and her sister had been forbidden to have close contact with their male servants, one of whom was whipped for unbecoming behavior toward them.[45] Parents were expected even to oversee their children's personal correspondence. For example, after Sir Thomas Coningsby's daughter received and read a letter in 1605, upon her father's orders she had to relinquish it to him.[46]

Despite fears that they might misuse their time, young women were encouraged to pray alone. As a child, Lettice, Viscountess Falkland, who

---

[42]Elizabeth Joceline, *The mothers legacie, to her unborne childe* (London: J. Havilan f. W. Baret, 1624), 33.

[43]Juan Luis Vives, *A very fruitfull and pleasant booke. Called the instruction of a christian woman*, trans. R. Hyrde (London: J. Danter, 1592), sig. C6, D2–3; Warnicke, *Women of the English Renaissance*, 33–35; Richard Brathwait, *The English gentlewoman, drawne out to the full body: expressing, what habiliments doe best attire her* (London: B. Alsop and T. Fawcet f. M. Spart, 1631), 49.

[44]Lady Mildmay's Journal, Central Library, Northampton, 10–11; see also Retha M. Warnicke, "Lady Mildmay's Journal: A Study in Autobiography and Meditation in Reformation England," *The Sixteenth Century Journal*, 20 (1989):55–68; for an edition of her meditations, see Linda Pollock, *With Faith and Physic: Lady Grace Mildmay, 1552–1620* (London: Collins and Brown, 1993).

[45]Lady Mildmay's Journal, 13–14.

[46]Historical Manuscripts Commission, *The Manuscripts of his Grace the Duke of Portland, preserved at Welbeck Abbey* (5 vols., London: H. M. Stationery Office, 1891–1919), II, 4.

lived at Tooley Park, near Leicester, often read a book in her closet when it was thought that she had gone to bed. The minister, John Duncon, who wrote an account of her life, also noted that she had been "constant" in her private prayers as a youth, and if visitors occupied the chamber to which she commonly retired for her devotions, "she would ask the steward for the key of some other room for that purpose, at her hour of prayer."[47]

With the center of their world in the household, these young Protestant females had their future mapped out for them in the words, "women to be married,"[48] for no other occupation was possible for them, the last of the English nunneries having been dissolved at the accession of Elizabeth. Although a certain number of women did remain single, since they were given some choice in the matter and could turn down parental candidates for their husbands, they were not permitted to live alone but had to reside in the households of their parents or married siblings. Whether children or servants of the family, unmarried females were expected to be watched closely and to be kept from frequent mingling in society. When they failed to marry, they doomed themselves to performing tasks that were described by their contemporaries as "servile," since they continued merely to work for someone else rather than to function as a mistress with authority over children and servants. The honorable future for them lay in marrying and assuming parental and spousal responsibilities.[49]

Wives, especially, were instructed to wear the home as a snail or tortoise wears his shell, for private family activities were their major concern or, as Thomas Gataker said, women were created for "domestical and houshold affaires."[50] Besides attending holy services, family business might well take wives, with their husbands' permission, into the public arena to sue for their family's estate, to purchase property, or to transact other private business. Even so, some authors were of the opinion that wives should venture abroad less often even than young girls.[51]

---

[47]*English Churchwomen of the Seventeenth Century* (Derby: Henry Mozley & Sons, 1845), 2–3; John Duncon, *Lady Lettice, Vi-Countess Falkland*, ed. M. F. Howard (London: John Murray, 1908), 3.

[48]Thomas Gataker, *A mariage praier*, 21; *The lawes resolutions of womens rights: Or the lawes provision for woemen* (London: assignes of J. More f. John Grove, 1632), 6.

[49]Francis Dillingham, *Christian oeconomy. Or houshold government* (London: J. Tapp, 1609), 4; Thomas Gataker, *A good wife Gods gift: And a wife indeed. Two mariage sermons* (London: J. Haviland f. F. Clifton, 1623), 19.

[50]Gataker, *Mariage praier*, 19, 21; Thomas Gataker, *Marriage duties briefly couched togither* (London: W. Jones f. W. Bladen, 1620), 20–21; Brathwait, *English gentleman*, 263; Gouge, *Of Domesticall*, 290.

[51]Gouge, *Of Domesticall*, 290; Vives, *A Very frutefull and pleasant boke.*

Women, whose lives were "more private" than men, were prohibited from holding public office, either civil, military, or church, although as the wife, child, or other kin of an officeholder, they might indirectly influence public action through manipulation of the male relatives.[52] When women were referred to as private people, then, the word private did not mean simply that they were confined to their households, although those areas were viewed as their special domains, but that they could not personally conduct public affairs. Even the queen consort of England, although technically a public figure, had merely a ceremonial role to play. An exception to this rule would be made only if she were appointed regent or if she were to inherit the crown.[53]

In their households, wives were given considerable authority. They had control of the religious and domestic education of their young children, who should never, it was warned, be treated with too much indulgence. They also supervised the training and work of all females, their servants as well as their offspring.[54] Husbands, who took charge of the male servants, could, but usually did not, interfere in their wives' housekeeping routine, although ultimately it was their duty to respond privately to the questions of their wives about religious matters and to see that the whole family attended household devotions and public services.[55]

It will be useful to review how some wives conducted their lives within this framework. Information about Lady Mildmay's married life can also he found in her autobiography. In 1567, when at the age of fifteen she wed Anthony Mildmay, she continued the daily religious meditations she had begun as a child under her mother's guidance. Ultimately, she bequeathed to her daughter and grandchildren more than one thousand manuscript pages along with her autobiography in which she instructed them about the desirability of relying on private religious devotions for comfort and help in dealing with the struggle of life. When she is compared to the other members of the Elizabethan and Jacobean Church of England, she must be judged extraordinarily religious. Christians regularly accounted privately for their daily sins and participated in religious

[52]Gataker, *Marriage Duties*, 21; for manipulation, see Mendelson, *Mental World*, 187.

[53]*The lawes resolutions of womens rights*, 6; Marion F. Facinger, "A Study of Medieval Queenship: Capetian France, 987–1237," *Studies in Medieval and Renaissance History*, 5 (1968):3–48.

[54]Francis Bamfort, ed., *A Royalist Notebook: The Commonplace Book of Sir John Oglander, Kt. of Nunwell* (London: Constable & Co., 1936), 250.

[55]Robert Prick, *The Doctrine of superioritie and of subjection* (London: f. E. Dawson and T. Downe, 1608), sig. K4.

devotions, but it was unusual for them to write down their meditations in such detailed fashion.[56]

Lady Mildmay's marriage was a particularly unhappy one. Her husband Anthony, the son of Sir Walter, Queen Elizabeth's Chancellor of the Exchequer, often traveled to court on business or abroad on diplomatic journeys, leaving her behind at the family estate in Northamptonshire. Consequently, her days were spent in "solitariness." This isolation was partly the result of her own decisions, for she refused invitations from women friends to attend court and to go to feasts, marriages, and plays, for fear that she would be unable to withstand worldly temptations. Authors and ministers did warn that women should be accompanied to social functions by their husbands, and Lady Mildmay contented herself with the answer that "God had placed me in this house, and if I found no comfort here, I would never seek it out of this house."[57]

During Anthony's absences, she insisted that she held no resentment toward him, but she also admitted that when he was home, he sometimes mistreated her. Having lived the life of a patient and silent wife according to the precepts of St. Paul, she confessed at his death, while she was meditating over his body, that she had

> carryed alwaye that reverent respect towards him, in regard of my good conceit which I ever had of the good partes which I knewe to be in him, that could not fynde in my harte to challenge him for the worst worde or deed whichever he offered me in all his lyfe.[58]

Lady Mildmay's life was especially isolated; others who attempted to follow the precepts set out by religious writers had less solitariness and were less homebound. One example is that of Lady Margaret Hoby, a Yorkshire resident, who between 1599 and 1605 kept the first known diary written in English by a woman. She may have begun it as part of her daily self-examination ritual, for she worried in 1599 that "the divell laboreth to hinder my profittable hearinge of the word." Earlier that same year she had characterized her headache and an upset stomach as God's "Just punishment" for her sins. The diary is mainly, however, a recitation of her daily activities and shows "no real capacity for self-knowledge or ability in self-analysis."[59]

---

[56]Warnicke, "Lady Mildmay's Journal," 63–68.

[57]Lady Mildmay's Journal, 39, 44–45.

[58]Ibid., 81.

[59]Dorothy M. Meads, ed., *Diary of Lady Margaret Hoby, 1599–1605* (London: George Routledge & Sons, 1930), 47, 64, 66.

Unlike Anthony Mildmay, who seems not to have been a particularly religious man, Lady Margaret's husband, a puritan, took care to perform the religious duties of a householder. He read the works of divines to her, prayed with her, educated her about theological issues, and maintained family prayers. In addition, she said personal prayers twice a day, read religious works with her maids, and attended church services. Her world was bound by this household routine, which was interspersed with public worship and occasional visits to friends and relatives. She also traveled to London at least three times in the company of her husband when his legal business drew him there. Her favorite public entertainment in the city was the hearing of sermons and the visiting of churches, although she attended court with her sister-in-law and bought a New Year's gift at the royal exchange. She refrained from going to fairs with her husband, however.[60]

Some women even lived alone. Modern misconceptions about the size of Stuart families notwithstanding, the mean was, as stated above, only 4.7 members. While some households were very large, others had single dwellers, and most aged widows, especially the poorest ones, must have spent many hours alone since they tended to reside alone. Very few over the age of forty remarried or resided with their adult children. Even in London where widows of craftsmen and tradesmen often remarried, 40 percent remained single.[61] In this, as in other social habits, London did not represent the provinces where the remarriage figures for women were lower.[62] Despite these numbers, the "enduring stereotype of the early-modern widow as a woman who anxiously sought a husband at any cost" prevailed.[63] This stereotype was an extension of the view that women were "biologically driven to intercourse" and the more lascivious of the sexes.[64] Affirming this worldview, ministers admonished women to spend their widowhood in solitary religious exercises and in honoring their dead husbands, who in some sense could be viewed as cuckolded if

[60]Ibid., 97, 118, 136, 139, 159, 163–167, 202, 214, 221.

[61]Lastlett, *Household*, 125–58; Laslett, *The World We Have Lost*, 5; Vivien Brodsky, "Widows in Late Elizabethan London: Remarriage, Economic Opportunity and Family Orientations," in *The World We Have Gained: Histories of Population and Social Structures: Essays Presented to Peter Laslett on his Seventieth Birthday*, ed. Lloyd Bonfield, R. M. Smith, and Keith Wrightson (Oxford: Basil Blackwell, 1986), 122–23, 130.

[62]Barbara J. Todd, "The Remarrying Widow: A Stereotype Reconsidered," in Prior, *Women in English Society*, 54–92.

[63]Linda Woodbridge, *Women and the English Renaissance: Literature and the Nature of Womankind* (Urbana: University of Illinois Press, 1984), 178.

[64]Patricia Crawford, "The Construction and Experience of Maternity in Seventeenth-Century England," in *Women as Mothers in Pre-Industrial England: Essays in Memory of Dorothy McLaren*, ed. Valerie Fildes (New York: Routledge, 1990), 6.

they remarried.[65] As late as the 1934 issue of Emily Post's *Etiquette*, in fact, elderly widows were advised about the different colors of clothing to wear for their required lifelong mourning; younger widows had to don mourning clothes for at least one full year.[66]

To the clerical advice about widowhood, women of the wealthy classes in early Stuart England had a myriad of responses, which do not seem to reflect a particular attitude toward the Church of England and its ceremonies. Many such as Anne Clifford, countess of Pembroke, who married Philip, third earl of Pembroke and Montgomery, after the death of her first husband, the earl of Dorset, and then was widowed a second time, led busy, productive private lives, overseeing their family estates or businesses. The second Englishwoman to have kept a diary that is extant, but only in her youth from 1602 to 1619, Lady Pembroke wrote of her struggles to regain control of her father's Westmorland estates that had descended to her uncle and his son. When, after the death of these relatives, she finally inherited the property, she spent the remainder of her life restoring the buildings of her ancestors, including some almshouses for poor women, and repairing places of worship. As a widow she dressed more humbly than before, stayed away from court, and even ate with the almswomen.[67] The custom of noble widows retiring from "worldly vanity and ostentation" and wearing plain apparel was practiced not only in England but also in other parts of Christendom, especially Catholic Spain.[68] At Lady Pembroke's death in 1677, her minister, Edward Rainbow, bishop of Carlisle, pointed out that some who were devoted to the Church of England had promoted the foundation of Protestant nunneries but that her example proved that "to overcome the world is more generous than to fly from it."[69]

Some women had more intriguing responses to widowhood. In 1623, Lucy, duchess of Bedford, wrote to her friend, Jane, Lady Cornwallis, about the reaction of Frances, duchess of Richmond and Lennox, to the expected death of her ailing husband Ludovic:

[65]Woodbridge, *Women and the English Renaissance*, 178.

[66]Warren Shibles, *Death: An Interdisciplinary Analysis* (Whitewater, Wis.: The Language Press, 1974), 198.

[67]V. Sackville West, *The Diary of Anne Clifford* (London: W. Heinemann, 1923), ix–xxix; Edward Rainbow, *A Sermon preached at the funeral of Anne, Countess of Pembroke, April 14, 1676* (London: f. R. Royston and H. Broom, 1677), 23, 24, 31, 41.

[68]Henry Clifford, *The Life of the Lady Jane Dormer, Duchess of Feria*, trans. E. E. Estcourt, ed. Joseph Stevenson (London: Burnes and Oates, 1887), 161.

[69]Rainbow, *A Sermon at the funeral of Lady Pembroke*, 54–55.

Her haire, in discharge of a vowe she had formerly made, she cutte off close by the rootes that afternoone, and told us of som other vowes of retirednes she had made if she should be so miserable as to outlive him, which I hope she will as punctually performe. For my part, I confesse I encouradged her to itt, which, som say, hereafter she will love me nothing the better for; but itt is the counsel I should take to myselfe in her case, and therefore I cannot spare to give it.[70]

Other examples of self-imposed retiredness can be found. When Lucius, Lady Falkland's royalist husband, died in battle in 1643, she feared that his death was a divine punishment for her sins.[71] Afterwards, according to the Reverend John Duncon, who wrote an account of her life, she led "a more strict course of life" at her home in Oxfordshire, dispensing with "vanity of apparel" and "all worldly pomp." One of her most cherished projects, which never came to fruition, was to establish a place for the retirement of widows and the education of young gentlewomen so they could have greater opportunity for worshiping God "without distraction." She, herself, sought lengthy private times for meditation. To prepare for Sunday services, she sequestered herself every Saturday and "seldom came out of her closet till towards evening." She did not always remain in her home, however, for it was noted, when she had cause to visit Oxford or London on business, her first inquiry was about attending church services there.[72]

One of the most interesting and most unusual Stuart widows was Jane Ratcliffe, a citizen of Chester, who died in 1638 on a visit to London. John Ley, prebendary of the Cathedral Church of Chester, who knew her well but who had not been given the opportunity to preach her funeral sermon, published an account of her life in 1640. He complained that the preacher who had officiated at her funeral had not given her the "discourse" she deserved and that some people were accusing him of being "a Traducer and contemner of Women-kinde." Observing that it was unusual for householders, and especially women, to die so far from their homes, Ley noted that she had been visiting her daughter in London.[73]

In her youth, he pointed out, she had liked dancing, stage plays, and other "publique vanities," but after her conversion:

---

[70]*The Private Correspondence of Jane, Lady Cornwallis, 1613–1644* (London: S. & J. Bentley, Wilson & Fley, 1842), 88–89.

[71]*English Churchwomen*, 7; Duncon, *Vi-Countess Falkland*, 44.

[72]*English Churchwomen*, 7, 12–14; Duncon, *Vi-Countess Falkland*, 57, 59.

[73]John Ley, *A Patterne of pietie: or the life a. death of Mrs. J. Ratcliffe* (London: F. Kinston f. R. Bostocke, 1640), 3–7, 10, 11.

by the immediate hand of God, who having taken away her first child (which she took much to heart) made that an occasion to make her apparently his owne child.[74]

Ley praised Ratcliffe's religious abilities, thereby ignoring the usual clerical convention of warning women against teaching others and of advising them to be instructed privately by their husbands and ministers. Praising her as a Priscilla and an Abigail, he pointed out that she performed private religious services for her servants and "secret" female friends. About her women friends he said,

they thought it some honour to themselves, that one of their owne sexe (so contemned by some both as weake and wicked) was graced by God with such an holy and excellent gift: and so in time ... it became a graduate from privat praise to a common fame of the truth.[75]

When she read the psalms, he recalled, he thought he had never heard David "with more effectuall feeling," and he had often but without success requested her to write down her "observations of the Bible." Shortly before her last trip to London, she had promised him she would turn to that project when she returned home. Unlike the vain *"Pharisaicall Puritans,"* who practice their religion publicly to win applause, she had attempted to keep her skills in scripture reading and teaching a secret. Her example predates the more daring activities of the women who participated in various radical religious sects during the civil-war period.[76]

The Protestant writers of early Stuart England, regardless of whether they were opposed to or approved of the Church of England's rituals and ceremonies, seemed to have agreed that women should have solitary moments alone for prayer, reading, and meditation. The importance to them of the religious experience, which had "contradictions" in its impact on women's lives, cannot be overstated.[77] Clerics did emphasize the inferior status of women and required them to be obedient to their fathers, masters, and husbands: "let him match with religious woman," Francis

---

[74]Ibid., 21, 24.

[75]Ibid., 27, 28, 42, 61, 62, 63; Gervase Markham, *The English Housewife*, ed. M. R. Best (Kingston, Can.: McGill-Queen's University Press, 1986), chap. 1/2; Gouge, *Of Domesticall*, 258.

[76]Ley, *Mrs. J. Ratcliffe*, 25–26, 69; for a cautionary note about how clerics viewed these radical women, see Patricia Crawford, "Historians, Women, and the Civil War Sects, 1640–1660," *Parergon*, new series, 6 (1988): 19–32.

[77]Gail Malmgreen, ed., "Introduction," *Religion in the Lives of English Women, 1760–1930* (London: Croom Helm, 1986), 7.

Dillingham said, "for religion teacheth her subjection."[78] And yet those same clerics also sought to convert women to sincere religious callings and to give them an important supervisory role in the family. Women's conversions, moreover, opened up to them a world of serious literature while at the same time affording them increased opportunities for teaching other females and for solitary moments for creative writing. Given the environment in which they functioned, it is no wonder that most of the works written and published by early-modern women were of a religious nature.[79]

That their lives were private does not mean that women never entered the public arena or never pursued family business outside the home. It did mean that they could only affect public policy in indirect ways through the manipulation of their male relatives who actually held community or royal office. Private sometimes referred to the activities of the whole family but could well refer to the solitary times an individual had for reading or writing. Private and public matters were organized somewhat differently than now but with distinctions that were just as obvious and definitive. The application to early-modern women of these concepts of public and private clearly resulted in social roles that differed greatly from those of their modern counterparts.

[78]Dillingham, *Oeconomy,* 8–9.
[79]Warnicke, *Women of the English Renaissance.*

NINE

Resurrecting the Author: Elizabeth Tanfield Cary

Donald W. Foster

The "Author" has been dead for a long time in literary studies, and in this postmodern period the canonical Author has had extra nails pounded into his coffin, to ensure that he *stays* dead. There is little nostalgia among us for those innocent times when Literature was read as a collection of great messages from great men. It is time, however, that our early woman writers be brought out of limbo and reconceived—as *authors*. The study of early women's writing requires that we find an alternative to the Oedipal model whereby the son-as-critic effaces the author-as-father in a contest for virile control of textual meaning. Roland Barthes, who first proclaimed the death of the author, follows others in viewing literary discourse as the offspring of a contest between father and son. For poststructuralists as for many of their critical predecessors, that contest is won hands down by the strong critic, the potent inheritor of the text. Barthes reduces the author to a cipher, joyfully killing off (or at least eloquently mutilating) those strong fathers who provide the (typically male) literary critic with his patrimonial inheritance. There is no thought, however, of the writer-as-mother, nor is allowance made for any critic who does not share Barthes's own Oedipal anxiety concerning the canonical author's claim to precedence.

Classical criticism, from Horace to E. D. Hirsch, privileges the author as the rightful father and proprietor of his literary works. Barthes rejects the author's claim to priority, but the author-critic relationship remains a strictly father-and-son affair. The cutting edge of meaning has merely changed hands, from the writer to the reader. For classical notions of the "Work" (as an inheritance to be understood and cherished), Barthes substitutes the "Text" (a methodological field of operation, one that allows the critic as son to inscribe his own name in the father's place). "The 'work'," writes Barthes, "is caught up in a process of filiation.... The author is reputed to be the father and the owner of his work.... The Text, on the other hand, is read without the Father's inscription. The metaphor of the Text is here again detached from the metaphor of the work; ... the

Text can be read without its father's guarantee."[1] That "we can at no moment identify [textual meaning] with the realistic novelist's castrating 'objectivity'" is illustrated at length, for example, in *S/Z*, where Barthes with considerable pleasure takes the balls from Balzac.[2]

Poststructuralists are not alone in defrocking the author as the honored sire of literature, or in dismissing the author's life as irrelevant to the writerly reader. For Michel Foucault, the author's fatherhood is bogus, having been belatedly conferred upon selected writers by our own ideology: "the author is not an indefinite source of significations which fill a work; the author does not precede the works, he is a certain functional principle by which, in our culture, one limits, excludes, and chooses; in short, by which one impedes the free circulation, the free manipulation, the free composition, decomposition, and recomposition of fiction."[3] Following Foucault, the new historicism has justifiably cut our canonical authors down to size, but they are usually whittled down to the same size and shape as more or less interchangeable illustrations of certain fixed historicist notions about power and culture. The author cannot escape or transcend the dominant ideology of the age in which he or she lives—or, to put it another way, there is no escape for the author from the historicist's own fictive reconstruction of that ideological system. Questions of biography and individual vision are largely precluded in historicist criticism as the author is paled within a discourse of power and privilege that is sought, and uncovered, in the author's text.

Arguing that literary discourse never belonged to the writer in the first place, historicists have typically pointed to the author's lack of seminal genius. Competition with the author *qua* father thus remains a persistent if implicit feature of historicist criticism, as is everywhere evident, for example, in the work of Stephen Greenblatt. Moreover, the author's personal history is generally the last place that historicists will turn for a source of meaning, except insofar as the biographical record shows the author to be a gull, slave, or advocate of the dominant ideology (unlike the potent and valorous critic-son who, as an armchair leftist, may harbor illusions of his own transcendence). Some authors, we learn, were oppressors: Guyon's destruction of the Bower of Bliss in Spenser's *Faerie Queene* (Book 2, Canto 12) is thus read as the product of a man who, as an English secretary in Ireland, "was involved intimately, on an almost daily

---

[1]Roland Barthes, "From Work to Text," in *The Rustle of Language*, trans. Richard Howard (Berkeley: University of California Press, 1989), 61.

[2]Roland Barthes, *S/Z* (Paris: Editions du Seuil, 1970). The quotation, however, is from Barthes, "The Death of the Author," in *Rustle of Language*, 50.

[3]Michel Foucault, "What is an Author?" trans. Joseph V. Harari in *Modern Criticism and Theory*, ed. David Lodge (London and New York: Longman, 1988), 209.

basis, throughout the island, in the destruction of Hiberno-Norman civilization." Other authors were deferential, glad to be of use: Shakespeare, although mostly innocent of Spenser's daily schedule of imperialist genocide, was a wage-earning performer dependent upon noble and royal patronage; and he therefore approached his culture "as dutiful servant, content to improvise a part of his own within its orthodoxy."[4] Thus is the "author" authored by his culture, and by the critic who most forcibly argues this hypothesis to be true.

Feminist criticism generally has had only limited success in escaping from this phallocentric, bardicidal position vis-à-vis the author. Granted, the issue at stake in feminist reading is not so much a competition for the phallus as it is a resistance to patriarchal domination. Much feminist criticism has, however, been shaped by a fundamental biologism in which male authors are shown, predictably, to be patriarchal ideologues, and female authors closet subversives (or even closed-caption subversives, whose message can be read only on a woman's receiver). The "male"—male anxiety, male creativity, male speech—is readily collapsed into the "masculine," and both into the "patriarchal"; while the "female" is frequently conflated with the "feminine," both of which are then homogenized as "feminist." In one strain of feminist discourse—of which Sandra Gilbert and Susan Gubar's *The Madwoman in the Attic* may be cited as paradigmatic—women's texts have been represented as if each were an authorless site of shrewdly concealed feminist rage; while the respective authors, when discussed at all, have been reconstructed as the invisible mouthpiece of an opposition that defines individual autonomy only in opposition to Patriarchy—which is itself conceptualized, all too often, as if it were an entity, a thing that ur-feminists could *see*, a monolithic structure against which an essentially "female" subjectivity always positioned itself.[5] Unfortunately, this monocular view, with or without a disclaimer concerning essentialist construction of gender, cannot accommodate such Renaissance essayists as Katherine Parr or Elizabeth Clinton, or such poets as Elizabeth Melville and Isabella Whitney, none of whom conceives her work as an argument against patriarchy.

The individual experience of the author, the relation of the author's life to his or her text (including the particularity of his or her relation to patriarchal values and institutions), has yet to be accepted within the purview of feminist critical discourse as a topic of interest. What I am calling

---

[4]Stephen Greenblatt, *Renaissance Self-Fashioning from More to Shakespeare* (Chicago: University of Chicago Press, 1980), 186, 253.

[5]Sandra M. Gilbert and Susan Gubar, *The Madwoman in the Attic: The Woman Writer and the Nineteenth-Century Literary Imagination* (New Haven: Yale University Press, 1979).

for here is not a return to old-fashioned notions of expressive realism. No thoughtful reader today wishes to resurrect notions of the literary text as a simple message about reality sent to the reader from the author, to be properly read and apprehended. Nor do I wish to invoke biography as the cause and origin of the literary work. I wish only to set aside our anxieties about proprietorship of the text, and our conventionalized fear of the intentional fallacy, so that we may attempt to reconstruct the lives of our early women poets, and of the vision and subjectivity that they brought to their writing, without greatly minimizing, exaggerating, or homogenizing their individual achievements; that is, to consider the ways in which the social and intellectual positions of the individual writer may have some bearing on both her writing and ours, on her *meaning* and ours. In our study of early women's literature, I should like to abandon the Oedipal model of reading (that of a will to power over the text), and to put in its place a model of mutually nurtured meaning, in which some allowance is made for the mother's vision of her own text without presuming that the mother's intended message is all that her text contains; one in which the author is no longer dead, but a participant, as it were, in an ongoing critical discussion.

Of the various critical approaches that have thrived in the past fifty years, none provides us with a language that facilitates the discussion of early women authors *as* authors. Catherine Belsey, for example, in surveying the contemporary critical scene, calls repeatedly and repetitively for "a genuinely radical critical practice," yet in her own *Critical Practice* she settles for a position that can only be described as deferentially Saussurean in its unwillingness to allow the author a place in the text.[6] Efforts to establish ties between the life and text of our women poets are thus consigned to the literary historian, to the custodian of cultural detritus. Yet the very fact that many Medieval and Renaissance women did write for a public (or at least for a sizable private) audience, in a society that discouraged women from making any public utterance, is one reason that we are coming to value their texts as objects of study. Moreover, those women who wrote the most remarkable texts generally led remarkable lives (Julian of Norwich, Margerie Kempe, Queen Elizabeth, Anne Askew, and Mary Wroth, to name just a few); and in such instances the author's life (as a different but related text) may be more pertinent to our interpretive work than is the case with those male poets who never had to struggle for the right to be heard by an attentive audience. To assume that the works of such women are best read without reference to the author's

---

[6]Catherine Belsey, *Critical Practice* (London and New York: Methuen, 1980), 7, 14, 33, 36, and passim.

life may be critically fashionable, but to efface the author in this way is a typically masculine (and today, one can almost say, a *traditional*) critical posture that should be reexamined, for the author's burial closes off as many meanings as it opens up. We shall therefore do well, in the years ahead, to reconstruct both the life and the work, the biographical and the literary text, of those women whose writings we have lately begun to read, thereby to arrive at a thoughtful understanding of women's stories that goes beyond the mere illustration of culturally produced ideology and subversion. And I should like to consider the life and works of Elizabeth Tanfield Cary as an exemplary instance.

Elizabeth Cary was a woman who refused the model of feminine virtue extolled by her society, choosing instead to fashion a self from the stuff of her own fiction. The motto that Cary chose for herself and passed on to her daughters—"Be and seem"—succinctly expresses the paradox of her own existence as a literary figure, for it was in and through literary discourse that Cary composed herself as a heroic woman—rewriting herself by turns as tragic hero, as avenging scourge, and as holy martyr.[7] In considering Cary's art we may resist that form of psychoanalytic criticism in which the text becomes history and each character a case study; I intend, however, to discuss Cary both as the constructor of literary texts and as the author of a self that came to mirror those texts. Such an approach may be said to violate the boundary between art and life; but in Cary's case, no such boundary is visible. Cary was the product of a continual interplay between her life and her art, as each was made to imitate the other in acts of self-conscious re-creation. Cary's life, I will argue, was a fiction in much the same sense as her extant literary works, and with much the same relation to the author: neither was wholly determined either by, or in opposition to, patriarchy; and each must be read in light of the other.

Most of what we know about the life and character of Elizabeth Cary—which is a good deal more than we know about either Shakespeare or Spenser—depends on a biography written between 1644 and 1649 by her eldest living daughter, Anne (in religion, Clementina), then a

---

[7]Cary's daughter Anne reports that her mother "did always much disapprove the practice of satisfying oneself with their conscience being free from fault, not forbearing all that might have the least show or suspicion of uncomeliness or unfitness; what she thought to be required in this she expressed in this motto (which she caused to be inscribed in her daughter's wedding-ring): *Be and seem*." In Anne Cary, *The Lady Falkland: Her Life. From a MS. in the Imperial Archives at Lille*, ed. Richard Simpson (1861; repr. London: Catholic Publishing Co., 1867), 16. All citations are to this edition.

Benedictine nun at Cambray.[8] The "Elizabeth Cary" set forth in "The Lady Falkland her Life" is, of course, a figure in a text, a comic-tragic heroine that exists only as metaphor, an imaginative substitute for the woman herself. Another biographer (her father, or her husband, or one of her creditors, or an Anglican bishop) would have given us a very different Elizabeth Cary. Yet it is difficult, after having read the "Life," to read Cary's surviving poetry, drama, translations, and letters as one would read those texts without the benefit of Anne Cary's fascinating biography. And it is the points of contact between the "Life" and Cary's own corpus that will interest me here.

The textual Elizabeth Cary of the "Life" and the author Elizabeth Cary who wrote *The Tragedie of Mariam* and *The History of the Life of Edward II* certainly have much in common.[9] Both are willful and assertive female figures. Both affirm their right to speak and to be heard. Yet both, finally, are profoundly conservative with respect to established gender roles. The moral precept that Cary impressed most strongly upon her own daughters (apart from the imperative to know and to love God) was that "wheresoever conscience and reason would permit," they "should prefer the will of another before [their] own."[10] It is a rule that Cary herself is said to have observed with penitential zeal. As a child, Elizabeth Tanfield (as presented in the "Life") was taught to be deferential; she rarely forgot that lesson, even as an adult:

---

[8]The authorship and date of the "Life" have not previously been noted, but it is clear from a collation of the internal and external evidence that the biography cannot have been written by anyone but Anne Cary. Anne Cary is an unsung hero of women's literary history. In addition to writing the "Life," she preserved many, perhaps all, of her mother's writings, some of which are extant. I have recently tracked down a copy, partly in Anne's hand, of what appears almost certainly to be the English translation of Blosius that Elizabeth Cary was working on during her last months (Colwich Abbey MS 36). Anne Cary appears also to be the scribe responsible for the most authoritative extant MS of the *Revelations* of Julian of Norwich (British Library MS Sloane 2499); and she appears to have played a role in the publication of the *Revelations* in 1670 (published by Anne's friend, Serenus Cressy). A more thorough search than I have made may reveal additional works written, translated, or transcribed by Anne Cary.

[9]E[lizabeth] C[ary], *The Tragedie of Mariam, the Faire Queene of Iewry. Written by that learned, vertuous, and truly noble Ladie, E. C.* (London: T. Creede for R. Hawkins, 1613); citations as edited in normalized text by D. Foster, from E[lizabeth] F[alkland], *The History of the Life, Reign, and Death of Edward II. King of England, and Lord of Ireland. With the Rise and Fall of his great Favourites, Gaveston and the Spencers. Written by E[lizabeth] F[alkland] in the Year 1627. And Printed verbatim from the Original* (London: J. C. for C. Harper, S. Crouch, and T. Fox, 1680); repr. (without Cary's preface and dedication) entitled, *The Parallel: Or the History of the Life, Reign, Deposition, and Death, of King Edward the Second* (London: R. Baldwin, 1689); all citations are to the first edition.

[10]A. Cary, "Life," 13.

> [H]er own father and mother she always used with much respect; so far as, for the most part, all her life to speak to her mother (when she was sitting) on her knees, which she did frequently for more than an hour, though she was but an ill kneeler, and a worse riser. She loved them both much, though her mother was never kind to her[.][11]

Young Elizabeth was similarly respectful to her authoritarian husband, Henry Cary, Lord Falkland (whom I will denote hereafter, for convenience sake, as "Falkland," although he was not actually granted that title until 1620). As represented in the "Life," Elizabeth Cary was a model of feminine self-denial, submitting herself to her husband's will in all things—even, at times, imperiling her own physical or financial well-being to do so.

> To her husband she bore so much respect, that she taught her children as a duty to love him better than herself.... He was very absolute; and though she had a strong will, she had learned to make it obey his. The desire to please him had power to make her do that that others could have scarce believed possible for her.... Where his interest was concerned, she seemed not able to have any consideration of her own.... [W]here she did but apprehend it would not please him, she would not do the least thing, though on good occasion; so as she seemed to prefer nothing but religion and her duty to God before his will.[12]

It is not without irony that this model of wifely submission was eventually renounced by her husband as a rebellious and wayward spouse, and abandoned to penury. But even after being cast off, when wholly destitute and fearing starvation, Cary remained deferential to her lord: she refused even to seek relief through the charity of her friends without first seeking his permission to do so (although he would give her nothing himself), lest she further provoke his wrath, or else prejudice his standing at court.[13]

Elizabeth Cary (the author) likewise struggles to affirm, and to conform to, a divinely established order that deprived women of free will. But unlike Anne Cary's almost-saintly heroine, Elizabeth Cary the author seems early on to have resented patriarchal authority. It is remarkable that Cary as a young bride—perhaps as early as 1604 when she was still in her teens—could put in the mouth of her female characters such forceful words as these, spoken by Salome in *The Tragedy of Mariam, the Fair Queen of Jewry*:

[11]Ibid., 22.
[12]Ibid., 14–16.
[13]Ibid., 43–44.

Are men than we in greater grace with heaven?
Or cannot women hate as well as men?
I'll be the custom-breaker and begin
To show my sex the way to freedom's door—

. . . .

I mean not to be led by precedent.
My will shall be to me in stead of law.

(I.iv.47–50, I.vi.79–80)

Much has been said of late about those male authors of the Renaissance period (Shakespeare among them) who tend to draw an absolute equation between marriage and cuckoldry; Cary's female characters, good and bad, tend rather to assume an equation between marriage and confinement. Mariam (Cary's protagonist) never challenges Salome's observation that women have yet to be shown the way to freedom's door; the queen of Jewry herself desires to be free. Married life is characterized for Mariam by capricious tyranny (when her husband is present), or by deputized tyranny and anxious uncertainty (when he is away). In comparison to such a life, widowhood (as the only virtuous alternative) looks to Mariam, in her most independent mood, like a vast improvement.

While trying to work up some tears for the reported death of her tyrannical spouse, Mariam remarks, "Yet had I rather much a milkmaid be / Than be the monarch of Judea's queen." (I.i.58–59) In longing for those days "When virgin freedom left me unconstrained" (I. i.72), Mariam seems to recall another famous queen who resisted both the temptation and the imperative to get married in the first place. In one of her most famous and famously equivocal speeches on marriage and the succession, Elizabeth remarked, "[I]f I were a milkmaid with a pail on my arm (whereby my private person might be little set-by [i.e., valued]), I would not forsake that poor and single state, to match with the greatest monarch."[14] If Elizabeth as a sovereign queen was to be matched with the

---

[14]From "The Queen's Most Excellent Majesty's Oration in the Parliament House, March 15, 1575/6." Normalized text by D. Foster, edited from Sir John Harington, *Nugae Antiquae* (1769–75), 2.149–54; repr. (1792) 3.170–78, (1804) 1.120–27. Cf. British Library MS Addit. 32379, fols. 22r–24r, and MS Addit. 33271, fol. 2r (with omissions, as transcribed by Robert Ascham). Elizabeth continues: "Not that I do condemn the double knot, or judge amiss of such as, forced by necessity, cannot dispose themselves to another life; but [I] wish that none were drawn to change but such as cannot keep honest limits. Yet, for your behalf, there is no way so difficult that may touch my private person, which I will not well content myself to take; and, in this case, as willingly to spoil myself quite of myself, as if I should put off my upper garment when it wearies me—if the present state might not thereby be encumbered." Elizabeth, in both public and private, was especially fond of comparing her state with that of a milkmaid; this speech is one instance among several that may have been known to Cary.

greatest of monarchs, it would be a match in comparable political stature, in her single state *as* monarch, and not in a marriage-match that would almost certainly have deprived her of her autonomy. Cary's Mariam is of Elizabeth's mind about marriage, but it is too late—Mariam has already been sentenced for life to wear the bonds of holy matrimony.

Directly upon being introduced to us, Cary's heroine expresses her mixed feelings about Herod, as she weighs her duty to her lord and husband against her checked ambition to be free:

> Oft have I wished that I from him were free;
> Oft have I wished that he might lose his breath; ….
> Hate hid his true affection from my sight
> And kept my heart from paying him his debt—
> And blame me not, for Herod's jealousy
> Had power even constancy itself to change:
> For he, by barring me from liberty,
> To shun my ranging, taught me first to range.
> But yet too chaste a scholar was my heart
> To learn to love another than my lord.
> To leave his love, my lesson's former part,
> I quickly learned; the other, I abhorred.

> > (I.i.16–30)

Mariam is not, like Salome, unfaithful to her spouse; but neither can she love her husband without ambivalence. Herod is a powerful, fatherly man, and sometimes a doting husband; but he is chiefly viewed by Mariam as her judge and jailer. Love, the debt of a wife, is an obligation that cannot be paid under Herod's exacting terms; and marriage is a debtor's prison.

Elizabeth Tanfield was contracted at age fifteen to a stranger, nine years her senior, whose sole motive was unabashed financial gain. Anne Cary in the "Life" writes sympathetically of her father, Lord Falkland; but she reports quite frankly that "he did not care for his wife"—Elizabeth was overly bookish and short and fat.[15] Falkland's Oxfordshire bride was, however, well-endowed as the only heir of a wealthy man. Nothing else mattered.

The Carys did not cohabit during the first years of their marriage. Elizabeth remained in Burford while Falkland dwelt either at Barkhamstead (his father's manor in Hertfordshire), or at court. Falkland then left for France and the Low Countries, perhaps without so much as visiting

---

[15] A. Cary, "Life," 6–9, 86.

his wife before leaving England.[16] Desiring, however, "to have her where she should be best content," his initial thought was that she should remain with her parents.[17] That plan was soon abandoned. Upon the insistence of his own mother (Dame Katherine, Lady Paget), Falkland ordered that his wife be taken from her family and friends in Burford in order to live thereafter with Dame Katherine at Barkhamstead.

> Her mother-in-law having her, and being one that loved much to be humoured, and finding [Elizabeth] not to apply herself to it, used her very hardly, so far as at last to confine her to her chamber; which seeing she little cared for, but entertained herself with reading, the mother-in-law took away all her books, with command to have no more brought her. Then she set herself to make verses. There were only two in the whole house (besides her own servants) that ever came to see her, which they did by stealth—one of her husband's sisters and a gentlewoman that waited on her mother-in-law.... From this time [Elizabeth] writ many things for her private recreation, on several subjects and occasions, all in verse (out of which she scarce ever writ anything that was not translations): one of them [*Mariam*] was stolen out of that sister-in-law's (her friend's) chamber, and printed, but by her own procurement was called in.[18]

Queen Mariam's opening speech about the prison-house of marriage acquires added resonance once we understand that it was written by a young woman for whom marriage had meant literal physical confinement, and estrangement from the books and people that she loved best. And while I do not wish to read *Mariam* as allegory or as autobiography, there can be no doubt that Cary's choice of materials was largely influenced by her own unhappy situation: Mariam's husband, like Cary's at the time of composition, has been long absent; Mariam, like Cary, has been jealously guarded in the interim; and Mariam, like Cary, struggles with her contempt and fear for a husband whom she feels she really *ought* to love.

[16]Falkland left England in 1604 with permission to travel for seven years. He was gone about three years, including one year as a prisoner of war after having been captured by the Spanish. He returned to England ca. 1606, following the payment of a costly ransom (a financial burden from which he never fully recovered). It is not certain that his marriage was consummated prior to his return. All of his children were born between 1607 and 1625 (eleven born alive plus an unspecified number that perished at birth or shortly afterward).

[17] A. Cary, "Life," 7.

[18]Ibid., 9. The sister-in-law mentioned here was actually Henry Cary's sister-in-law, Elizabeth (n. Bland) Cary, the wife of Philip Cary. And it was to her that Cary dedicated *The Tragedie of Mariam*, with a sonnet addressed "To Diana's earthly deputess, and my worthy sister, Mistress Elizabeth Cary."

Nor is Mariam's predicament, or Cary's, simply that of an independently minded woman struggling against patriarchy. The matriarchal figures in Cary's life and work are no less oppressive than her fathers, husbands, and kings. Mariam, like Cary, must contend with an imperious and unsympathetic mother (respectively Alexandra, and Lady Elizabeth Tanfield); and Mariam, like Cary, is engaged in a bitter struggle with a woman who holds a prior claim on her husband's affection (respectively Doris, and Falkland's mother, Dame Katherine). In the "Life," Cary's mother and mother-in-law compete with Falkland for the role of chief oppressor in Cary's life just as Alexandra and Doris, in Cary's play, are ranged with Herod against Mariam. The obsessive tyranny of these female figures, in Cary's life as in Cary's text, may be dismissed, perhaps, as an inevitable and compensatory by-product of their own oppression by patriarchal authority. But to view Cary's literary and biographical conflicts as a singular struggle against "patriarchy" is to look at the evidence with one eye closed. The domestic authority of the privileged matriarch is nearly as problematic for Cary (and for Mariam) as the authority of husband, father, and king.

The conflict between Mariam and Herod, as set forth by Cary, has less to do with feminine obedience or masculine jealousy than with the right to speak and to be heard, while the conflict between Mariam and Salome is one of the right *way* for a woman to speak. Salome and Mariam receive fundamentally the same warning from all of the most powerful male and female characters in their world: they are told to keep quiet. Married women especially must remain silent. Constabarus speaks words of patriarchal wisdom when he admonishes his wife Salome that "A stranger's private conference is shame." (I.vi.3) Similarly, as Sohemus remarks (albeit sympathetically), "Unbridled speech is Mariam's worst disgrace, / And will endanger her without desert." (III.iii.65–66)

No one in Cary's play has any doubts about the *power* of women's speech. Salome, for one, has an almost shamanistic faith in the power of her words, as when she remarks to herself on the inconveniences of having a live husband: "Had I not begged his life, he had been dead. / I curse my tongue, the hinderer of his doom" (I.iv.59–60); and again, of her lover Sylleus: "Sylleus said / He would be here—and see, he comes at last. / Had I not named him, longer had he stayed." (I.iv.62–64) Salome's confidence in her own witty tongue is largely borne out by the narrative: it is her speech, not physical strength or hard work or beauty, whereby Salome attains her ends; but her speech is also quite fatal to goodness, and her ends, in Cary's construction, are wicked—not because women's speech is by nature untrustworthy or threatening (as, say, in many Shakespearean texts), but rather because Salome has assumed the right to speak, as it were, like a man. Like most of Cary's male characters, Salome says what she thinks without restraint. She will speak deceitfully, or lustfully, or aggressively, to whomever she pleases—without much concern for those traditional feminine virtues in which Queen Mariam, and the author Elizabeth Cary, are fully vested.

Salome guards her speech only in the presence of Herod. Martha Slowe has shown that "Mariam fails, and Salome (on the surface at least) achieves success in her attempt to subvert the patriarchal symbolic code, precisely because the former resists and the latter appears to accept the implication of [the patriarchal] conjunction of the sexual and the symbolic." In Herod's court as in Cary's England, "patriarchal control of the order of language implies the inscription of silence as the sign of female chastity, the confinement of woman's discursive place to the private sphere, and the definition of woman's speech as a male property category."[19] But Salome—most notably in the scene that decides Mariam's death—simply manipulates Herod while appearing to accept his authority:

> Salome … appears perfectly willing to allow Herod to take possession of her speech as a reflection of his wishes. Actually, her strategy entails some subtle modifications of his ideas, but her speeches to Herod disguise these intentions. Guilty of the adultery which she persuades intermediaries to attribute to Mariam, and extremely radical in her ideas, Salome is a skillful verbal negotiator. At the same time that she subverts the patriarchal symbolic order she claims, and, from Herod's perspective, appears to uphold it. Salome is fully cognizant of Herod's absolute sequential and discursive precedence in Judea, and she defers entirely to his word in his presence.[20]

Here is Gilbert and Gubar's shrewd feminist from *The Madwoman in the Attic*, disguising her resistance to achieve her ends while appearing to submit to patriarchal authority. But we should keep in mind that the strategy is Salome's, not Elizabeth Cary's. Salome is condemned from all sides—even from her own mouth—as a shameful strumpet. As a female without "femininity," Salome is a type familiar in the work of male

[19]Martha Slowe, "Speech Crimes in *the Tragedy of Mariam*," unpublished paper, Shakespeare Association of America (Philadelphia, 1990), 2.

[20]Slowe, 4. Slowe concludes that Salome by toying thus with Herod is "disowning her discourse," so that Salome "sacrifices her individuality and integrity as a speaker." Salome, clearly, has not appropriated Julia Kristeva's discourse—but to say that Salome sacrifices her "individuality" and "feminine heterogeneity" through her encounter with Herod is to view Salome as a failed feminist, in full disregard of the heterogenous figure in Cary's Jacobean text, who lays no claim to having anything like "integrity as a speaker."

authors; she hardly illustrates an essentially "female creativity." What we might term the "feminist" side of Elizabeth Cary may indeed find veiled expression in Salome, but Salome stands condemned for her inconstancy, willfulness, promiscuity, impudence, and loose speech. Granted that the creation and scapegoating of Salome may have been necessary, if only as a strategy for opening up another kind of space in which Cary herself could speak as someone *different*, as a woman not-like-Salome. Salome nevertheless remains an Iago-like villain, one whose tongue engineers the death of every reasonably virtuous character in the play; and her proto-feminism finally proves more threatening to Mariam, and to Cary's own sense of moral virtue and right order, than to Herod.

I am inclined, for all that, to say of Elizabeth Cary what Blake said of Milton: she is of the devil's party without knowing it. Crafty, witty, and irrepressible, Salome shoulders most of the play's dramatic energy. Moreover, her opening line ("More plotting yet?") implicates not just Mariam and Salome as female plotters, but Cary herself, as a maker of plots; even as Salome's final line in the play ("'Tis no time / To purge me now, …") raises the question of whether she is to be shriven, or whether she is herself something to be purged (either from the court of Herod the tyrant or from the breast of Elizabeth Cary the virtuous and submissive wife). These lines, and all that passes in between, suggest that Salome as a feminist demon is invoked by Cary partly as an act of self-exorcism. The return of the repressed finds expression here, with a vengeance, in a character who wages war upon all that obstructs her will (including other women), and whose energy drives the play to its tragic conclusion. Granted that Mariam finally obtains a spiritual or symbolic victory—that of marching in silence to her death, with "a dutiful, though scornful smile"—and granted that Mariam's speechless victory is represented as superior to Salome's Machiavellian triumph. It is nonetheless Salome, not Mariam, who survives Herod's wrath to continue breathing and smiling and plotting within the play's fictive future. (V.i.52) Nor was that lesson lost upon Cary herself, a woman who eventually traded in her own dutiful smile for a willful if sanctified rebellion.

It is clear from the "Life" that Cary in her later years enjoyed combating those powerful men and institutions that had ruled her life, more or less successfully, until her open rebellion in 1626, when she was formally received into the Catholic Church. In other words, Cary's Salome may have been partly responsible for the eventual subversion of Elizabeth Cary—but if we wish to read Cary's Salome as a shrewd subversion of patriarchal values, we can do so only by refusing to hear Cary's own voice as a young married woman and aspiring author who dared to speak with a public voice. Cary, like Salome, was a "custom-breaker" who looked for freedom's door; but Cary, as the author of *Mariam*, is not a feminist, even insofar as that modern term may be applied to Renaissance women who entertained a vision of liberty and equality under the law. This may be disappointing to some readers. Still, to recognize that there were certain feminine (i.e., culturally defined) perimeters around Cary's female ambition is not to diminish the value of her play (except, of course, as a diminished confirmation of our own values); nor does that recognition preclude a reading of *Mariam* that finds in Salome a forceful repudiation of patriarchal order.

In Cary's good-woman, bad-woman paradigm, wicked Salome serves as a foil to the virtuous Mariam, the fair queen of Jewry. The problem presented to Mariam is much the same as that which engages Salome: How is a woman to find personal freedom, and a measure of self-expression, in the court of Herod the tyrant? How is a woman to find her *breath* (a multivalent term that in Cary's play comes to stand, not just for life itself, but for speech, vitality, spirit, and liberty)? Against Salome's vicious, even murderous tongue, Cary has set the speech of chaste Mariam. The integrity of Mariam's words, the identity of her speech with womanly virtue, distinguishes Mariam from her villainous counterpart—and it is not Mariam's death per se, but the ruthless suppression of Mariam's speech, that provides for Cary the central meaning of her tragedy.

Cary's heroine can speak as well as Salome, and she shares Salome's confidence in the power of her woman's tongue. But Mariam prefers (she says) to remain silent rather than to manipulate her husband and lord with self-serving speech:

> I know I could enchain him with a smile
> And lead him captive with a gentle word;
> I scorn my look should ever man beguile,
> Or other speech than meaning to afford—
> Else Salome in vain might spend her wind;
> In vain might Herod's mother wet her tongue;
> In vain had they complotted and combined
> (For I could overthrow them all, ere long).

(III.iii.45–52)

There is no doubt that Mariam likes to speak her mind. Her attempt to do so is the focal point of the play, beginning with her opening exclamation, "How oft have I with public voice run on ..." (I.i.1); but this remark, spoken solus, contains a familiar note of self-reproach, an ambivalence about her own speech that haunts Mariam throughout the play. It is tempting for us to overstate Mariam's outspokenness. Martha Slowe, for example, remarks that Mariam "will not allow [Herod's] wishes to direct or mediate her speech." In speaking of Mariam's "public openness," Slowe observes that "Herod knows that Mariam and her reported lover, Sohemus, have had private conversations, and he is aware that Mariam speaks freely to strangers." Mariam is also said to have "maintained her outspokenness throughout the play."[21] But this is to read Mariam through the eyes of the chorus and of the male characters, chiefly Herod, who accuse Mariam of habitual looseness. In point of fact, Mariam and Sohemus have only one private conversation that we know of, nor is Mariam ever seen to speak with strangers. On at least two occasions in the play's fictive past, Mariam's male guardians have broken with Herod's confidence in order to provide for Mariam's safety in the event of Herod's death. But Mariam's silence and restraint belie the accusation brought against her of verbal promiscuity. Most of her lines are spoken solus or to her husband, and most of the rest are addressed to women—to Alexandra (her mother), Doris (Herod's former wife), and Salome (Herod's sister). Her one unguarded moment comes with Sohemus. When Mariam is surprised with the shocking news that Herod is not dead after all, she suddenly blurts out her contempt for Herod as her husband and king. Sohemus, having brought the news, is startled by Mariam's speech. But unless we include Mariam's final message to Herod, as delivered offstage to Nuntio, this exchange with Sohemus in III.iii is the only time in the play that Mariam speaks, even briefly, to a man other than her own lord.

Rather than speak like Salome, Mariam has always taken refuge in her innocence, assuming (quite wrongly, as it turns out) that her innocence will speak for itself. (III.iii.53–62) She learns otherwise:

> *Mariam.* Am I the Mariam that presumed so much
> And deemed my face must needs preserve my breath?
>
> . . . .
>
> But I did think, because I knew me chaste,
> One virtue for a woman might suffice—
> That mind for glory of our sex might stand.
>
> (4.8.1–2, 35–39)

Mariam's original assumption, "That mind for glory of our sex might stand," proves doubly false: care for her chastity, the glory of her sex, fails to preserve Mariam's "breath"; nor can "mind," or intellect, stand for the glory of women in a society that commands women—especially married women—to remain silent.

Mariam's fate is sealed in the moment that she speaks to a male character (Sohemus) other than her own husband. Upon hearing Mariam speak, Sohemus promptly intuits doom. The chorus then enters, and reproaches an innocent but incautious Mariam for having sought "to be by public language graced." In Mariam's world, glory is reserved for that

---

[21]Slowe, 3–4.

woman who voluntarily refrains even from lawful public utterance. She who shares her mind with any "second ear" (other than her husband's) is thereby made common, a woman of "blotted" glory. The speech is worth quoting in its entirety as a succinct statement of patriarchal ideology:

> *Chorus.* 'Tis not enough for one that is a wife
> To keep her spotless from an act of ill,
> But from suspicion she should free her life
> And bare her self of power as well as will.
>   'Tis not so glorious for her to be free,
>   As by her proper self restrained to be.
> When she hath spacious ground to walk upon,
> Why on the ridge should she desire to go?
> It is no glory to forbear alone
> Those things that may her honor overthrow.
>   But 'tis thankworthy if she will not take
>   All lawful liberties (for honor's sake).
> That wife her hand against her fame doth rear,
> That (more than to her lord alone) will give
> A private word to any second ear—
> And though she may with reputation live,
>   Yet though most chaste, she doth her glory blot
>   And wounds her honor, though she kills it not.
> When to their husbands they themselves do bind,
> Do they not wholly give themselves away?
> Or give they but their body, not their mind,
> Reserving that (though best) for others, pray?
>   No, sure, their thoughts no more can be their own,
>   And therefore should to none but one be known.
> Then she usurps upon another's right
> That seeks to be by public language graced;
> And (though her thoughts reflect with purest light)
> Her mind, if not peculiar, is not chaste.
>   For in a wife it is no worse to find
>   A common body than a common mind.
> And every mind (though free from thought of ill)
> That out of glory seeks a worth to show,
> When any's ears but one therewith they fill,
> Doth (in a sort) her pureness overthrow.
>   Now Mariam had, but that to this she bent,
>   Been free from fear, as well as innocent.

(III.iii.97–132)

Cary's patriarchal chorus reacts as if Mariam has sullied her purity simply by unfolding her private thoughts to a third party. In doing so, she has made herself "common" (III.iii.126). The kindhearted Sohemus will not repeat Mariam's remarks; but by having spoken at all, Mariam has blotted her virtue. Mariam's dilemma, as articulated by the chorus, is not unlike that faced by Mariam' s author. Catch 22: Women cannot have both honor and a public voice. To seek one is to lose the other.

The loss of Mariam's voice is central to the meaning of the tragedy that bears her name. Whether or not Cary acquiesces in the verdict of the chorus—that a wife's mind "should to none but one be known" (and the very existence of *Mariam* suggests that she does not)—it is clear at least that women's speech cannot be stifled without tragic consequence. Martha Slowe concludes that "the play presents a strong case for the suppression of a woman's speech." That is certainly true if the Chorus is allowed to speak for the entire text. The figure of Salome, and the Chorus's commentary, might easily have confirmed the Renaissance gynophobe's worst fears concerning the liberation of women's speech. And yet it seems to me that the speech and intellect of a virtuous woman are affirmed in *Mariam* as a source of value and meaning, in that the suppression of Mariam's speech is shown to be catastrophic.

When Herod, Cary's patriarchal avatar, silences Mariam by stopping her breath, he is driven to the brink of disintegration as a subject, suffering "an intolerable and almost frantic passion for her death" (as Cary notes in "The Argument"). The moral (as set forth in the final choric speech) is that, when "The guiltless Mariam is deprived of breath," chaos is come again (V.i.272):

> Had he with wisdom now her death delayed,
> He at his pleasure might command her death;
> But now he hath his power so much betrayed,
> As all his woes cannot restore her breath.
>> Now doth he strangely, lunaticly, rave,
>> Because his Mariam's life he cannot save.

>   (V.i.283–88)

Herod has always valued Mariam's beauty, not her wit. When the tyrant finally appears, in Act IV, his first words are of Mariam; and it is immediately clear that Mariam is for Herod an object to be seen. (IV.i.1–40) Herod professes to read (and then to have misread) Mariam's face (IV.iv.17–20, 31–34, 39–68), but without attending to her words. When in his rage he commands the royal guard to seize his wife for having deceived him, he remarks still that "Her looks alone preserved your sovereign's breath" (IV.iv.96); and he fears, after his sentence of death, that he "cannot live without her sight." (IV.vii.30) It is not until Mariam has been sentenced to death that Herod first thinks of his wife's "world-amazing wit"—but (as prompted by Salome) he shortly concludes that "She's unchaste: / Her mouth will ope to every stranger's ear. / Then let the executioner make haste...." (IV.vii.77–79)

When Mariam has been silenced, Herod begins to realize what he has lost by having stopped the "breath" of a virtuous wife. He hangs on every word of Mariam's message from the scaffold, as reported to him by Nuntio:

> *Herod.* Oh say, what said she more? Each word she said
> Shall be the food whereon my heart is fed.
> *Nuntio.* "Tell thou my lord thou saw'st me lose my breath—"
> *Herod.* Oh that I could that sentence now control!
>
> (V.i.70)

Having sought to control Mariam's speech during her life, and unable to control his own, Herod's sentence of death returns to plague him now that she is silent:

> *Herod.* But art thou sure there doth no life remain?
> Is't possible my Mariam should be dead?
> Is there no trick to make her breathe again?
> *Nuntio.* Her body is divided from her head.
> *Herod.* Why yet methinks there might be found, by art,
> Strange ways of cure— 'tis sure rare things are done
> By an inventive head and willing heart.
> *Nuntio.* Let not my lord your fancies idly run.
> It is as possible it should be seen
> That we should make the holy Abram live,
> Though he entombed two thousand years had been,
> As breath again to slaught'red Mariam give.
>
> (V.i.87–98)

Herod's crime is not altogether irremediable. As the text seems to recognize, Elizabeth Cary's own "art," her own "inventive head and willing heart," will eventually provide "[s]trange ways of cure" for Mariam's silence. After being "entombed two thousand years," Mariam the fair queen of Jewry will again be given "breath"—by Elizabeth Tanfield Cary, a woman who will resuscitate the queen of Jewry in the interests of her own will to speak, like Mariam, with a public voice. The silent audition of the written text is thus presented in *Mariam* as a possible resolution of the conflict between woman's desire to speak and man's desire to keep her quiet: a woman may take up the pen, and write.

Salome, when thinking to preserve herself from Herod's wrath and from public shame, remarks of Mariam, "Yet ... I of Mariam will keep me mute, / Till first some other doth her name detect." (II.ii.1098–99) Cary, in a sense, has it both ways: Her "I" of *Mariam* can safely dramatize a scene of female resistance while Cary herself remains physically mute. But this solution, too, is fraught with problems. Free-speaking Salome recognizes that "'Tis long ago / Since shame was written on my tainted brow." (I.iv.22–23) The fundamental problem for Mariam, and for Cary at the time of *Mariam*'s original composition, is their mutual desire to write a text that will reach other eyes besides those of their respective husbands, yet without reducing their respective texts—Cary's play and Mariam's face—to a text of shame like that of Salome. Cary conceives her play, and Mariam her face, to be silent but self-validating declarations of virtue (and each takes considerable pride in the finished product). Aware of the dangers, and anxious to please their respective lords, both women clearly desire to eliminate in their respective texts any discrepancy between signified and signifier: "I cannot frame disguise," boasts Mariam, "nor ever taught / My face a look dissenting from my thought. " (IV.iii.59–60) Herod's deferred reply is that "I might have seen thy falsehood in thy face!" (IV.iv.61)

Mariam's face may be a text of female honor, but Mariam in the course of the play comes to recognize that she has no control, is allowed no authority, over the signification of that text. The message that she wishes to convey is never identical with its received meaning. Sohemus is the kind of admiring, unpossessive, and sympathetic reader whom Mariam covets most. He finds that Mariam's brow is a "table" (i.e., a writing tablet) "to the modest law, / 'Yet, though we dare not love, we may admire.'" (III.iii.93–94) Other readers, however, have less regard for Mariam's authorial intention: Antipater, for example, accepts Herod's reading rather than Mariam's: "foul adultery blotteth Mariam's brow." (II.iii.64) Because men may read, as they please, the face of any woman who is seen, a woman's silent text is not her own: it becomes the reader's "methodological field of operation" (Barthes's phrase), and a site of contested ownership. Herod, having appropriated Mariam's text as his private property, fears that Mariam's ambiguous "I" may communicate to other men meanings over which he has no control: Mariam's "eyes can speak, and in their speaking move." Most fearfully, "Pretty tales of love / They utter, which can human bondage weave." (IV.vii.89–92) Rather than allow other men to read in Mariam's face a tale of love, Herod simply destroys the text, hardly caring at the time that he must destroy along with it the author's signifying and signified self.

When Herod has agreed with Salome to take Mariam's breath, the two of them wile away Mariam's final hour by marking, remarking on, and marking up Mariam's face:

> *Herod.* But have you seen her cheek?
> *Salome.*   A thousand times.
> *Herod.* But did you mark it, too?
> *Salome.*   Ay, very well.
> *Herod.* What is't?
> *Salome.*   A crimson bush, that ever limes
> The soul whose foresight doth not much excel.
>   *Herod.* Send word she shall not die! Her cheek a bush!
> Nay, then I see indeed you marked it not.
>   *Salome.* 'Tis very fair— but yet will never blush,
> Though foul dishonors do her forehead blot.
>   *Herod.* Then let her die! 'Tis very true indeed….
>
>   (IV.vii.40–51)

When it is too late to save her breath, or to erase the blots that he has himself placed on Mariam's forehead, a remorseful Herod decides that "fictions" of Mariam "are void of sense"; after all is said and done, "They neither can offend, nor give defense, / And not by them it was my Mariam fell." (V.i.235–37) Mariam has perished rather as a result of Herod's own deadly misreading.

Unable ever to restore Mariam's breath, Herod concludes that he will himself become a text. After his death, his life will become grist for another writer who will stand in a position to pronounce the meaning of his existence. Herod intuits that when he is dead and buried, someone will place an inscription upon the vault, "And these shall be the words it shall contain: / 'Here Herod lies, that hath his Mariam slain.'" (V.i.258) That speaker is of course Elizabeth Cary, whose *Mariam* exposes the lies of Herod and of any other reader who dares to misread or to suppress the text of a virtuous woman.

Sadly, Mariam's fate foreshadows that of the tragedy that bears her name: the prompt recall of Cary's play following its publication in 1613 suggests either that Cary lacked Mariam's resolve to face the tyrant's wrath, or else that she was silenced against her will. According to the "Life," the manuscript of *Mariam* was stolen from her sister-in-law's chamber and published without Cary's consent.[22] That version of events—variations of which are found in literally hundreds of Renaissance tracts, to deflect criticism of the author—is perhaps doubtful. Anne Cary reports also that *Mariam* was promptly and voluntarily recalled by the author. This too is doubtful. Whether or not Cary was involved in the original publication, it seems incredible that this woman in particular

---

[22]A. Cary, "Life," 9.

should have recalled her own work, and silenced her own voice, without pressure from her in-laws. It is of course possible that Cary, having been advised by her own fictive chorus, felt that she had no choice but to muffle up her public voice for the sake of her "honor." But either way, the net result is that our first woman playwright was quickly and effectively silenced.

It was seventeen years before any of Cary's subsequent work was printed. In 1630, following her conversion to Catholicism, Cary published a translation of Davy du Perron's *Replique a la response du serenisme roy de la Grande Bretagne*. Cary's translation, "The Reply of the Most Illustrious Cardinall of Perron," was dedicated to Queen Henrietta Marie, Charles's Catholic queen, as the figure "fittest to protect a woman's work."[23] But the entire impression, printed at Douay and smuggled into England, was seized and burned by Archbishop George Abbot. Only a few copies escaped the flames. Undaunted, Cary pushed on with a translation of Perron's complete works intended for the students at Oxford and Cambridge, but she was never able to print it.[24] This monumental labor likewise came to nought: no manuscript copy is extant. Nor do we have a surviving copy of Cary's earliest drama, a Sicilian tragedy.[25] "The Life of Tamburlaine," said to have been her best work, is lost as well. So, too, are Cary's verse biographies of St. Magdalene, St. Agnes Martyr, and St. Elizabeth of Portugal, along with countless devotional verses. Also lost is a volume of moral precepts written for her children, a theological discourse, most of her private correspondence, and "many things" that she wrote "for her private recreation, on several subjects and occasions, all in verse."[26] I have recently discovered a funeral elegy on the Duke of Buckingham that was written by Cary, as well as her lost translation of Blosius and what I think may be her lost translation of Seneca's Epistles.[27] Other-

---

[23]Elizabeth Cary, *The Reply of the Most Illustrious Cardinall of Perron, to the Answere of the Most Excellent King of Great Britaine. The First Tome* (Douay: M. Bogart, 1630), prelim. sig. [a]2r.

[24]A. Cary, "Life," 39.

[25]Cary's Sicilian tragedy was written before *Mariam* and dedicated to her husband. The play is mentioned by Cary in her dedication of *Mariam* to her sister-in-law, Elizabeth Cary, sig. A1r, and by John Davies of Hereford in *The Muses Sacrifice, or Divine Meditations* (London: T. S[nodham] for G. Norton, 1612), sig. prelim. [a]3v.

[26]For mention of Cary's lost works, see "Life," 4, 9–10, 13, 34, 39. For the extant correspondence, see Simpson, 130–176 passim, and Lady Georgiana Fullerton, *The Life of Elisabeth Lady Falkand, 1583–1639* (London: Burns and Oates, 1883), 84–93, 104–8.

[27]Cary's funeral elegy for the Duke of Buckingham is a poem of fifty lines known hitherto only as a fragment ("Reader stand still and look, lo, here I am ..."). The first six lines of Cary's elegy were widely circulated in seventeenth-century manuscripts, the least corrupt of which is British Library MS Egerton 2725, fol. 60r ("An Epitaph upon the death of the Duke

wise, the only original literary works to have survived are *The Tragedy of Mariam* and *The History of the Life of Edward II*. Nothing more remains, apart from her translation of the *Reply* (of which some dozen copies escaped the flames) and a juvenile translation of a geographical treatise.[28]

Some twenty-five years after she wrote *Mariam*, and some fourteen years after it was published, Elizabeth Tanfield Cary was formally received into the Catholic Church. It was a move that she had contemplated for several years. Anne Cary informs us that her mother as a younger woman had been persuaded by various churchmen, chiefly Dr. Neale, Bishop of Durham, that she might remain within the English church in good conscience, "never questioning, for all that, but that to be in the Roman Church were infinitely better and securer." Cary deferred to their priestly judgment, for "she had learned in the fathers and histories of former Christian times to have a high reverence to the dignity they pretended to." In the eyes of some observers, however, Cary's high reverence for the fathers' pretensions was not wholly convincing:

> She was in the house of the same bishop [Dr. Neale] divers times at the examinations of such beginners or receivers of new opinions as were by them esteemed heretics, where some, strangers to her, wondering to see her, asked the bishop how he durst trust

---

of Buckingham by the Countesse of Faulkland"). The complete text of the elegy, not hitherto identified, appears in Beinecke Library MS Poetry Box VI/28. In addition, Bodleian Library MS Rawl. poet. 103 may represent Cary's Seneca. It contains a translation into English verse of Seneca's treatises *De vita beata* ("Lucius Annaeus Seneca the Philosopher His booke of a Blessed life translated into verse," sigs. 3r–31v) and *De otio aut secessu sapientis* ("Lucius Annaeus Seneca his Book / of the rest or retirement of a Wiseman," 32r–38v). The first begins, "All (brother Gallio) blessednesse would find ..."; and concludes, "And after burned downe againe as fast?" The second begins, "It is agreed by all that vice is taught ..."; and ends, "That I should not imbarke, I thinke, intends." Both are written in end-stopped blank verse, after the manner of Cary's *History of the Life*. I have not made a close inspection of the texts for internal evidence (vocabulary, incidentals, and so on) of Cary's authorship, but the Senecan treatises bear many superficial similarities to Cary's work. For example, that "vice is taught," and not hereditary, is a characteristic Cary theme, as in the opening paragraph of *The History of the Life* ("He [Edward II] could not have been so unworthy a Son of so noble a Father, nor so inglorious a Father of so excellent a Son, if either Vertue or Vice had been hereditary," 2). The Senecan works are preceded by an anonymous preface ("To the Reader," 1v–2v), beginning "This tract was written by Seneca ...." The manuscript was inscribed on January 25, 1677, as "James Elyott his book"—which is roughly contemporaneous with the sale of Cary's manuscript *History of the Life* and the Falkland manuscript of the *Most Unfortunate Prince*. The text is in what I take to be a feminine hand, earlier than, and different from, Elyott's signature. For Cary's lost translation of Blosius, see n.8, above.

[28]Abraham Ortelius, "The mirror of the Worlde translated out of French," trans. Cary (Burford, Oxfordshire: Burford Parish Library MS); holograph. For *The Reply*, see n. 23, above.

that young lady to be there? who answered, he would warrant she would never be in danger to be a heretic; so much honour and adherence did she ever render to authority where she imagined it to be, much more where she knew it to be.[29]

The bishop was of course mistaken in his young catechist. Already as a young woman, Cary's apparent reverence for patriarchal authority was a text that was undergoing silent revision.

Cary left Dublin and her husband in 1625, ostensibly to escape the danger of the pending Irish wars and to further her husband's suits at court—Lord Falkland then being in danger of losing his entire estate, at discount, to pay off his enormous debts. Finding that his wife's efforts at court were ineffectual, and fearing lest she complicate his already delicate position in Ireland, Falkland made every thinkable effort to have his wife confined to her mother's home in Burford, Oxfordshire. Cary, however, now found herself (after more than twenty years of marriage) at liberty to pursue her own intellectual interests. Upon finding new friends at court (mostly Catholic women, among whom were the Duchess of Buckingham and Queen Henrietta Marie), Cary refused to settle for a dreary life in Burford with her difficult and sometimes tyrannical mother. Instead she remained in London, contrary to Falkland's expressed desire; and, after a period of renewed religious inquiry, she took steps to fulfill her long-suppressed ambition to be received into the church of Rome. By December 1626, Elizabeth Cary was confirmed as a Roman Catholic.

Cary's conversion might be interpreted as one more act of feminine submission—reflecting her submission to God in matters of faith, and her deference, in all lesser concerns, to Harry the husband. This, certainly, is the interpretation offered by Cary's worshipful daughter. But Cary's conversion to Roman Catholicism also represented a profound rebellion, a refusal to substitute, for her own conscience, the voice of her king or prelate or husband. As a result, the last thirteen years of Cary's life were a continual struggle against almost impossible odds. When Falkland received word of his wife's conversion, he responded with unmitigated rage. Elizabeth's allowance was immediately cut off. All of her children were taken from her, and all of her servants as well, except for the faithful Bessie Poulter. Her house was stripped of almost everything that could be moved, including food and fuel. She was then forcibly confined to her lodgings by a royal injunction that was engineered by her own husband. For at least the second time in her married life, Elizabeth Cary was made a literal prisoner.

---

[29]A. Cary, "Life," 10–11.

By the summer of 1627, Cary was still confined indoors, neglected by her friends and family, and forgotten by King Charles, who had ordered her confinement. Wholly destitute, Cary was kept from starvation only by the sparse charity of a few faithful friends and by Bessie Poulter's gleanings from the dinner table of Lord Ormond.

Barred from her liberty, Cary turned once again to her writing. It was during this time of privation that she undertook to write *The History of the Life, Reign, and Death of Edward II*. Cary's principal source for this work was a manuscript entitled *The History of the Most Unfortunate Prince, King Edward the Second*, an anonymous chronicle tentatively ascribed, in its first printed form, to Cary's own husband, Henry, Lord Falkland.[30] The two narratives are often—in fact, usually—confounded. The first critical discussion of the two versions is by D. A. Stauffer, who supposes *The History of the Life* to represent an earlier draft of *The History of the Most Unfortunate Prince*, to which it is closely related.[31] But the two texts are clearly the work of two individuals, each with a distinctive lexicon and with a unique set of stylistic fingerprints—and the *Unfortunate Prince* was written first. In the most recent article devoted to the two *Edwards*, D. R. Woolf offers to supply "The True Date and Authorship of Henry, Viscount Falkland's *History of the Life, Reign and Death of King Edward II*," but he only multiplies the confusion.[32] From its unwittingly ironic title to its closing sentence, Woolf's "true" account is hopelessly muddled; Woolf gets almost everything wrong for *both* texts, including authorship, date, sequence, textual transmission, occasion, and topical allusions.

Then, too, one *Edward* or the other (and sometimes both) has been described as an unfinished closet drama by Elizabeth Cary. But both are clearly finished products, and neither is a dramatic text. The *Unfortunate Prince* is a prose narrative written on the model of Plutarch's *Lives*. The *History of the Life*, written principally in end-stopped blank verse, is a verse biography—the only extant example of a form that Cary appears to have favored—and it comes complete with a dated preface in which the

---

[30]*The History of the Most Unfortunate Prince, Edward the Second. With choice Political Observations on him and his unhappy Favourites, Gaveston & Spencer: Containing Several Rare Passages of those Times, Not found in other Historians. Found among the Papers of, and (supposed to be) Writ by, the Right Honourable Henry Viscount Faulkland, Sometime Lord Deputy of Ireland.* (London: Playford, 1680); repr. in *Harleian Miscellany*, 10 vols., ed. Thomas Park (London: White and Murray, 1808–11); I (1808):92–127. Citations are, regrettably, to the sometimes unreliable Harleian text; I do not have the 1680 text at my present disposal. For *The History of the Life*, see n. 9, above.

[31]D. A. Stauffer, "A Deep and Sad Passion," in *The Parrott Presentation Volume*, ed. Hardin Craig (Princeton: Princeton University Press, 1935), 289–314.

[32]D. R. Woolf, "The True Date and Authorship of Henry, Viscount Falkland's *History of the Life, Reign and Death of King Edward II*," *Bodleian Record* 12.6 (1988):440–452.

author herself validates the work as finished. Nor is there any doubt that *The History of the Life* was written by Elizabeth Tanfield Cary. The internal evidence—the form, vocabulary, sentiments, pattern of alliteration, and so on—are strongly indicative of Cary's hand. The "E. F." on the title page is not a problem—Cary from 1620 signs herself "E. Falkland," not "E. Cary."

Authorship of the *Unfortunate Prince* is less certain. John Playford's copy-text for the 1680 quarto is said to have been found among Falkland's own papers. Whether or not this was the same copy used by Cary in 1627 when she wrote her *History of the Life* is impossible to say; but there is no reason for us to doubt that such a manuscript actually belonged to the Falklands, nor is there any evidence that such a manuscript ever belonged to anyone else during their lifetime. Whether Falkland was himself the author of the *Unfortunate Prince*, as assumed by Playford, has not yet been investigated in a careful attributional study. As for its date, the *Unfortunate Prince* is certainly earlier than Cary's *History of the Life*; and there are numerous indications in the text (such as an apparent reference to the death of James I) that it may have been written ca. 1626–27, at a time when many of the peers were anxiously warning Charles I to stop showering favors on his beloved "Steenie," the Duke of Buckingham. It could have been written earlier, as a Plutarchan parallel with the life of King James, whose own escapades with Buckingham had been a source of widespread resentment; but the best bet, I think, is ca. 1626, only weeks or months before Cary used it for her *History of the Life*.

The *Unfortunate Prince* focuses on King Edward's improvidence, especially with respect to the "depraved and vicious inclination" that he showed toward his favorites, Gaveston and Despenser. The narrator of the *Unfortunate Prince* is presented as a sage counselor who warns against the mistakes of an earlier age; and he leaves no doubt that Despenser, as the chief villain of the piece, is a stand-in for Buckingham:

> Let the favourite taste the king's bounty, and enjoy his ear; but let him not engross it wholly, or take upon him the sway and governance of all the affairs of his master.... As kings ought to limit their favours, so ought they to be curious in the election; for persons of baser or meaner quality, exalted, are followed at the heels with a perpetual murmur and hatred.[33]

Similar glances at Buckingham's career appear on almost every page of the narrative.

---

[33]*Unfortunate Prince*, 120.

In the latter half of the *Unfortunate Prince*, the narrative focus shifts from Edward's failure as king, to the success of Edward's abandoned Queen (the historical Isabella).[34] Forsaken and neglected by her lord, and confined to her chambers, the Queen finally steals away to France, taking her son, Prince Edward, with her. When she returns, she returns as a conqueror, deposing her husband and crushing her former adversaries.

When Cary wrote *The History of the Life*, she was ill and destitute, and dependent for her very survival on the intermittent charity of a few old friends (including the Duchess of Buckingham, whom Falkland heartily despised as a bad influence on his wife). Cary also wrote with considerable haste—"at the worst," as she says in her preface, "'twas but one Month mis-spended; which cannot promise ought in right Perfection."[35] These factors may partly account for the artistic inferiority of Cary's *History of the Life* relative to *Mariam*, and perhaps also for the extraordinary degree to which Cary has plagiarized her source material: in writing *The History of the Life*, Cary simply incorporates *The History of the Most Unfortunate Prince*, and with only minimal alteration except in those long stretches where she casts the text into irregular blank verse.

Cary's motives for writing *The History of the Life* are not easily reconstructed. Struggling with debt and hunger, it may be that Cary took up the pen in hopes that she could sell her finished chronicle to a stationer. (If so, no one wanted it: her work was not published until 1680.) It may be that she took the *Unfortunate Prince* as her source for this new writing-project only because most of her other books and manuscripts had been confiscated during her confinement. (But in that case, it would have been easier, and more profitable given the high cost of writing paper, for Cary merely to have sold the *original* manuscript to a stationer, without revision.) The artistic motive is likewise obscure. There are many indications—the most obvious of which is the recasting of prose into blank verse—that Cary thought of her redaction as an improvement over the original. Yet the texts are remarkably similar at first glance, on account of Cary's excessive borrowing (which is why the two versions are so often confounded). Indeed, even the shift from prose to verse is easily overlooked: in our only extant textual authority—the folio text of 1680—Cary's entire narrative, including the verse, is printed as prose.[36]

---

[34]After her initial introduction, Isabella is not usually mentioned by name in either version.

[35]E. Cary, *History of the Life*, sig. A2v.

[36]Irregularities in the verse suggest that the printer found the lines thus arranged in his copy-text. Perhaps Cary's poverty at the time forced her to conserve paper by printing her verse as prose; but since the text is considerably less readable when rearranged as verse, future editors will do well, I think, to follow the folio text in printing the entire work as prose.

It is not, however, difficult to see why a story of Edward II and his queen had special significance for Elizabeth Cary in 1627. When she first selected this tale of a woman's revenge as a fitting subject for her own pen, Cary no less than Edward's queen had been abandoned by a proud, haughty, and cruel spouse. Like Edward's queen, Cary was confined to her quarters and forced to rely on her wits for a remedy. One might suppose, then, that Cary's text would look very different from her source, at least with respect to Edward and his forsaken queen—and indeed, some readers have already seen, or thought they saw, some antipatriarchal rage in Edward's Queen.[37] Curiously, however, Cary in rewriting the story simply transported, into her own narrative, the thoroughly patriarchal ideology of the *Unfortunate Prince*—including even many of the narrator's misogynistic or gynophobic remarks. Disappointingly, Cary's text appears as anxious as its predecessor—at every level of English society, both domestically and politically—to preserve patriarchal order. To read *The History of the Life* as a woman's text is thus especially problematic.

Some of that difficulty may be erased if we can think of Cary's *History of the Life* as three texts in one. First there is the narrative source, about 90 percent of which resurfaces in Cary's redaction, much of it copied verbatim. Second is Cary's completed text, which is considerably longer than the original (and, it must be confessed, more tedious in its exposition). Neither of these works has much intrinsic interest either as literature or as a political or historical discourse. Cary's *History of the Life* also contains within it, however, a third text of considerable interest, one that is more or less invisible to ordinary reading. This other text is a basket of fragments, for it consists of the *difference* between Cary's completed text and the orig-

---

[37]For example, in a paper recently presented at the annual meeting of the Shakespeare Association, the author mistakenly assumed that Cary wrote *The History of the Most Unfortunate Prince*. The author of the paper was blissfully unaware that there are two versions, and Cary's text is the one that she had not read. Thinking the *Unfortunate Prince* to be Cary's work, this author then compared the text with Holinshed's *Chronicles*, which she took to be Cary's source for the narrative, and found in Cary's supposed departures from Holinshed evidence of Cary's feminist sensibilities—even though the author of *The Unfortunate Prince* was almost certainly a male with little interest in women's rights. Another contributor to the same seminar discussed, with some ingenuity, the report in Josephus that Mariam was charged with "criminal conversation," i.e., adultery. But her quotations from Josephus were taken from "Flavius Josephus, *The Life and Works of Flavius Josephus*," trans. William Whiston [n.d.]. Mariam's source was the 1602 translation of Thomas Lodge, in which the euphemistic phrase "criminal conversation" does not appear. Lodge repeatedly uses the word "adultery." See Lodge, trans. *The Famous and Memorable Workes of Josephus* (London, 1602), bks. 15–16. Such are the pitfalls of reading our own critical ideology into the text when we have not first done a little old-fashioned research.

inal *Unfortunate Prince*.[38] The difference is not altogether obvious, even (for example) with respect to the Queen. Neither Cary's Queen, nor that of her source, is especially villainous or heroic. There is no sense in which Cary turns a femme fatale into a feminist, or vice versa. The narrators of both *Edwards* are surprisingly fair-minded, at least with respect to both Edward and the Queen. Nevertheless, in the interstices of Cary's text there appears a Queen that is more complex—at once more vengeful and romantic, expressive and histrionic, and (in my own reading, anyway) more like Elizabeth Cary—than either the original Queen or Cary's composite figure.

In her wholesale borrowing, Cary took few pains to change her author's conventional sentiments concerning the role and nature of women; yet her tinkering with the source material illustrates her imperfectly suppressed identification with the Queen, and her fascination with

---

[38]Compare, for a fairly representative example, the following. First, from the *Unfortunate Prince*, with Cary's principal omissions stricken: "Love and jealousy, ~~two powerful motives,~~ spurred her on to undertake it. She saw the king a stranger to her bed, and revelling in the embraces of his wanton minions, without ~~so much as~~ a glance or look on her deserving beauty. This contempt had begot in her impressions of a like, though ~~not so wanton and licentious a~~ nature. She wanting a fit subject for her affections to work on ~~(her wedlock being thus estranged)~~ had fixed her wandering eye upon ~~the goodly shape and beauty of~~ the gallant Mortimer. He was not behind-hand in the reception ~~and comely entertainment of so rich and desired a purchase.~~ But his last act had lodged him in the tower, which was a cage ~~too~~ strait ~~to crown their desires with their full perfection.~~ Yet there is a sweet correspondency continued; letters and many loving messages bring their hearts together, ~~tho' their bodies were divided~~" (*Unfortunate Prince*, 109).

Second, from *The History of the Life*, with Cary's principal additions emphasized here in bold type: "Love and Jealousie, **that equally possest the queen**, being intermixed **with a stronger desire of Revenge**, spurs her on **to hasten on this Journey.** She saw the King a stranger to her bed, and revelling in the wanton embraces of his **stoln** pleasures, without a glance on her deserving Beauty. This contempt had begot a like change in her, though **in a more modest** nature, her **youthful** Affections wanting a fit subject to work on, **and being debarr'd of that warmth that should have still preserv'd their temper,** she had cast her wandering eye upon the gallant *Mortimer*, **a piece of masculine Bravery without exception; had those his inward Gifts been like his outside, he had** not been behinde-hand in reception, **but with a Courtly, brave respect, full meets her Glances. A silent Rhetorick, sparkling Love, findes quick admittance; such private trading needs few words or brokage**: but his last Act had mew'd him in the *Tower*, **where he was fast from sight of his great Mistress' Love, that makes some men fools, makes others wary: had** *Mortimer*'s **designe been known, his head had paid for't; which** *Spencer*'s **malice long and strongly aim'd at, but that the Queen had begg'd a solemn respite, which** *Edward* **would not break at his intreaty. The** cage of his restraint was strong, and guarded; **yet 'twas too weak to cloyster his Ambition, which did suspect, but never fear'd his Freedome; which he attempts, but yet was not so sure, that he durst trust it.** In the mean time, with a sweet Correspondencie, and the interchange of many amorous Letters, their hearts are brought together, **and their several intents perfectly known**; ..." (E. Cary, *History of the Life*, 90–91).

the Queen's empirical conquest over her male adversaries. For example, in relating the Queen's summary execution of the earl of Arundel, the *Unfortunate Prince* informs us that "we may not properly expect reason in women's actions, whose passions are their principal guide and mover."[39] In Cary's text this reads, "we may not properly expect Reason in Women's actions: It was enough the incensed Queen would have it so, against which was no disputing."[40] Throughout the latter half of her narrative, Cary subtly (or timidly, or hastily) rewrites the Queen's revenge as springing, not from a feminine subjection to irrational passions, but from a potent female will (notwithstanding the unchallenged sentiment about women's supposed unreasonability). Cary's interstitial Queen also learns, however, that literal revenge is an evil to be avoided. In the additions, the abandoned wife suffers remorse for harboring hostile thoughts of her unloving lord, as when Cary reports that "The Queen, who was guilty but in circumstance, and but an accessory to the Intention, not the Fact" of her husband's death, nevertheless "tasted with a bitter time of Repentance, what it was but to be quoted in the Margent of such a Story."[41] Cary thus adds to the source-Queen a spiritual refinement that is scarcely visible in the composite sketch of her completed *History of the Life*.

The Edward that dwells in the difference between these two narratives is likewise distinct from both the original king and Cary's composite Edward. In the interstitial Edward of Cary's revision, homosexual desire is not really at issue; but Cary's additions and omissions repeatedly underscore the likeness of King Edward to her own Lord Falkland, whose private life was now marked by the abandonment of a virtuous wife and who as Lord Deputy of Ireland had cruelly oppressed an entire nation—a nation of Catholics with whom Elizabeth Cary had greatly sympathized.

I cannot say how conscious Cary was of the way in which the changes that she imposed on the *Unfortunate Prince* subtly altered the text as an analogue for her relations with Falkland. But there are indications in the text that Cary's revising hand may have had a precise motivation that went beyond either financial or aesthetic concerns. And if—as seems entirely plausible—the original manuscript of the *Unfortunate Prince* was not just owned, but written, by her husband, then even Cary's excessive borrowing may be read in a more sympathetic light: Cary's redaction on the *Unfortunate Prince* may represent a deliberate appropriation and rewriting of her husband's text as a mirror whereby he might view his own monstrous image. There are, at least, frequent moments in Cary's

---

[39] *Unfortunate Prince*, 119.
[40] E. Cary, *History of the Life*, 130.
[41] Ibid., 155.

narrative that lend themselves to such a reading, for her Queen repeat-edly rewrites the text of her adversaries. In Cary's source, for example, the Queen attempts to escape from her confinement. But "seeing herself deluded, and this opportunity stolen from her by those whom she before so mortally hated, [she] sets her own brains a-working, to invent a speedy remedy. She was therein so fortunate, as to pretend a journey of devotion and pilgrimage to St. Thomas, of Canterbury, which by her overseers was wholly unsuspected."[42] In Cary's narrative, this passage becomes a site of more-than-usual revision:

> Yet *Edward* would not give consent she should be a gadding; time past away; she labours hard, but fruitless, till at length she found she was abused. *Guien* must be rather lost, than she should wander. Her heart so strongly fix'd upon this Journey, was torn as much with anger as with sorrow: Reason at length o'recame her Sexes weakness, and bids her rather cure, than vent her Passion. The opportunity thus snatch'd from her hopes, she seems well pleased, and glad to stay at home; no inward motion seem'd to appear, that might beget suspicion. *Spencer*, that was as cunning as a Serpent, findes here a female Wit that went beyond him, one that with his own Weapons wounds his Wisdome, and taught him not to trust a Womans Lip-Salve, when that he knew her breast was fill'd with rancour. When the nap of this Project was fallen off, and *Spencer* with the king were seeking for some other bush to stop this gap, her judgment was so fortunate as to pre-tend a Journey of Devotion to St *Thomas* of *Canterbury*; which by her jealous Overseers (being a Work of Piety) is wholly unsus-pected.[43]

If it was Cary's intent to appropriate and to rewrite a discourse that was not just owned, but *written* by her husband, and to cast it back in his teeth with new meaning as an ostensible "Work of Piety," then Falkland, like Spencer, found here a female wit that went beyond him, one that with his own weapon wounded his wisdom. It is of course not certain that Play-ford was correct in ascribing the *Unfortunate Prince* to Falkland. But if the *Unfortunate Prince* was indeed Falkland's—even if he did not write it, but sent it to his wife as part of his ongoing effort to drive a wedge between her and the Duchess of Buckingham—then Cary's *History* looks less like an instance of mindless plagiarism than like a piece of marital mischief—like a narrative that simultaneously relates, and enacts, a symbolic

[42]*Unfortunate Prince*, 109.
[43]E. Cary, *History of the Life*, 90–91.

revenge on her oppressive lord. Falkland's manuscript (whoever the author) points to a mote in the eye of Buckingham and the king; Cary's *History of the Life* suggests that there is a beam in the eye of her husband. Those readers who hold that an author's biography is irrelevant to our interpretive activities will of course be unwilling to consider such a hypothesis; but such readers are left with a narrative that is far less interesting.

Whatever it was that Cary thought she was doing in her *History of the Life*, she seems to have spoken with a prophetic voice. Two years later, in 1629, her husband was recalled from Ireland in disgrace and forced to defend himself against grievous charges concerning his conduct as Lord Deputy; his financial condition worsened year after year; and in 1633 he suffered a death that was almost as gruesome as that of King Edward. Yet Falkland, like King Edward, was largely responsible for his own demise. His banished wife lacked the resources, if not the will, to effect his overthrow (and even her conversion to Catholicism cannot have injured him as much as he liked to think that it did). Nor is it likely that Cary wished consciously to get even with her husband for his cruelty. According to the "Life," Elizabeth Cary preserved, till the hour of her husband's death, a posture of dutiful concern for his spiritual, material, and political welfare. Anne Cary allows no possibility that her mother resented the brutal treatment that she received as a forsaken spouse; Anne suggests even that her mother won the ultimate victory—that her father on his deathbed submitted, in silence, to his wife's superior understanding of divine truth.

Be all that as it may, Cary this time was not fully content with a symbolic victory over those patriarchal institutions and individuals that sought to control her life. She was, perhaps, able to sustain an attitude of loving servility to her peremptory spouse, and that may be due partly to the satisfaction that she took in her Queen's fictive victory as a metaphorical substitute for a literal revenge. Yet in the two decades between the writing of *Mariam* and the writing of *The History of the Life*, Elizabeth Cary had fashioned herself into a woman who was no longer satisfied simply to amuse herself with the imaginative textual triumphs of Mariam, Queen Isabella, St. Mary Magdalene, St. Agnes Martyr, St. Elizabeth of Portugal, or Cardinal Davy du Perron. No longer was she willing to bear her cross in silence, with "a dutiful, though scornful smile." Elizabeth Cary in the interim had become a woman who insisted upon a *spiritual* (and thus, to her mind, an altogether *literal*) triumph over her male adversaries. Literary endeavor, even if gratifying, lacked the power of redemption; literary discourse was at best a glass through which to behold a path of true virtue.

The History of the Life is less remarkable as literature than for its apparent role in shaping the central event of Cary's subsequent biography: the kidnapping of her sons in 1636, and the safe delivery of her children to Catholic houses in France. Cary's greatest ambition, during the final decade of her life, was to reenact—literally—a portion of her Queen's triumph. The Queen in Cary's narrative empowers her revolt by taking to France her only child, Prince Edward, without whose abduction the Queen's subsequent victory in England could not have taken place. Not long after her retelling of that story, Elizabeth Cary hit upon the madcap plan of following her fictive Queen's example. She was not able to do so while her husband was yet living; but within three years after his death, Cary plotted the successful abduction of her two youngest sons from the home of her eldest, Lucius (a rationalist who, if he was not already beyond hope of eternal salvation, was at least beyond all hope of kidnapping). The abduction of her sons coincided with a virtual kidnapping of her three youngest daughters—with a visit to their mother's house, authorized by Lucius, from which they never returned. Elizabeth's plan was to send her children to France to be raised as Roman Catholics— and her plan succeeded despite enormous obstacles, not the least of which was a nearly complete lack of ready cash. Anne Cary attributes the success of this unlikely plot to God's Roman Catholic providence. To the secular reader its success appears rather to have depended almost entirely on the extraordinary resolve of Elizabeth Cary, who successfully prosecuted her scheme, long after the abduction was discovered, in open defiance of the King's Privy Council, Chief Justice Bramston, and Archbishop Laud—all of whom joined hands with Lucius Cary in demanding the immediate return of the children, and not one of whom was able to restrain her, even with threats of imprisonment.[44] Threats of confinement no longer daunted Cary as they had when she was a child. Unintimidated, Cary took every opportunity to defend her actions, even before the King. Clearly, Cary's attempted reconciliation of public utterance with feminine virtue had ceased to be a problem—except for her frustrated adversaries. Cary's triumph over England's legal and ecclesiastical authorities, as described by Anne Cary in the "Life," was not unlike that of the Queen's triumph in her mother's own *History of the Life*: "[T]hey, to justifie themselves, profess it freely the Queen had gone beyond them with their Cunning; ... Thus Womens Wit can sometimes cozen Statesmen."[45]

Cary's abduction of her children, and her subsequent self-defense before the combined powers of institutionalized patriarchy, were

---

[44] The story of Elizabeth Cary's abduction of her children is told in the "Life" and corroborated by letters and court papers in the Public Record Office. See Simpson, 80–111, 182–89.

[45] E. Cary, *History of the Life*, 109.

supremely literal triumphs by a woman whose literary efforts for thirty years had been recalled, burned, ignored, or forgotten. In this artful domestic drama, Elizabeth Cary cast herself, Elizabeth Cary, as her own crafty protagonist. It cannot, of course, be proven that Cary's abduction of her children was prompted by her own fictive Queen's successful abduction of a fictive Prince Edward. But *The History of the Life* makes it abundantly clear that Cary, living and writing in dire poverty, identified strongly with her Queen's suffering; and given the extraordinary act of kidnapping her own sons, I think there is little doubt that Cary came also to identify with her Queen's triumphant victory. Cary, like all successful authors, wrote from her private experience; but Cary's work, to an uncommon degree, seems to mirror her life both coming and going. Unwilling to accept the "feminine" role of a selfless woman, unable to conform to the rule established for a virtuous Anglican wife, Cary instead shaped a self that was partly modeled upon her own fiction, drafting fictive heroines that came to shape her own biography.

Except for the obstinate rationalism of her eldest son, Elizabeth Cary in her last days could relish a complete and gratifying triumph over her adversaries. Cary's children were taken from her in 1626; she wrote *The History of the Life* in 1627; her husband died in September 1633; she kidnapped her sons in 1636; and she managed to spirit six of her eight children to France before her death in 1639. Before she died, she saw those six become Catholics (her four daughters as Benedictine nuns). Her tyrannical husband was dead, and (as she thought) he may have died as a Catholic: the best of both worlds. There was even some hope that her eldest son, Lucius, would convert. He did not, but she died happy anyway. Anne writes that her mother was garrulous to the end, a woman who in her last days, as always, "spake very much, and earnestly."[46] "[I]n her last sickness ... she was very quiet, pliable, and easily ruled, which were not very natural to her," and her audience, never very large, was diminished in the end to a few faithful friends.[47] There is no indication that she expected any of her original writings to be read or valued after her death, except perhaps by her own children. And indeed, until the recent revival of interest in her work, the voice of Elizabeth Tanfield Cary has been silent. It may have been more satisfying, for us, if Cary had invested more of her inexhaustible energy in her literary endeavors than in the making over of her children into images of herself. But Elizabeth Tanfield Cary was a woman with a mind of her own. Her last public and creative act, before she died, was to rename herself after the mother of God.[48]

---

[46]A. Cary, "Life," 115.
[47]Ibid., 121.
[48]Ibid., 39, 117.

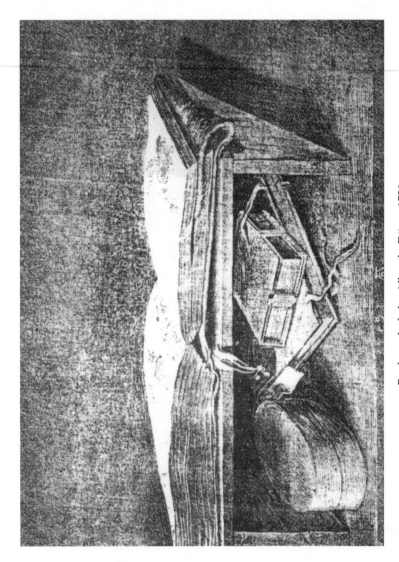

Book on desk, by Albrecht Dürer, 1521, 198X 280. Wein, Albertina [Winkler 791]

TEN

Dictionary English and the Female Tongue

Juliet Fleming

> *I am supposing that in every society the production of discourse is at once controlled, selected, organised and redistributed according to a certain number of procedures, whose role is to avert its powers and its dangers, to cope with chance events, to evade its ponderous, awesome materiality.*
>
> *Michel Foucault, "The Discourse on Language"*

I

> *Speech is not merely the medium which manifests—or dissembles—desire; it is also the object of desire. Similarly ... speech is no mere verbalisation of conflicts and systems of domination, but ... is the very object of man's conflicts.*
>
> *Michel Foucault, "The Discourse on Language"*

What is arguably the first dictionary of vernacular English was published by Robert Cawdrey as *A Table Alphabeticall, conteyning and teaching the true writing and understanding of hard usuall English wordes, borrowed from the Hebrew, Greeke, Latine, or French, &. With the interpretation therof by plaine English words, gathered for the benefit and helpe of Ladies, Gentlewomen, or any other unskilful persons* (London, Edmund Weaver, 1604).[1] The three dictionaries that followed it, John Bullokar's *An English Expositor* (1616), Henry Cockeram's *The English Dictionarie* (1623), and Thomas Blount's *Glossographia* (1656), were also directed at least in part to women. This essay investigates the configurations of the relationship between the feminine and the vernacular at the inception of the English dictionary, and argues

---

[1]For a description of the fifteenth- and sixteenth-century bilingual lexicographic activity which precedes Cawdrey see Gertrude Stein, *The English Dictionary before Cawdrey* (Tübingen: Niemeyer, 1986); and Jürgen Schäfer, *Early Modern English Lexicography: A Survey of Monolingual Printed Glossaries and Dictionaries 1475-1640* (Oxford: Clarendon Press, 1989).

for the importance of this association in the creation of the national "standard."

For it is a curious fact that female difference is regularly evoked in the early history of English lexicography, through the production of, and further proposals for, dictionaries "for women." Since in England the emergence of the vernacular as a prestige language, and its concomitant representation in a fairly standard printed form, coincided with and reflected the beginnings of national capitalism, one might expect early prescriptions of English to address themselves in the first instance to those class divisions out of which seventeenth-century Britain was produced—divisions which have certainly determined all subsequent descriptions of standard English. And *A Table Alphabeticall* does indeed claim to have been "gathered for the benefit ... of Ladies, Gentlewomen, *or any other unskilful persons*" (emphasis added), while succeeding dictionaries accord an ever diminishing importance to women among those "unskilful" people whose existence justifies the lexicographic project. It is however not until the publication in 1658 of Edward Phillips's *New World of English Words* that the English dictionary falls, for the first time, completely silent on the subject of women; and even after this the ladies' dictionary continues its uncanny irruption into the field of English lexicography, appearing now as a joke, now as a threat, and now as an intimation of the chaos that lies beyond the pale of national linguistic regulation. There may then be something to be gained in following the inclination of the earliest English dictionary, and according primacy to the difference made by sex.[2]

Commenting on the importance, to the project of nationalism, of developing a common language, and a literature based on it, Max Weber pointed to one typical, but typically overlooked, resource,

> namely, women. They contributed specifically to the formation of national sentiment linked to language. An erotic lyric addressed to a woman can hardly be written in a foreign language, because then it would be unintelligible to the addressee. The courtly and chivalrous lyric was neither singular, nor always the first literature to displace Latin by the national language, as happened in France, Italy, Germany, or to displace Chinese, as happened in

---

[2]For a brilliant and provocative essay on the politics of early lexicography and its present effects, see Allon White, "The Dismal Sacred Word: Academic Language and the Social Reproduction of Seriousness," *LTP: journal of literature, teaching, politics,* 2 (1983): 4-15. While I also credit the early English dictionary with a stern and serious cultural *effect,* I argue that at a local level—the level at which it is addressed to women—its intention is, precisely, less than serious.

opportunity for the official extension of gender norms into the realm of language. Claiming that personally he had "long lamented that we have no lawful standard of our language set up, for those to repair to, who might chuse to speak and write it grammatically and correctly," Chesterfield congratulated Johnson on having put himself forward as the linguistic "dictator" of English, and professed his own readiness to be instructed in its proper use.[9] The flippancy which characterizes Chesterfield's approval (and doubtless contributed to Johnson's sense of having been ill-served by it) constructs Johnson's project as a work of menial seriousness in contrast to Chesterfield's more aristocratic levity. What interests me here, however, is that Chesterfield's arrogation of a politesse that will, after all, not be able to take Johnson too seriously finds its fullest expression in his concern for the ladies. Pretending to hold that language is "indisputably the more immediate province of the fair sex," Chesterfield represents women as talking more, coining words at need, extending established words "to various and very different significations," and finally eschewing the "dry crabbed rules of etymology and grammar" in favor of a polite, "auricular" spelling that relies on "the justness and delicacy of the ear." The problem that Chesterfield then poses for Johnson is where to contain within his dictionary "those words and phrases which, hastily begot, owe their birth to the incontinence of female eloquence."

---

fatti sono maschy, Wordes they are women, and deeds they are men. But let such know that *Detti* and *fatti*, wordes and deeds with me are all one gender. And though they were commonly feminine, why might not I by strong imagination (which Physicians give so much power unto) alter their sexe?" Florio is alluding here to Montaigne's essay "Of the power of the imagination," which tells the story of a girl whose strenuous jump caused "masculine organs [to come] forth"; and about which Montaigne observes, "It is not so great a marvel that this sort of accident is frequently met with. For if the imagination has power in such things, it is so continually and vigorously fixed on this subject that in order not to have to relapse so often into the same thought and sharpness of desire, it is better off if once and for all it incorporates this masculine member into girls." For a discussion of this passage and the "one sex" model of human biology that it suggests see Thomas Laqueur, *Making Sex: Body and Gender from the Greeks to Freud* (Cambridge: Harvard University Press, 1990), 126-130. Johnson knew Florio's *Montaigne*, and may be citing it here: his refusal to sustain its playful claim that the two sexes are versions of each other may reinforce Laqueur's claim that human sexual nature was reconceptualized during the eighteenth century, and aligned with the proposal that the two sexes were incommensurable. (Laqueur, 5)

[9]"Toleration, adoption, and naturalization have run their lengths. Good order and authority are now necessary. But where shall we find them, and, at the same time, the obedience due to them? We must have recourse to the old Roman expedient in times of confusion, and choose a dictator. Upon this principle, I give my vote for Mr Johnson to fill that great and arduous post. And I hereby declare, that I make a total surrender of all my rights and privileges in the English language, as a free-born British subject to the said Mr Johnson during the term of his dictatorship." *The World*, 100, 1754.

Chesterfield's "serious" advice to Johnson in this imaginary dilemma is to publish "by way of appendix to his great work, a genteel Neological dictionary, containing those polite, though perhaps not strictly grammatical words and phrases" affected by women. He claims two advantages for this course. First, by affording space to their words, Johnson might contain the threat that women pose to the lexicographer: "By such an act of toleration, who knows but he may, in time, bring them within the pale of the English Language?"[10] Second, by compiling a woman's supplement, the lexicographer provides himself with a key to polite society:

> I must also hint to Mr Johnson, that such a small supplemental dictionary will contribute infinitely to the sale of the great one; and I make no question, but that under the protection of that little work, the great one will be received in the genteelest houses. We shall frequently meet with it in ladies dressing rooms, lying upon the harpsicord, together with the knotting bag, and signor Di Giardino's incomparable concertos; and even sometimes in the powder-rooms of our young nobility, upon the same shelf with their German flute, their powder-mask, and their four-horse whip.

Implying that there is something "ungenteel" about Johnson's project as it stands, Chesterfield proposes a modification that has a curious series of effects. For the "neological appendix" would mark Johnson as an over-sexed drudge who looms dangerously close to the wives and daughters of his aristocratic patrons; it would also mark the dictionary itself as a common thing, frequently met with as it circulates in the market or lies undistinguished among other attributes of female or dandiacal pleasure.

---

[10]Chesterfield's metaphor, extant in the eighteenth century largely in the context of the English attempt to "settle" Ireland, is one instance of a regularly evoked analogy between lexicographic practice and the internal politics of colonial Britain. For other examples consider Chesterfield's claim that he has "rights and privileges in the English language as a free-born British subject" (see n. 8, above); and Johnson's famous admonition in his *Preface to the Dictionary* (1755): "Tongues, like governments, have a natural tendency to degeneration; we have long preserved our constitution, let us make some struggles for our language." Chesterfield's claim that "toleration" will eventually bring women "within the pale" of standard English may appear to have some predictive power, for within the history of the English dictionary female difference is first "specially" catered to, and then assimilated, officially disappearing from the field of lexicography by the beginning of the eighteenth century. That this assimilation is not tied to the political reality of women should remind us that, although as an arena within which social discriminations are enforced, language serves as a particularly powerful metaphor for social organization, to assert a *necessary* connection between the linguistic and the political spheres is always to be arguing from within the very heart of national politics.

However, the humiliation of Johnson which is Chesterfield's joke is not supposed to be absolute: the lexicographer exposes himself to the dangers of the marketplace (dangers which include both class derogation and an effeminizing contact with women) only to triumph over them. For just as a "proper" man may be produced out of and in contradistinction to his immersion in the company of women, so too the ladies' appendix serves to provide a secondary term (here a profusion of "polite" words) out of which a primary term—"standard English"—may be produced. But it is important to observe that if the feminine is used to mark the nonstandard out of which the standard may be born, the nonstandard provides in its turn an opportunity for the introduction of the notion of femininity, and consequently masculinity, into standard English.

It is my assumption in this essay that women were interpellated as users of hard word lists not because they cared to ascertain the correct use of English, but because they could be used to represent its problems. The early English dictionary is then, among other things, a type of colonialist discourse, one which produces a disruptive other as the grounds on which to assert its own adequacy, proceeding first by the full exhibition of that which is to be effaced or repressed.[11] The choice of woman to represent the lexical extravagance that would justify regulation is facilitated in early modern England by the traditional association of maleness with form and femaleness with matter that informs Johnson's later comment; but it may also have had a more local determinant. In western Europe standardization of a national language was usually preceeded by a *questione della lingua*, in which rival dialects competed to become the basis for the standard. But South East Midlands, the dialect associated with London and its environs, had reigned more or less unchallenged as the synecdochic dialect of England since its adoption as the language of Chancery by Henry V.[12] In the absence of regional contests, and within a linguistic community that had not yet officially attached the question of language to that of class, sexual difference may have appeared to be the obvious place in which to erect those distinctions which would enable the division of English into its standard, and consequently nonstandard forms.

---

[11]For a description of this process of exhibition followed by exclusion, and a brief discussion of its functioning in the linguistic community of early modern England, see Steven Mullaney, *The Place of the Stage: License, Play, and Power in Renaissance England* (Chicago: University of Chicago Press, 1988), chap. 2. Patricia Parker has already suggested that "the dilation and control of a copiousness figured as female might be seen as the gendered counterpart" of this process of containment through rehearsal; see *Literary Fat Ladies*, 31.

[12]See John Earl Joseph, *Eloquence and Power: The Rise of Language Standards and Standard Languages* (London: Frances Pinter, 1987), 58-60.

III

No language (language) is capable of speaking (the) truth without submitting to the common or proper terms that mould it into adequate, that is to say essential terms.

Luce Irigaray, *"The Language of Men"* [13]

In his account of language standardization in western Europe, John Earl Joseph argues that the process typically began when the stable functional division between Latin and a native vernacular (a division within which Latin was superposed as the language of prestige) began to break down.[14] The development of the vernacular into a language which could itself perform all official functions then typically proceeded according to two phases, which may have overlapped in time, but which are functionally and ideologically distinct. In the first phase, attention to the perceived "inadequacy" of a native tongue gave rise to a period of rapid elaboration, during which structural or lexical elements were added to make the language adequate to new needs. In the second or restrictive phase of standardization regulations were introduced to stop unsupervised elaboration and make variation less a matter of choice than of fixed rules.[15] It is this second phase, during which an apparently random vari-

[13]Luce Irigaray, "The Language of Men," in *Cultural Critique* 13 (Fall 1989): 191-202. In Irigaray's work "the language of men" is opposed to a female speech (or mother tongue) that resists the tyranny of the "proper."

[14]See Joseph, 48-56: his argument is more nuanced that my summary suggests. Joseph argues that while language standards (that is, linguistic value judgments) exist in every linguistic community, "standard languages" represent a specifically European concept, whose defining criteria are based on the attributes of the European languages and European cultural values. These criteria include the presence of nonstandard dialects against which the norm can be articulated: the codification of standard norms in written forms such as dictionaries and grammars; and the use of the standard language in prestige functions such as the writing of national literature, science, technology, medicine, religion, and law, the keeping of historical records, and the development of a unified philosophical tradition.

[15]Joseph connects elaboration and restriction in a diachronic sequence, with restriction following and responding to elaboration. There is certainly evidence to suggest that the standardization of English was *experienced* according to this model, so that, for example, sixteenth-century theorists felt that their language was "unruled" and unruly, while eighteenth-century grammarians and lexicographers believed they possessed a vernacular that was more nearly perfect and "fixed." But such perceptions may represent political rather than linguistic judgments, and the story of the standardization of English to which they correspond should be treated with caution. We could for example evoke a different, synchronic model for standardization, one in which regulation *produces* elaboration, and, in so doing, produces itself. For a brief description of the attempt to institute grammatical control of linguistic "abundance" in early modern England which relies on this synchronic model see Patricia Parker, *Literary Fat Ladies*, 114. My own account draws from both models since I hold: 1) that English as it standardized produced and thrived on the threat that women and

ation is replaced with one that is hierarchically organized, that produces the standard language as a terrain on which linguistic and social distinctions may be drawn.

In the case of English, the elaborative phase occupies the second half of the sixteenth century, and is most memorably manifest in the production of the national literature that was its aim and sign, while the restrictive phase of standardization can be located in the seventeenth century. Consequently, when Cawdrey published his *Table Alphabetical* in 1604, English was not yet the patriarchal monolith against which some modern feminisms have tilted. In the first half of the sixteenth century it had been overshadowed by Latin (and to a more limited extent by French) and had enjoyed the reputation of being a rude, inadequate, and unpolished tongue, best fit for instruction of the unlearned.[16] Translations and other vernacular works offered prefatory apologies for the inadequacy of their medium, and thereby asserted the superiority of Latin, French, and those who could speak them, even while marking the beginning of the end of their domination.[17] The middle of the sixteenth century then saw an extraordinary period of elaboration, during which the lexicon was nearly doubled through the addition of words borrowed, coined, and revived, until the old anxiety that there are "moe things, then there are wordes to express things by" had apparently been quieted. By the end of Elizabeth's reign the vernacular success of her poets had proved that English was, after all, an "eloquent" tongue, whose geographic and social mar-

---

the principles of linguistic elaboration could be assumed to pose to it; and 2) that there *was* a brief moment in the early modern period when English was beyond the pale of the newly born impulse towards grammatical and lexical regulation.

[16]For a useful summary of sixteenth- and seventeenth-century opinions on the English vernacular see Richard Foster Jones, *The Triumph of the English Language: A Survey of Opinions Concerning the Vernacular from the Introduction of Printing to the Restoration* (Stanford: Stanford University Press, 1953), whose work I am summarizing here. Jones concludes (168): "The fact that the native language was associated with the rude multitude, in contrast to the learned few, that it was the medium through which the former were to be enlightened, that it could be employed in books by those unblessed with a classical education, that it had to be used in a simple, plain, 'ineloquent' manner to achieve its ends, and that it was an 'unruled' tongue with an irrational orthography—all these facts led to the conclusion that the language itself was rude, or barbarous."

[17]See for example the introduction to Ascham's *Toxophilus* (London, 1545), a guide to archery written in English "for the benefit of the unlatined": "And as for the Latin or Greke tongue, everything is so excellently done in them that none can do better: In the English tongue, contrary, every thinge in a manner so meanly, both for the matter and handelynge that no man can do worse." Quoted in Jones, 14.

ginality was coming to an end.[18] But it was still "unruled," lacking a grammar, a lexicon, and a standardized spelling; where Sir Philip Sidney, who lived and died while the elaborative stage of English was at its height, had considered it one of the strengths of the vernacular that it was not subject to grammatical regulation, seventeenth-century England seems to have suddenly felt the need for a vernacular that could operate as a stable register of the authority and the distinctions that were to define the Stuart age.[19] The slow movement of English into the second or restrictive stage of standardization can be plotted by the gradual yielding of sixteenth-century works on rhetoric to the grammars, orthographies, and dictionaries of the seventeenth century.

William Bullokar was the first person to call for an English grammar and dictionary and predict their stabilizing effect in his *Booke at Large, for the Amendment of Orthographie for English Speech* (1580). His appeal was seconded two years later in Richard Mulcaster's *Firste Part of the Elementarie* (1582):

> It were a thing verie praiseworthy in my opinion, and no less profitable than praiseworthie, if somone well learned and as laborious a man, wold gather all the words which we use in our English tung, whether naturall or incorporate, out of all professions, as well learned as not, into one dictionarie, and besides the right writing, which is incident to the Alphabete, wold open unto us therin, both their naturall force, and their proper use: that by his honest travell we might be as able to judge of our own tung, which we have by rote, as we are of others, which we learn by rule. The want thereof, is the onelie cause why, that verie manie men, being excellentlie well learned in foreign speche, can hard-

---

[18]Ralph Lever, *The Art of Reason* (London, 1573), quoted in Jones, 126. See also John Horsfal whose English translation *The Preacher, or Methode of Preachinge, written in Latin by Nicholas Heminge* (London, 1574) testifies at once to the inadequacy of the vernacular vocabulary and to its capacity for expansion: "Nowe it is not unknowen howe hard a thing it is to translate an arte written, either in the Latyne, or in the Greeke tongue, especially into our Englishe and vulgare tongue, in the which we have wordes, neither sufficient, nor yet apt enough to declare and express the same: that is to saye, the termes and proper names of arte ... yet the example of other wise and learned men (who before me have brought into our tongue the artes of Grammar, Logicke, Rhetoricke, Astronomie, Geographie, etc.) did not a little encourage and embolden me hereunto." Quoted in Jones, 74.

[19]I draw this conclusion from the wealth of examples compiled by Jones, who also notes the terms with which Sidney expressed his favorable opinion of the "unruled" vernacular: "Sidney considered his mother tongue capable of any excellence such as the power to express thoughts freely and properly, freedome from the cramping rules of grammar, and felicity in compounding words, the last of which he considered the greatest of linguistic beauties." (Jones, 198).

lie discern what theie have at home, still shooting fair, but oft missing far, hard censors over other, ill executors themselves.

The dictionary Mulcaster imagines is our own authoritative handbook to explain the "proper use" of "all the words … which we use in our English tung." Mulcaster displays the same readiness to be told the "right" use of English by one "well learned and laborious man" that accounts for the authority enjoyed by Johnson a hundred and fifty years later. During the sixteenth and seventeenth centuries regular appeals were made to encourage the King, the Court, Parliament, the Universities, or a specially created Academy to ascertain and legislate the "correct" use of English, but the language continued to lack an external or absolute authority until Johnson, who himself opposed the idea of an Academy as counter to "the spirit of English liberty," established his dictionary on that untheorized and unexamined notion of consensus according to which it still operates today.[20]

That the consensus producing the list of words of "common" use has always operated according to a highly restricted franchise is demonstrated by John Cheke's letter to Sir Thomas Hoby concerning his 1557 translation of Castiglione's *Book of the Courtier*. For Cheke, whose stated prescriptive aim was an English "cleane and pure, unmixt and unmangeled with borrowing of other tunges," offered Hoby suggestions for changing some of the words, "which might verie well be let alone, but that I am verie curious in mi freendes matters, not to determin, but to

---

[20]"In absolute governments there is, sometimes a general reverence paid to all that has the sanction of power, and the countenance of greatness. How little this is the state of our country needs not to be told. We live in an age in which it is a kind of publick sport to refuse all respect that cannot be enforced. The edicts of an English academy would, probably, be read by many, only that they might be sure to disobey them." Samuel Johnson, *Lives of the Poets* (London, 1779), III, 16, 1. But for an example of the desire for an authoritarian ratification of English see George Snell, *The Right Teaching of Useful Knowledge* (London, 1649). Snell called for education in the vernacular, a grammar, and a dictionary of words "in use among the English" to be secured by an act of Parliament or Royal edict, "everie word henceforth to be used, by any native of *England*, contrariant to the edict for the English language, [will] bee adjudged and condemned for non-English, barbarous, non-significant, and of none effect, and void to all intent and purpose." Quoted in Jones, 296. The year in which Mulcaster published *The Elementarie*, 1582, also saw the establishment of the Italian Academia della Crusca; the Académie Française was founded in 1635. For an account of the founding of the Académie Française, and its role both in the centralization of the French arts and in the production of the certain *je ne sais quoi* used to characterize the official "genius" of the French writer see Timothy Murray, "The Académie Française," in *A New History of French Literature*, ed. Denis Hollier (Cambridge: Harvard University Press, 1989), 267-273.

debaat what is best."[21] This image of the lexicon as a small matter between Cheke and his friends anticipates Johnson's validation of words as they are used by himself and his literary and social peers; in such contexts standard English is necessarily registered as that dialect which is common among the "best" speakers, and not among the "ladies, gentlewomen, or other unskilful persons," for whose benefit it is written down. And here we may begin to understand the function of women as people who are not, and may never be, full members of the language community: that it is precisely at the scene of their instruction that the "rules" of English may be articulated.[22]

Experimental works, the early English dictionaries provide a forum within which the conditions and possibilities for a linguistic "consensus" are first noticed and debated. Each is consequently directed to a double audience: first to the lexicographer's political peers, who are invited to join him in discussing "what is best," and then to those "unskilful persons" whose uncritical belief is necessary to validate a term's "currency."[23] The woman's lexicon is the proving ground for male words and, more importantly, for the whole male project of lexicography. But while women (and foreigners) may be permitted to lend their assent to the new

---

[21]Sir John Cheke, letter to Sir Thomas Hoby, July 24, 1557; quoted in Jones, 102. See also the conclusion of John Bullokar's prefatory letter to *An English Expositor*: "But as for you (judiciall or courteous reader) whose favour I desire, and whose counsell or friendly correction I will not refuse, if to you (I say) any thing herein shall occurre, which seemeth by me omitted, mistaken, or not fully satisfactory to your expectation ... I promise that upon warning hereof given to me or the Printer, at a second Impression it shall be amended." This could be argued to be an instance of the characteristic defensiveness of the Jacobean writer going to press. But see also the entry for *crampe* in Richard Huloet's English Latin dictionary, the *Abecedarium Anglo-Latinum* (1552): "a defecte of the synnowes and muscles, wherby somtyme the whole bodye, and sometyme parte therof is stretched, if it be in parte of the bodye, then it is Englyshed, crampe: if it be in the entier body (which is rare) the name therof in our mother tongue is not known. Conuultio. onis, Spasmus ... Some learned man maye Englyshe it."

[22] For the use of a female audience as pretext for the explanation of a rule that is otherwise alleged to be common practice see Puttenham's description of the figure of "Parenthesis or the Insertour" in *The Arte of English Poesie* (London, 1589), 180: "The figure is so common that it needeth none example, nevertheless because we are to teach Ladies and Gentlewomen to know their schoole points and termes appertaining to the Art, we may not refuse to yeeld examples even in the plainest cases."

[23]See in this context Patricia Parker's description of Wilson's *Rule of Reason* as being characterized by "a contradiction within the conception of order itself: that it is both legitimated as a representation of something existing and 'natural,' and, in the anxious as well as the more confident passages of such texts, presented as a form of construction, one that institutes rather than simply reflects." (Parker, 118). I am arguing that early English lexicographic texts disguise this contradiction by relating it to the simple "fact" that men and women have different pedagogical needs.

authoritative functions of English, they are not expected to use it authoritatively themselves—indeed the adequately "ruled" English turns out to be the exclusive possession of men. The early English dictionary is thus marked by an irony that is characteristic of conduct literature in that it functions to exclude from a general franchise precisely those people to whom it is addressed.

IV

Language is indisputably the more immediate province of the fair sex.

Lord Chesterfield, 1754.

A Table Alphabeticall was dedicated to five sisters, "the right honourable, Worshipfull, vertuous, and godlie Ladies, the Lady Hastings, the Lady Dudley, the Lady Mountague, the Ladie Wingfield, and the Lady Leigh." The Harington sisters were second cousins both to the translator of Ariosto and, through their mother Lucie Harington, to Sir Philip Sidney. Cawdrey had apparently enjoyed the friendship and patronage of Lucie Harington since "your Ladyships brother was my scholler, (and now my singuler benefactor) when I taught the Grammer schoole at Okeham"; and it is in consideration of this debt, "and also for that I acknowledge my selfe much beholding and indebted to the most of you, since this time," that Cawdrey ventured to make the Harington sisters "all joyntly patrons ... and under your names to publish this simple worke."

Since dictionaries are texts that are always heavily dependent on those that precede them, the address to women that characterizes the first four English word lists could be argued to be merely conventional: Blount having copied it from Cockeram, Cockeram from Bullokar, and Bullokar from Cawdrey.[24] But Cawdrey himself had the idea from John Florio, whose recent translation of the *Essais* of Montaigne had been dedicated to six women in three separate prefaces: Anne Harington and her daughter Lucie, the Countess of Bedford; Elizabeth, Countess of Rutland and Penel-

---

[24]The mutual involvement of *The English Dictionarie* and *An English Expositor* provides another example of the interrelatedness of lexicographic texts. The first edition of *The English Dictionarie* (1623) contained extensive borrowings from *An English Expositor* (1616), while later editions of the *Expositor* borrowed in turn from the *Dictionarie*. The last edition of the *Dictionarie* (1670) then took over the new features and the old name of its rival, announcing itself as "The English Dictionary; or an EXPOSITOR of Hard English Words." For an account of the interrelatedness of these and the other early English dictionaries see Starnes and Noyes, *The English Dictionary from Cawdrey to Johnson 1604-1755* (Chapel Hill: The University of North Carolina Press, 1946).

ope Rich (the daughter and the mistress of Sir Philip Sidney); Mary Neville (daughter of Thomas Sackville, Lord Buckhurst) and Elizabeth Grey. And in Florio's case the address to women was not coincidental, but part of the stance that characterized his long and successful career.

An accomplished courtier and language tutor (whose *Worlde of Wordes, Or, most copious and exact dictionarie in Italian and English* [London: Edward Blount, 1598] was the last dictionary published in English before the appearance of *A Table Alphabeticall*), Florio worked throughout his career to associate himself with the interests of women, and to link those interests with the status and practice of the European vernaculars. Dedicating his translation of the essays of Montaigne to six women of the Bedford-Harington family (five of whom he had tutored in French and Italian), he had extravagant praise for the linguistic facility of women:

> French hath long time beene termed the language of Ladies: So doth it grace your tongues; so doe your tongues grace it; as if written by men it may have a good garbe, spoken by you it hath a double grace: for so have I heard some of you speake it, as no man, few women, could come near their sweete-relisht ayre of it. That as *Tullie* averred of his Roman Ladies for Latine, so not onely for our mother-tongue, but also for the principall, Italian and French, not onely our princely Mother of Majestie, Magnificence, omnisufficiencie, but (for instance) I avowe, you my five honoured Schollers (whom as ever in heart, so would I honor now by these my laboures) are the purest, finest, and clearest speakers.

Uncoupling speech from writing, Florio here opens the possibility that a language "written by men" may be differently realized in the mouths of women—a claim that corresponds to Lord Chesterfield's more anxious description of the ways in which women elaborate the standard English script. Florio's assertion that women make the best vernacular speakers had been inherited by the English humanists from Cicero. During the sixteenth century, when the prestige activities of English culture were carried out in Latin or French, the claim that women guard the wellspring of vernacular purity may have appeared to be beside the point of the reproduction of that culture. However, the rise in the status of English that characterized the turn of the seventeenth century made Cicero's remark newly problematic, and gives added piquancy to Florio's reminder that the vernacular spoken by Cicero's mother-in-law was, after all, Latin.[25]

---

[25]From *De Oratore*, Book III, 44-46, trans. H. Rackham (Cambridge: Loeb Classical Library, 1982), 37. Cicero's character Crassus holds that women guard the wellspring of pure Latin: "For my own part, when I hear my wife's mother Laelia—since it is easier for women

A propitious moment for the extravagant compliment to women comprised by Florio's translation of Montaigne arrived in 1603, for the Bedford-Harington women were chosen by Queen Anne to form her own inner circle after the accession.[26] Florio himself went on to become Italian instructor to the Queen, after whom he renamed his dictionary.[27] Cawdrey's dedication of *A Table Alphabeticall* to the five Harington daughters, nieces of Florio's dedicatee Anne Harington, in the year of the accession was then a particularly happy thought, for in following Florio through the mazy politics of patronage Cawdrey was able to draw on and appear to strengthen that connection between women and the vernacular from which Florio's career had so considerably profited. It is a connection further exploited by John Bullokar, author of the second English dictionary, whose *English Expositor* (1616) is once again dedicated to one of the five Harington sisters, the "Singular Good Ladie, the Ladie Jane Vicountesse Mountague."

Published during the early years of James's reign, when the flowering of the European arts in England was being overseen by Queen Anne, these two earliest English dictionaries speak of a particular and newly privileged association between women and vernacular English. It is an association with a history, for fifteenth- and sixteenth-century disdain for the vernacular had often left women as the patrons and audience for English texts. Indeed, Walter J. Ong has suggested that the learning of Latin in early modern England functioned as a male puberty rite that marked the adolescent's entry into the adult world, dividing him from that of his mother and sisters.[28] The "natural speach, which together with

---

to keep the old pronunciation unspoiled, as they do not converse with a number of people and so always retain the accents they heard first—well, I listen to her with the feeling that I am listening to Plautus or Naevius: the actual sound of her voice is so unaffected and natural, that she seems to introduce no trace of display or affectation; and I consequently infer that that was how her father and her ancestors used to speak."

[26] I owe this observation to a talk given by Leeds Barroll at the annual conference of the Renaissance Society of America, Duke University, North Carolina, April 1991.

[27] The dictionary was reissued as *Queen Anna's World of Words* (London: Edward Blount, 1611). Florio's attitude to women should be contrasted to that of Montaigne, to whom the belief that his essays were read by women gave little apparent pleasure: "It vexeth me, that my Essayes serve Ladies in lieu of common ware and stuff for their hall ... I love their society somewhat private; their publicke familiarity wants favor and savor." (III, 5, "Upon Some Lines of Virgil").

[28] Walter J. Ong, S. J., "Latin Language Study as a Renaissance Puberty Rite," in his *Rhetoric, Romance, and Technology* (Ithaca, 1971), 130 ff. Ong begins his investigation with the observation that in early modern England Latin enjoyed a currency and prestige far in excess of its function. Actually the authority exercised by a prestige dialect is always in excess of that which can be explained by its ostensible linguistic and social functions, but puberty rites, which function to produce the adult male within a particular group, are a good

their Nources milk they sucked," and the right to define it, was of course later to become an object of desire to the denizens of English culture.[29] But it is tempting to imagine that an earlier masculine disregard for the "mother tongue" left space for a female-specific vernacular activity; albeit one that left no better record than that which is recorded in the hard word lists that men produced, after the fact, "for women."

The existence of a time or place beyond the pale of linguistic regulation is of course a chimera: one that in this instance is produced and thrown into the past—and into the domain of women—by precisely that lexical regime whose origins I am interested to chart. For language does not exist except as a set of rules: it can appear "unruled" only if the validity of the techniques according to which it is regulated are denied. In the sixteenth century English appears to have been not unruled, but ruled differently—perhaps in accordance with a rhetorical, rather than grammatical, lexical, and orthographic order.[30] The identification of this "other" order as a period of misrule, and its concomitant association with women, is, I think, largely the work of that impulse towards a reorganized vernacular that forms part of the project of seventeenth-century English nationalism.[31] The male-authored representations of women speaking differently

---

example of that apportionment of cultural capital which operates behind the scene of linguistic hierarchies to produce such apparent overvaluations. For an illustration of the pedagogical production of this division between Latin and English, male and female, see Will Page's Latin lesson in *The Merry Wives of Windsor*, IV, i, a scene that is discussed in Parker, *Literary Fat Ladies*, 27.

[29]The quotation is from E. K.'s letter to Gabriel Harvey in commendation of "the new Poete" that stands as preface to *The Shepheardes Calender* (London: Hugh Singleton, 1579). This letter, which was probably written by Harvey himself, praises Spenser for his commitment to the vernacular, and in particular for his having "laboured to restore, as to theyr rightfull heritage, such good and naturall English words, as have be long time out of use and almost clear disinherited." Harvey is obviously aligned here with those who invest their cultural ambitions in the "mother tongue."

[30]I owe this suggestion to Margreta de Grazia.

[31]Thus in 1589, when writing the first appraisal of English vernacular poetry, George Puttenham became suddenly and significantly anxious about his commitment to rhetorical ornament. His solution was to claim somewhat belatedly that while ornament is "not unnecessarie to all such as be willing themselves to become good makers in the vulgar, or to be able to judge of other men's makings ... our chiefe purpose herein is for the learning of Ladies and young Gentlewomen, or idle Courtiers, desirous to become skilful in their owne mother tongue, and for their private recreation to make now and then ditties of pleasure" *The Arte of English Poesie*, 170-171. See also Montaigne's 1580 essay "Of the Vanity of Words," in which Montaigne dissociates himself from at least the terms of rhetoric with the improbable claim that they pertain to the conversation of women: "Doe but heare one pronounce *Metonymia, Metaphore, Allegory, Etimologie,* and other such trash names of Grammar, would you not thinke, they meant some forme of a rare and strange language; they are titles and words that concern your chamber-maids Tittle-Tattle." *The Essayes*, trans. John Florio (London: E. Blount, 1603), Book I, 51.

—gossiping, telling old wives tales, or speaking euphuism—that appear towards the end of the sixteenth century are then best understood as attempts to *produce* a vernacular that is "in need of" rules; and the female-specific linguistic practices to which they attest may have little historical basis.[32] But to show that men have both scripted and had something to gain from female specific discourse is not to prove that women did not, in their turn, implement those scripts: my point is only that the relation between male script and female practice cannot be assumed. During the elevation of the vernacular at the turn of the century it does seem that, briefly retaining their association with English, women found themselves at the center of the nation's new cultural enterprise. It was of course a promotion that was circumscribed in scope, and of brief duration. Anne was not involved in the preparation of the 1611 King James Bible, and was quickly replaced as leading patron of the arts by her two sons. At the same time the distinction between masculine and feminine which had once corresponded to that between Latin and English was moved inside the vernacular pale; and while English could now be spoken either in a "manly" or in an "effeminate" way, its virtues were understood to be "masculine," and its best speakers consequently men.[33] But this is a coincidence that may lead us to suspect that the masculinity that became a hallmark of British high culture was in part designed to contain, and in part produced itself in the act of containing, the epiphenomenon of Queen Anne's influence on the arts.

[32]On gossip see, for example, Samuel Rowlands, *Tis Merry When Gossips Greet* (London: W. W., 1602), a work Rowlands describes as a female supplement to *The Canterbury Tales*; and the Clown's description of "tittle-tattling ... among maids" in *The Winter's Tale* (IV, iv, 244-250). For old wives tales see the preface "To the curteous Reader" of Florio's *Montaigne*, where he defends translations against those who hold "it is not wel Divinitie shoulde be a childes or an old wives, a coblers, or clothiers tale or table-talke." On the vogue for euphuism and its reputation as a woman's dialect see the printer's preface to John Lyly's *Six Court Comedies* (London: Edward Blount, 1623).

[33]The assertion of the masculine qualities of the vernacular was aided by the discovery of and insistence on the teutonic origins of English, which was itself the product of the antiquarian movement of the early years of James I's reign. See Jones, 214-271.

V

All words, good and bad, are there jumbled indiscriminately to-
gether, insomuch that the judicious reader may speak, and write
as inelegantly, improperly, and vulgarly as he pleases, by and
with the authority of one or other of our WORD BOOKS.

Lord Chesterfield, describing the early English dictionary in
The World 1754

A *Table Alphabeticall* announced itself as a collection of "hard usuall English wordes," gathered out of Hebrew, Greek, Latin, and French. In this context "usual" denotes not words of common use, but those terms that are specific to a certain practice or customary among a certain group. It is this meaning that is employed by Thomas Blount when he glosses the word "Embargo" as "an usual word among our Merchants, when their ships or Merchandizes are arrested." Usual words are terms of art, and it is these, together with the strange, marvelous, and sometimes bitterly disputed words that had recently been imported from other languages to supplement the perceived paucity of the vernacular, that comprise the word store of the earliest English dictionaries, capitalizing on and making articulate that association of women with the elaborative principle of language that Chesterfield was to elevate into the Achilles heel of the polite lexicographer.[34]

It is notable, however, that this association is made in English somewhat after the fact, as the language is entering its restrictive phase, and elaboration consequently acquiring a negative value. As a hard word list "for women" the early English dictionary stages itself as representing at once the problem of and a solution to the unregulated vernacular, so that at the very point where it is first "officially" made, the association of women with the principle of elaboration is cast as an aspersion. The proverbial facility of the female tongue had of course long been a cause for anxiety and complaint; from this point, however, it becomes easier to say exactly what is wrong with it, and in what it is wrong. The early alliance of women and hard word lists is then remembered in such Restoration works as the bitterly misogynist and self-parodic *Fop Dictionary; OR, An*

---

[34]For a reading of Cawdrey which understands his term "usual" to mean, after all, "common" see Gertrude E. Noyes, "The First Dictionary: Cawdrey's *Table Alphabeticall*," *Modern Language Notes* 63, 600-5. For other examples of the association between women and linguistic elaboration see Puttenham (n. 30, above); and the later *Academy of Compliments. Wherein Ladyes Gentlewomen, Schollers, and Strangers may accomodate their courtly practice with most Curious Ceremonies, Complemetall, Amorous, High Expressions, and forms of speaking and writing. With the Additions of witty Amorous Poems. And a TABLE expounding the hard ENGLISH words* (London: T. Badger, 1639). A brilliant and extended exploration of the phenomenon can be found in Parker, *Literary Fat Ladies*, chap. 2.

Alphabetical Catalogue of the Hard and Foreign Names and Terms of the Art Cosmetick, etc. Together with their interpretation, for Instruction of the Unlearned (London, c. 1680). Designed to display the aberrance of women's vocabulary, *The Fop Dictionary* marks the triumphant emergence of a restrictive standard associated with the linguistic practices of men: the fact that it was written by Mary Evelyn is a reminder of the cultural gymnastics that a woman would now have to perform in order to align herself with the interests and practices of standard English.[35]

Cawdrey's promise to teach his female readers to "better understand many hard English wordes, which they shall heare or read in Scriptures, Sermons, or elsewhere, and also be made to use the same aptly themselves" is reiterated in his offer to teach the "true writing" of such words.[36] The generosity of this offer requires scrutiny. For while it is true that correct spelling empowers those who know it, Cawdrey's publication of a list of words that he says women do not know *creates* the gap it ostensibly tries to bridge—a gap which is in future experienced as a distinction between those who already know how to spell, and those who must learn. Thus in 1623, dedicating *The English Dictionarie* to the Earl of Cork, Henry Cockeram is careful to assure the Earl that it is "intended only to serve you, not to instruct you." Cockeram's work, which offers to teach "the speedy attaining of an elegant perfection of the English tongue," divides its audience into those whose speech is already elegant, and those who will use the text to aspire to be like them. And here the usefulness of the address to women may be the consolation that inheres in the fact that even if she successfully acquires the attributes of class distinction, a woman is still not a man.

The words on Cawdrey's list are certainly "hard" enough, 40 percent of them appearing in only slightly different form in Thomas Thomas's

---

[35] *The Fop Dictionary* appeared as an appendix to the pamphlet whose full title runs *Mundus Muliebris: or the ladies' dressing-room unlock'd and her toilette spread. Together with the fop-dictionarie compiled for the use of the fair sex* (London: Richard Bentley, 1690, 2nd. ed.). Mary was the daughter of diarist John Evelyn. When she died in 1685 her bereaved father attributed the pamphlet to her in his diary, noting that "she could not indure that which they call courtship, among the Gallants," and herself "writ not onely most correct orthography, but with that maturitie of judgement, and exactnesse of the periods, choice expressions, and familiarity of style, that some letters of hers have astonish'd me." *The Diary of John Evelyn*, ed. John Bowle (Oxford: Oxford University Press, 1985), 324-25.

[36] Much of Cawdrey's prefatory material, including this promise, is taken almost verbatim from Edmund Coote's *English Schoole-maister*, which the author claimed would teach "a direct course, how any unskilful person may easily both understand any hard English words, which they shal in Scriptures, Sermons, or elsewhere heare or reade: and also be made able to use the same aptly themselves." To this end, Coote "set downe a Table contayning and teaching the true writing and understanding of any hard English word, borrowed from the Greek, Latin, or French." Quoted in Starnes and Noyes, 14.

popular Latin-English dictionary, the *Dictionarium Linguae Latinae et Anglicanae* (1588). The *Table Alphabeticall* includes many words for which it is the first English source: and while some of these enjoyed a brief and limited currency, such as *agnition* (knowledge), *calliditie* (craftiness), and *obnibulate* (to make dark); others, such as *agglutinate, hemisphere,* and *horizon,* are still current—a fact that may cast doubt on the attractive suggestion that Cawdrey, Bullokar, and Cockeram wilfully coined hard "English" words by anglicizing the lemmas of Latin-English dictionaries.[37] Because of the extraordinary linguistic crisis within which they were composed it is impossible to recover the precise status of the individual terms that make up the early English hard word lists; but whatever the provenance and status of Cawdrey's "hard words," it is impossible to square his lexicographic practice with his letter "To the reader."[38] There Cawdrey inveighs against "over fine or curious" speech, the affectation of "strange inkhorne termes," and those who "pouder their talke with over-sea language"; instead he advocates "the plainest and best kind of speech," "such words as are commonlie received," and a "plaine manner":

> Do we not speak, because we would have other to understand us? or is not the tongue given for this end, that one might know

[37]A suggestion that was first made by Starnes and Noyes when they discovered the extensive debt that Cawdrey, Bullokar, Cockeram, and Blount owed to Thomas, to Cooper's *Thesaurus Linguae Romanae et Britannicae,* and to John Rider's *Bibliotheca Scholastica* (1589). See Starnes and Noyes, 13-47. A second explanation for presence of scarcely naturalized Latin words in the early English dictionary is that even as it yielded its prestige functions to English, Latin remained a powerful source and companion for the standardizing tongue, so that compilers of the hard word lists turned to the Latin lexicon to check the definitions of words that were, as they claimed, newly current in English. (On this see Jürgen Schäfer, *Early Modern English Lexicography,* 2.) But the assertion of Thomas Blount that he was citing contemporary authorities for the use of words "that I might not be thought to be the innovator of them" (*Glossographia,* 1656) suggests that the early hard word lists did encounter contemporary accusations that they had been wilfully padded. It is an accusation repeated and elaborated by J. K. in the introduction to his *New English Dictionary* (London: Henry Bonwicke, 1702) which censures his immediate predecessor Elisha Coles for having "in his elaborate Work, inserted several Words purely Latin, without any alteration, as *Dimidietas* for a half; *Sufflamen,* for a Trigger, and some hundreds only vary'd with an *English* Termination, which are scarce ever us'd by any." That is, there is evidence that the earliest English lexicographers taught as "hard English" words terms which they had themselves newly coined out of Latin.

[38]For discussion of another occurrence of the contradictory injunction that women speak both naturally and in a refined and elegant manner see Ann Rosalind Jones, "Nets and Bridles: early modern conduct books and sixteenth-century women's lyrics" in Nancy Armstrong and Leonard Tennenhouse, eds. *The Ideology of Conduct: Essays in Literature and the history of sexuality* (New York: Methuen, 1987), 42-48.

what another meaneth? Therefore, either wee must make a difference of English, and say, some is learned English, and othersome is rude English, or the one is Court talke, the other is Country-speech, or els we must of necessitie banish all affected Rhetorique, and use altogether one manner of language.

Actually, it is the legislation of "one manner of language" that permits not only the distinction of court from country speech, but also the production of a far more intricate range of social differences within a single national language. But what is particularly interesting, because puzzling, about Cawdrey's advice to "banish all affected Rhetorique" is its obviation of the reasons for which the female reader was ostensibly offered the dictionary—that she might understand and use hard English words.[39]

Cawdrey continues his advocacy of a speech that is both uniform and "common" with an appeal to an authority that has become curiously bifurcated between female and male:

Some men seek so far for outlandish English, that they forget altogether their mothers language, so that if some of their mothers were alive, they were not able to tell, or understand what they say, and yet these fine English Clearkes, will say they speak in their mother tongue; but one might as well charge them, for counterfeyting the Kings English.

Re-inflecting the passage from Cicero of which Florio had made recent use, Cawdrey implies that women, once the guardians of pure and traditional English, have now lost control, either of their language, or of their sons (who speak any "outlandish" phrase and call it English). Cawdrey recommends recourse to the protection of the monarch when he activates the traditional claim that "the king ... is lord of this language."[40] Published in 1604 Cawdrey's assertion that English is the *King's* is at least topical, for the accession of James I had brought to an end a half century of

---

[39]The apparent inconsistencies in Cawdrey's lexicographic practice, reproduced in this letter, result in part from his heavy dependence on Cicero's *De Oratore*. For Cicero's speaker is able to assume that the orator is in full possession of a correct and adequate Latin "imparted in education by boyhood and fostered by a more intensive and systematic study of literature, or else by the habit of daily conversation in the family circle, and confirmed by books and by reading the old orators and poets." (*De Oratore* III, 48) It is precisely this confidence—and the insouciance possessed by the practitioners of a "standard"—that eludes Cawdrey, who is involved in the task of insisting on those qualifications for English.

[40]As first recorded in the preface to Chaucer's *Treatise on the Astrolabe* (1391), a work on astronomy compiled and translated from Latin into "light Englissh" for Chaucer's son Lewis. See *The Complete Works of Geoffrey Chaucer*, ed. F. N. Robinson (Oxford: Oxford University Press, 1957), 546.

female rule during which English had been under the aegis of the Queen.[41] Combined with his suggestion that women are no longer fit guardians of English, but are themselves implicated in its elaboration and corruption, Cawdrey's record of a historical fact speaks also of a wish that in future English might be secured within the province of men. His service to women thus involves him in that logic of supplementarity that repeatedly overturns the diachronic account of the role played by gender in the history of the English lexicon, for at the moment that he asserts the involvement of women with the vernacular, Cawdrey produces the image of an English from which women have been and will be excluded.

The second monolingual English dictionary announced itself as *An English Expositor: Teaching the Interpretation of the Hardest words used in our Language. With Sundry Explications, Descriptions, and Discourses, by J. B., Doctor of Physicke* (London, John Legatt,1616). In two prefatory letters (which draw both on Florio's representation of the text as an "inknown infant" seeking godparents, and on his justification of the democratizing effects of translation), Bullokar represents the publication of his work, its translation from manuscript to print, as corresponding to a movement from a private male space to the wider sphere of women. For as he tells the Vicountess Mountague, its dedicatee:

> Being perswaded (Right Noble Ladie) by some friends, for pub-like benefit to make this Collection of words common, which at first was intended onely for private use, (as written in my youth, at the request of a worthy Gentleman, one whose love prevailed much with me) ... I am emboldened to present this little Pamphlet unto your Honour, with hope that by your Patronage it shall not only bee protected from injuries, but also finde favourable entertainment, and perhaps gracefully [be] admitted among greatest Ladies and studious Gentlewomen, to whose reading (I am made beleeve) it will not proove altogether ungratefull.

Representing a circle that is both restricted and common, the company of aristocratic women provides a forum within which the particular combination of humility and arrogance that characterizes Bullokar's publication of his text is recast, so that he registers his decision to serve a market economy as a decision to serve women—to give them, as he reminds the Vicountess Mountague in terms that could elsewhere be a threat, what it is that they "want."

---

[41]See for example Thomas Nashe's invective against Gabriel Harvey: "It is not enough that he bepist his credite, about twelve yeeres ago, with *Three proper and wittie familiar letters*, but he must still be running on the *letter*, and abusing the Queenes English without pittie or mercy." (*Strange Newes*, London, 1592)

Bullokar searched not only for hard, but as he says, "the hardest words used in our language," and he seems to have intended his word list, compiled through years of "observation, reading, study, and charge," as a guide to contemporary vernacular literature. His list is characterized by its ready embrace of the exotic and by its long, anecdotal definitions. It includes, as he says, neologisms from Latin, Greek, Hebrew, and the European vernaculars; "sundry old words now grown out of use," which are marked with an asterisk; "divers termes of art," with specifications as to the field of knowledge to which each belongs, such as logic, philosophy, law, medicine, divinity, and astronomy; and the terms of an unnatural natural history, for which Bullokar cites authorities such as Pliny and Avicenna. A shadowy delineation of the dictionary of common use makes its appearance in Bullokar's own description of what text is not, for in his "Instruction to the Reader" he warns "if a word bee of different signification, the one easie, the other more difficult, I onely speake of interpretation of the hardest, as in the wordes *Tenne, Girle, Garter,* may appear." According to Bullokar's text a *girle* is a roe buck of two years, while *tenne* and *garter* are terms of heraldry—an anecdote which demonstrates how dictionaries for women provide for the arrogation (and profitable realization) of male knowledge.

The dictionary that followed was published in 1623 with the following title page:

> *The English Dictionarie*: or *An Interpreter* of hard English Words. Enabling as well Ladies and Gentlewomen, young Schollers, Clarkes, Merchants, as also Strangers of any Nation, to the understanding of the more difficult Authors already printed in our Language, and the more speedy attaining to an elegant perfection of the English tongue, both in reading, speaking, and writing. Being a Collection of the choicest words contained in the Table Alphabeticall and English Expositor, and of some thousand words never published by any heretofore.
> By H[enry] C[ockeram] Gent. (London, Edmund Weaver, 1623)

Like Bullokar before him, Cockeram is interested to facilitate the reading of "Authors already printed in our language," a reminder that English lexicography began, as it has since developed, in tandem with the project of a national literature.[42] But Cawdrey has other plans as well, and divides

---

[42]See Jones, 183: "Literature was considered instrumental to language, not language to literature. Writers are more frequently praised for what they have done for the medium of their expression than for the intrinsic view of their compositions." For an illuminating discussion of the concomitant development of the disciplines of English and the specific type of historical linguistics that informed preparation of the Oxford English Dictionary see Tony

his book into three parts. The first is the by-now-familiar hard word list comprising "the choicest words themselves now in use, wherin our language is inriched and become so copious, to which words the common sense is annexed." Part two, however, is a thesaurus where "vulgar" words are glossed by the terms of a "more refined and elegant speech," including "the mocke-wordes which are ridiculously used in our language ... by too many who study rather to be heard speake, than to understand themselves"; and part three is an encylopaedia of "severall persons, Gods and Goddesses, Giants and Devils, Monsters and Serpents, Birds and Beasts, Rivers, Fishes, Herbs, Stones, Trees and the like," included so that "the diligent learner may not pretend the defect of any helpe which may informe his discourse or practice." Following the earlier suggestion of Cawdrey, Cockeram is here offering a guide to a "speedy attaining of an elegant perfection of the English tongue"—that is, a book of self-help.

The importance that the dictionary was later to assume in patrolling the channels of social mobility is suggested in Cockeram's dedicatory letter to Richard Boyle, Earl of Cork. Cockeram was unknown to Boyle, and justified his dedication with a curious non sequitur: "as I have done my best to accomodate discourse with the choicest language, so I desire that my ambition of being knowne unto your Lordship may not be imputed unto an error of impudence, or an impudence in erring." This can be glossed either as a claim that linguistic decorum may replace other forms of social observance; or more simply as the statement "as I am trying hard, so am I not impudent." In either case it functions as a comment on Cockeram's own social ambition, lodging his text within a paradoxical terrain of class difference where to try hard is, precisely, to be impudent. And similarly, to learn something from a book, as by an "easy" method, is not to gain immediate access to the power of the people who know it without a book.

The English Dictionarie is prefaced by seven poems which are divided over the nature of Cockeram's achievement. John Ford, Bartholomew Hore[?], and John Webster are of the opinion (expressed perhaps with some irony) that Cockeram's text is of value because it adds to the store of "hard" English words. Thus Ford suggests that continental travel will no longer be necessary for gallants seeking "new fashions of complementall phrases"; Webster assures Cockeram that his text will be read "while

---

Crowley, *Standard English and the Politics of Language* (Urbana: University of Illinois Press, 1989) for a discussion of: "In a precise sense, literature had to come before the language since without written records there could be no history of the language" (Crowley, 120). The citation of authorities to validate the definition of a word did not originate with Cockeram, for Latin glosses had regularly adduced verses or sentences from reputable authors (see Stein, 129).

Words for paiment passe at court"; and Bartholomew Hore underlines the connection between linguistic elaboration and women by associating neologisms with luxury goods as he tells Cockeram's reader "The *Adage* is far sought, deare bought, please ladies, / You must yield to this Maxime or prove babies."[43]

However, Nicholas Smith, Thomas Spicer, and John Day are each prepared to credit Cockeram with having begun the legislation that was to make English not only a "refined" but also a restricted language. Nicholas Smith attributes to Cockeram's legislative function the future avoidance of "critical disasters"; Thomas Spicer congratulates him on having naturalized the neologisms that his work contains; and John Day believes that Cockeram has fixed the vernacular through having "taught us all good language," reduced "a rude pile / Of barbarous sillables into a stile / Gentle and smooth," and from a "rough speech / taught us all to speake / A perfect language." The seventh and final poem, by John Crugge, is itself divided. Crediting *The English Dictionary* with having contributed both to the elaboration and to the restriction of English, Crugge's poem begins that conflation of the categories "choice" and "common" that determine the later political operations of the English dictionary.

Cockeram's own "Premonition from the Author to the Reader" is characterized by an extraordinary confidence. Acknowledging that the "praise-worthy labours" of others laid the foundation for his own work, he holds that his endeavors may still "bee truly termed rather a necessity … than an arrogancie in doing. For … what any before me in this kinde have begun, I have not onely fully finished, but thoroughly perfected." Having explained the advantages of alphabetization, "by which the capacity of the meanest may soone be inlightened," and the different uses of the three books that comprise his text, Cockeram summarizes his own achievement in terms that demonstrate ambitions beyond the compilation of a hard word list:

> I might insist upon the generall use of this worke, especially for Ladies and Gentlewomen, Clarkes, Merchants, young Schollers, Strangers, Travellers, and all such as desire to know the plenty of

---

[43]For other examples of this proverb see Barnaby Rich, *Faultes, faults, and Nothing else but Faults* (London, 1606): "farre fet, and deare bought (they say) is fit for Ladies"; and Puttenham's example of the figure of metalepsis: "as when we had rather fetch a word a great way off then use one nearer at hand to expresse the matter aswel and plainer. And it seemeth the deviser of this figure, had a desire to please women rather than men: for we use to say by manner of Proverbe: things farrefet and deare bought are good for Ladies." *The Arte of English Poesie*, 193.

the English; but I am confident, that experience will be the truest herauld to publish to the world on my behalfe, how my debt to my Countrie is to bee challenged, so my Country shall not altogether boast of any impunity from being indebted to my Studies.

Unlike Cawdrey, Cockeram does not pretend that his work was only "gathered for the benefit ... of Ladies, Gentlewomen, or any other unskilful persons"; indeed, as its function becomes more overtly legislative the English dictionary displays increasing indifference to those pedagogic needs of women that had been its earliest justification.

The final dictionary in the unbroken chain of works making reference to the needs of women is Thomas Blount's *Glossographia: or, a Dictionary, Interpreting all such Hard Words, Whether Hebrew, Greek, Latin, Italian, Spanish, French, Teutonick, Belgick, British, or Saxon; as are now used in our refined English Tongue. Also the Terms of Divinity, Law, Phusick, Mathematics, Heraldry, Anatomy, War, Musick, Arcitecture; and of several other Arts and Sciences Explicated. With Etymologies, Definitions, and Historical Observations on the same. Very useful for all such as desire to understand what they read* (London: Thomas Newcomb,1656). Like *The English Dictionarie*, the *Glossographia* claims for itself a variety of motivations and effects. Blount portrays himself as a plain, representative English man who has been "gravelled" in his reading both by an "affected novelty of speech" (of which he disapproves), and by the quantity of foreign and specialist words with which "our best modern Authors ... have both infinitely enriched and enobled our Language ... I beleeved myself not singular in this ignorance, and that few, without help of a Dictionary, would be able to understand our ordinary English books." It is this supplemental function that is celebrated in the dictionary's prefatory poem, which asks what is due to Blount for his "industrious observation:"

> And re-acquainting our self-stranger *Nation*
> With its disguised self; what's merited
> By rendring our hard *English* Englished;
> What, when our Tongue grew gibbrish, to be then
> National *Interpreter* to Books and Men;
> What ever praise does such deserts attend,
> Know, *Reader*, 'tis thy debt unto my friend.

According to this honorific by J. S., Blount reduced the horrid confusion of English ("Our *Tongue*, grown *Labyrinth*, and *Monster* too") to an order correspondent to that of the British nation. Thus Blount emphasizes the consensus from and for which he speaks; the written works he consulted; and "the Enclopeadie of knowledge and concurrence of many learned heads" and the help of "some very learned and noble my friends" necessary to the completion of his project.

It is interesting then that Blount's second and perhaps more overt purpose is the compilation of those terms that it befits a gentleman to know. His ideal reader is the man of leisure whose interests are encyclopaedic, shallow, and disinterested; someone who has no need for the detailed knowledge of specialist terms that would suggest an intelligence mired in a particular trade or business. Instead the *Glossographia* provides

> such and so many of the most useful law terms as I thought necessary for every Gentleman of Estate to understand, not intending anything for the studied Professors of that noble Science ... as also the names and qualities of at least ordinary Diseases ... I held it no less necessary for every Gentleman to be so far seen in Heraldry, as to know (at least) the most usual Terms ... that he may by consequence be able at least to blazon his own Coat ... and the terms of many Sciences unfolded; as of Logicke, Astrology, Geometry, Musick, Architecture, Navigation, etc., with those of our most ingenious Arts and Excercises, as Printing, Painting, Jewelling, Riding, Hunting, Hawking, etc.... I will not say I have met with all that might require Explication.... But I have inserted such as are of most use, and best worth knowledge.

Encompassing in this "wide survey" that which is now "best worth knowledge," Blount is frankly catering to "Gentlemen of Estate": men whose wealth elevates them above the serious details of labor and trade, and makes them fit members of a linguistic as well as a political franchise.[44] This, however, is a project that may easily represent itself as having democratic credentials. In Blount's final direction educated women, insouciant men, and the ignorant meet, if not on equal terms, at least in the same volume, with "scholars":

> It chiefly intended for the more-knowing women, and the less-knowing men; or indeed for all such of the unlearned, who can but finde in an Alphabet, the word they understand not; yet I

[44]The phrase "wide survey" is from John Barrell's *English Literature in History 1730-1780: An Equal Wider Survey* (New York, St. Martin's Press, 1983). I am indebted to Barrell's description of the way in which the differentiation of types of knowledge and ways of possessing it was made to reflect class difference in eighteenth-century Britain; and have also profited from his description of how grammatical regulation confirmed the divisions it pretended to heal: "how the authority of the gentleman, and of the ruling class, was re-enforced at the level of language; how, that is, a 'correct' English was defined in such a way as to represent it as the natural possession of the gentleman, and to confirm that possession, too, as a source of his political authority."

think I may modestly say, the best of Schollers may in some part or other be obliged by it.

It is important then to notice that if Blount's dictionary groups together the members of the nation that it serves, producing an apparent unity out of the disparate interests whose terms it glosses, this is a grouping which may allow old distinctions to be redrawn. By multiplying the available choice among apparently synonymous terms, the extension and regulation of the lexicon creates opportunities for new social and linguistic discriminations; and an increasingly complicated set of rules for its "correct" use will function to produce exclusion clauses within the general franchise that the national standard seems to offer. And finally the dictionary becomes the ground on which this new inequality may be staged: for *how* one uses it can now function as an integer of status.

VI

> There is, I believe, a third group of rules serving to control discourse. Here, we are no longer dealing with the mastery of the powers contained within discourse, nor with averting the hazards of its appearance; it is more a question of determining the conditions under which it may be employed, of imposing a certain number of rules upon those individuals who employ it, thus denying access to everyone else.
>
> Michel Foucault, "The Discourse on Language"

With the exception of such texts as the parodic *The Fop Dictionary compiled for the use of the fair sex* (1690), and *The Lady's Dictionary* (London: John Dunton, 1694), a sort of encylopaedia for women "in all relations, Companies, conditions and states of life," Blount's *Glossographia* was the last dictionary to mention the needs of women until the publication of J[ohn?] K[ersey?]'s *New English Dictionary* (London, 1702). Announcing itself as a "Compleat Collection Of the Most Proper and Significant Words, Commonly used in the Language," this work marks a watershed in the history of English lexicography since it represents the first attempt to list

> all the most proper and significant *English* Words, that are now commonly us'd either in Speech, or in the Familiar way of Writing Letters &c; omitting at the same time such as are obsolete, barbarous, foreign or peculiar to the several Counties of *England*; as also many difficult, abstruse and uncouth Terms of Art.

J. K. is aware that "no other book of the same nature, is as yet extant"; though he mentions "a little Tract first set forth by John Bullokar ... under the title of *An English Expositor*," as one of two works that pretend "to come near our present Design," while in fact "abound[ing] with difficult terms" and containing "few of the genuine and common significant Words of the *English* Tongue" that comprise his own enterprise. For *The New English Dictionary* is a dictionary of "common" use, which offers to "explain such *English* Words as are genuine and used by persons of clear Judgment and good Style."

That such words are chosen on political grounds, as representing the diction already in use among those people who have authority to legislate a desire for its continuance, is indicated by *The New English Dictionary*'s description of its intended audience:

> The usefulness of this Manual to all Persons not perfectly Masters of the *English* Tongue, and the assistance it gives to young Scholars, Tradesmen, Artificers and others, and particularly, the more ingenious Practitioners of the Female Sex; in attaining to the true manner of Spelling of such Words, as from time to time they have occasion to make use of, will, we hope procure it a favourable Reception.

Reinflecting Blount's notion that the audience for a dictionary comprises "the more-knowing women and the less-knowing men," J. K. suggests that women and the unskilful have a weak grasp not of the "hard" but rather of "the genuine Words of their own Mother-tongue." It is telling that at this moment of disjunction, when the lexicographic tradition is adapting itself to a new practical and ideological function, the ignorance of women is re-evoked to form the ground on which that function may be justified. It is however a strictly vestigial evocation, surviving here only under the pressure of lexicography's new turn. For as English has become coterminous with a "common" national good the special status of women has been dispersed through the more powerful register of class difference as that now appears on the field of a common language: and here, at last, the English dictionary falls silent on the subject of women.

It is a silence that puzzled James Murray, founding editor of the Oxford English Dictionary and the first to remark English lexicography's early appeal to women:

> It is noticeable that all these references to the needs of women disappear from the later editions, and are wanting in later dictionaries after 1660; whether this was owing to the fact that the less-knowing women had now come upsides with the more-knowing men; or that with the Restoration, female education went out of fashion, and women sank back again into elegant illiteracy, I leave to the historian to discover.

Assuming that the early English dictionary's marked interpellation of a female audience was motivated "largely [by] a consideration of the educational wants of women," Murray interprets its later indifference to women as reflecting either the fulfillment, or the abandonment, of this pedagogical aim.[45] It is important to notice, however, that the shift in audience for the English dictionary can be read as a symptom or instance of the larger epistemological shift which Foucault has wrestled to describe.

Localized within the subject of discourse itself, this shift corresponds to a movement away from the "awesome materiality" of language, to a concern with a new "will to verifiable and useful knowledge."[46] The anxiety that once concerned itself with language per se is thus rearticulated as anxiety concerning the division of the social goods generated by its *use*. While the historical status of language, and in particular the possibility that it once functioned differently, both needs to be asserted and is extraordinarily difficult to ascertain, the appearance of the early English dictionaries can be made to speak of such a shift. For the first page of Cawdrey's *Table Alphabeticall* stages, at least for our criticism, both its own control procedures and the escape of matter from under them. Thus while *abbreviat* and *abbridge* are bracketed together and glossed by a single explanation "to shorten, or make short"; the lemma *aberration*, "a going astray, or wandering," appears twice, once near the top and again at the bottom of the page. The hard word list has here an apotropaic function, for it stages the materiality of words even as it ushers in the order that will destroy them both. The development of the dictionary of common use out of lists of hard words can now be understood as the production of a "how to" manual out of a set of texts that had originally *represented* the problem to which they were also addressed; the problem that Foucault summarized as the simple fact "that people speak, and that their speech proliferates." But we can now add to this the observation that while in early modern England anxieties concerning the *materiality* of discourse were articulated through the register of gender, those concerning a will to knowledge are expressed (and expressed later) through the register of class.

---

[45]James Murray, *The Evolution of English Lexicography* (Oxford: Clarendon Press, 1900), 32. Suzanne Hull recently followed Murray both in noticing that the early English dictionary is addressed to women, and in attributing this fact to some real "want" on their part: "little attention has been given to the fact that these earliest English dictionaries … were actually published with women's needs in mind." Suzanne Hull, *Chaste, Silent, and Obedient: English Books for Women 1450-1640* (San Marino: Huntington Library, 1982), 64.

[46]See Michel Foucault, "The Discourse on Language," 215-237.

I would like to thank Andrew Garrett, Gwynne Kennedy, Maureen Quilligan, Matthew Rowlinson, Seth Schwartz, and Peter Stallybrass, who all commented on earlier versions of this essay, and Margreta de Grazia, who read it first and last.

ELEVEN

Re-Gendering Individualism: Margaret Fell Fox and Quaker Rhetoric

Judith Kegan Gardiner

An attractive, talkative, and rich middle-aged widow marries a charming, even more loquacious younger man without much money; her only son tries to dispossess her and take over the property. He succeeds in having her thrown into jail as a religious fanatic. The plot sounds as though it belongs in a seventeenth-century comedy with either one of the younger men as the hero. Since he died young, the disinherited son George Fell has not had his viewpoint heard. The other man, described in song "with his leather britches and his shaggy, shaggy locks," became a folk hero who figures more in tracts and histories than in Restoration comedy. George Fox, the weaver's son who became the rich gentlewoman's second husband, had a revelation when in his twenties, and, like many other talented, ambitious, and uneducated young men in England during the turbulent 1640s, took up the life of an itinerant preacher, converting mostly women and poor men to his doctrine of the inner light.

An important early leader of this religious group, called the Society of Friends or Quakers, the gentlewoman Margaret Askew Fell Fox (1614–1702) has usually been treated as an ancillary figure to this colorful early history. Confined first by the institutions of marriage and childbearing, then by Charles II's jails, Margaret Fell has been more effectively silenced by the historians who enclose and diminish her accomplishments within the stories of her husbands, her religion, and the economic changes of the late seventeenth century.[1] Not the butt of a Restoration comedy, neither is

---

[1]Throughout this essay I will refer to its subject by the name Margaret Fell. For biography, see Bonnelyn Young Kunze, "The Family, Social, and Religious Life of Margaret Fell" (Ph.D. diss., University of Rochester, 1986); and Isabel Ross, *Margaret Fell: Mother of Quakerism* (London and New York: Longman, Green, 1949). Earlier sources include Sarah Fell, *The Household Account Book of Sarah Fell of Swarthmoor Hall*, ed. Norman Penney (Cambridge: Cambridge University Press, 1920), and the autobiography and letters listed below.

she simply the saint of Quaker hagiography nor her second husband's bourgeois handmaiden, as some Marxist and feminist historians represent her. Freed by her widowhood from the enclosure of early-modern patriarchal marriage, she engaged in commercial agriculture as a member of the northern gentry. With partial success, she lobbied Charles II on behalf of her group and its ideology, which she helped shape, of a pacifism that might be considered more revolutionary than the radical sectarians' call to arms, and she defended women's rights to speak and write through gendered and familial rhetoric that helped create an affective public community. By refusing to pay tithes or take oaths, and by harboring what her gentry neighbors thought of as seditious lower-class rabble, she made herself vulnerable to repeated imprisonment. While in prison she wrote *Women's Speaking Justified*, a liberating foray into the public sphere on behalf of herself and other godly women. Her second marriage renounced obligations of both sex and money.[2] When married to Fox, she continued to act as a northern organizer for her group in concert with her daughters but largely independent of her husband. Maneuvering within, and sometimes transgressing, the boundaries of her class position, the culturally available metaphors for her femininity, and the ideology of the Society of Friends, Margaret Fell created a new role for herself, not only as her sect's "nursing mother" but also as a women's organizer.

The most prolific Quaker woman writer, she wrote letters encouraging fellow Quakers; tracts soliciting, warning, and condemning public officials; and treatises about theology and women's roles. Her career and her writings demonstrate some inadequacies in the traditional historical dichotomies of public/private, conformist/subversive, male/female, and communal/individualist. Her familial rhetoric both enlarges upon and sometimes repudiates patriarchal feudal family structures based upon subordination and authority, and, despite her economic activity, her case shows that interpretations of the Quakers as protocapitalist Protestant individualists are too simple. Particularly among Quaker women, we see images of an expanded and altered familial community neither exclusively patriarchal nor individualistic. In these terms, Fell is both an idiosyncratic leader and a representative figure.

Married at seventeen to a man about twice her age, the kindly Parliamentarian and Lancaster landowner Thomas Fell, Margaret Askew spent the next twenty-six years bearing his nine children, eight of whom—

---

[2]Kunze, and Barbara Ritter Dailey, "The Husbands of Margaret Fell: An Essay on Religious Metaphor and Social Change," *Seventeenth Century* 2(1987):55–71, leave open the question of whether the marriage was celibate.

seven daughters and one son—lived. In 1652 she first met the charismatic George Fox, then twenty-six years old and ten years her junior. Years later, she described the ambivalent emotions attending her conversion, which already signaled some autonomy from her husband and conventional role. When she heard Fox preach in church, she said later, "this opened me so, that it cut me to the heart," and she wept in her pew because she was worshipping in the conventional way rather than from an indwelling spirit of God. Then Fox visited her home and converted her, her children, and many of the household servants: "I was stricken with such sadness, I knew not what to do," she wrote later, "my husband being from home. I saw, it was the truth, and I could not deny it ... and it was opened to me so clear, that I had never a tittle in my heart against it."[3] She followed up her conversion with activity on behalf of the new creed. She was an active organizer from the year of her conversion through her marriage to George Fox in 1669, and thereafter until her death—a period of fifty years. Her house, Swarthmoor Hall, became a center of the Society of Friends as it defined itself through preaching and practice. She organized and acted as treasurer for the group's Kendall Fund, which supported itinerant preachers, including women, and as a corresponding secretary, coordinating between seventy and one hundred preaching Quaker men and women of all classes who traveled throughout England and to Europe, the Americas, and sometimes farther. In their first decade, the Quakers were the largest group of Protestant dissenters in England and may have approached thirty-five thousand to sixty thousand people, making them as numerous as Roman Catholics.[4] They were perceived as dangerous and seditious fanatics by both Puritan and Royalist authorities and by most of their neighbors, and they were subjected to considerable popular and official abuse.

Although she thereby lost Judge Fell's valuable protection against discriminatory laws and hostile neighbors, widowhood in 1658 brought Margaret Fell considerable property to use for the cause. The period of her first widowhood from 1658 to 1669 was especially active. As a widow of means and one of the most socially prominent early Quakers, she traveled, wrote, and lobbied in behalf of the group. In 1660 she went to London to persuade Charles II to release George Fox and other Quakers from jail, and she there presented Charles with the first Quaker declaration of pacifism. She later said, "I was moved of the Lord to go to the King

---

[3]Margaret Fell, "The Testimony of Margaret Fox concerning her late husband George Fox," in George Fox, *A Journal or Historical Account of the Life, Travels, Sufferings ... of ... George Fox* (London: Thomas Northcott, 1694), ii, iii.

[4]Barry Reay, *The Quakers and the English Revolution* (New York: St. Martin's Press, 1985), 11.

at Whitehall; and take with me a declaration, and information of our principles."[5] After months at court lobbying the king and council and other members of the royal family, her mission proved partially successful. She herself later suffered fines, trials, and other harassments and served two jail sentences, one of about a year, another of four years' duration. During the latter imprisonment, she wrote and published extensively, including her tract *Women's Speaking Justified*, 1667. Released from prison in 1668, she soon married George Fox. "At Bristol, he declared his intentions of marriage with me; and there also was our marriage solemnized," she wrote laconically in her autobiography. (vii) After the marriage, she rarely lived with him in the twenty-two years until his death, later excusing her unusual behavior by attributing it to her "concern for God" and "for the ordering and governing of my children and family, so that we were very willing both of us, to live apart some years upon God's account.... I was willing to make many long journeys, for taking away all occasion of evil thoughts." (ix) That is, instead of becoming a conventional wife by marrying Fox, she continued to act as the matriarchal center of a Northern activist cadre into her second widowhood and until her death at age eighty-eight.

Isabell Ross, a descendent of Fell, wrote the standard, still-cited biography in 1949. Her approach is reverential, making Fell not only an important religious figure, virtually a saint, but also a Victorian lady bountiful "with grace of body and mind, a woman winning the love and respect of great numbers of men and women by her understanding sympathy, her wisdom and her power to encourage and inspire."[6] Ross reports Fell heroically traveling on horseback and visiting prisoners into her old age but makes such activity seem merely wifely, motherly, and supportive. In the same vein Margaret Hope Bacon begins her *Mothers of Feminism: The Story of Quaker Women in America*, 1986, with the platitude, "if George Fox was 'the father of Quakerism,' Margaret Fell his *helpmeet* ... was its 'nursing mother.'"[7]

---

[5]Fell, "Testimony," vi. Further citations follow in text. The text is very similar in Fell, *A Brief Collection of Remarkable Passages and Occurrences ... of ... Margaret Fell* (London: T. Sowle, 1710), 8. I quote Fell's work from this edition, referred to hereafter as "1710," when I have not been able to consult earlier editions or manuscripts. The 1710 edition conforms Fell's usage to eighteenth-century standards of punctuation, capitalization, and so on. In her holographic letters, spelling tends to be erratic, punctuation light, and paragraphing almost nonexistent. I have regularized all quotations from seventeenth-century writers in this essay into modern spelling and capitalization and deleted some italics.

[6]Ross, v. Further citations in text.

[7]Margaret Hope Bacon, *Mothers of Feminism: The Story of Quaker Women in America* (San Francisco: Harper and Row, 1986), 7.

In her recent biography of Margaret Fell, Bonnelyn Young Kunze disputes these hagiographic versions of Fell's life and uncovers some additional information on which to judge it. Kunze sees Fell as a strong, effective, but not always admirable character who enjoyed a companionate, not patriarchal, relationship to her first husband and who sometimes complemented and sometimes undermined Fox, her "great love."[8] Kunze emphasizes Fell's dominion over her family: "after 1658 she was the matriarchal locus of authority in the Fell clan." She surrounded herself at trial with her young daughters and sometimes traveled with them, but she also fostered their autonomy. Unusually for her time and class, she did not arrange any of her daughters' marriages, and her support apparently made their relatively long spinsterhoods attractive to them, while they retained close emotional ties. "If we should be always from you outwardly, there was a pretty hard time with us," one daughter wrote her from Swarthmoor when she was on her travels. (49)

Kunze sees Fell as the chief architect of the separate women's meetings that gave Quaker women a limited separate sphere within the Quaker movement, and she praises Fell's organizational skills. Fell helped establish women's meetings over the objections of the more male-supremacist wing of the Quakers, creating an organizational format that worked on a practical level. Over fourteen hundred letters to and from Fell are included in the Swarthmore documents.[9] Kunze stresses the millenarian and radical ideas in Fell's theology, and her parallel concern for women's public ministry and for other outsiders, especially Jews. Spinoza translated and may have been influenced by one of her tracts. Contemporaries saw Fell as a "powerful, dominant, argumentative, and somewhat distant authority figure," Kunze argues. "Fox was the great idealist while she was of a more practical nature." (4) Despite the consensual and democratic Quaker ideals, Fell could be "manipulative, dictatorial, and opportunistic," using her social position, connections, skills, and wealth to contribute to Fox's "kingship" of the sect and her own local power. (388) Fell's worldliness, Kunze speculates, may have resulted from a loss of mystical belief in her later years, and it is reflected in her twenty-year-long acrimonious dispute with her former iron steward.[10] At the same time, however, she employed and helped poor women and established the model for an authoritative female public ministry, and she was highly instrumental in turning Quakers from a diffuse movement to

---

[8]Kunze, 1. Further citations in text.

[9]Kunze, 15–16.

[10]Kunze, 286-329, considers Fell guilty of unethical behavior and describes this controversy in detail. My guess is that Fell believed herself to be in the right, as in her property controversies with her son.

a coherent organization, insisting, for example, that Quakers record their marriages with the civil authorities.

Leftist historians, including leftist feminist historians, have their own standards for what is truly revolutionary and therefore commendable. In *The Quakers and the English Revolution* (1985), Barry Reay argues that the Quakers of the 1650s were a revolutionary and radically egalitarian social movement based in the poor rural classes; then George Fox organized them into a more conservative sect espousing pacifism in the 1660s. Reay does not mention Fell.[11] Similarly, A. L. Morton bemoans the "aggressive radicalism, the underlying materialism, and the hope of a new life for all" that was lost when the early, revolutionary Quakers separated themselves from the Ranters, "retreat[ed] from Revolution," and "decline[d] into apolitical nonconformity."[12] Christopher Hill claims that George Fox attained leadership of the Quakers in part by longevity, since other charismatic leaders like James Naylor died young; he does not include Fell as one of the long-lived Quaker pioneers.[13] Margaret George admires the revolutionary zeal of elderly Quaker preacher Elizabeth Hooten but looks down on the "respectable ... bourgeois" Margaret Fell for giving only "private support" to the cause before she was widowed in 1658: "clearly this estimable lady had considered first the duties of her marriage," George sneers, claiming that Fell played a "mostly background role" as "Fox's supporter and late-life wife." George apparently resents Fell's "unshakable social assurance," but it was part of what made her effective in the law courts and King's court, and it was startlingly unusual for one of her sex.[14] Basing her own account on Ross's depiction of Fell, the popular biographer Antonia Fraser takes an approach similar to George's, comparing Fell negatively with more colorful Quaker women who were whipped in public squares or who traveled as missionaries abroad.[15]

In the flighty, affected Francophile Melantha of *Marriage à la Mode*, Dryden satirized the bourgeois woman who wanted to appear at court. Such satires abound in seventeenth-century literature, especially when, as with Ben Jonson and John Dryden, the satirist was himself an ambitious parvenu. Critics like George fall prey to the same kind of snobbishness in scorning Fell for her trips to court as though they were a vain, upper-class

[11]Reay, 11.

[12]A. L. Morton, *The World of the Ranters: Religious Radicalism in the English Revolution* (London: Lawrence & Wishart, 1970), 18–19.

[13]Christopher Hill, *The Experience of Defeat: Milton and Some Contemporaries* (New York: Viking, Penguin, 1984), 166.

[14]Margaret George, *Women in the First Capitalist Society: Experiences in Seventeenth-Century England* (Urbana and Chicago: University of Illinois Press, 1988), 93, 101, 102.

[15]Antonia Fraser, *The Weaker Vessel* (New York: Alfred A. Knopf, 1984), 356–73.

affectation rather than a laborious and frustrating form of political action, and one of the few in which women could take part.

Moreover, I would argue that Quaker pacifism can be seen as more revolutionary than the Ranters' militarism, and Fell was one of its earliest and most vigorous proponents. Not quietism, Quaker pacifism required active resistance to the imperialist state, including nonpayment of some taxes and tithes, noncooperation with the military, and, as the doctrine evolved, opposition to slavery. Other Quaker practices, like objecting to oaths and tithes and refusing gestures of respect, also characterized some Ranters and other Reformation English radicals, but pacifism was more distinctive of the Quakers. Christopher Hill calls those Quakers with pacifist ideas before 1661 "premature pacifists" and sees the doctrine emerging directly from Fox's spiritual crisis at the failure of his millenarian beliefs to materialize in 1660.[16]

After Fox's and Richard Hubberthorne's "Declaration against Plots and Fightings" was stopped in the press in 1660, Margaret Fell "went to the King," and, in Fox's words, "told him what sad work there was in the city and nation, and showed him we were an innocent peaceable people, and that we must keep our meetings."[17] Fell presented Charles her statement, "A Declaration and an Information from the people of God called Quakers, to the present Governors, the King, and both Houses of Parliament," which was signed by Fox and twelve other male Quakers, as in agreement with what she said. Ross says that Fell "drew up" this document and the others "subscribed" to it. (127–28) Andrew Parker wrote concerning Fell's mission to Charles in 1660 that she "had a full and large time to lay all things before him concerning Friends' sufferings."[18] Commenting that Fell took "great labour, travail, and pains" to talk to the king, Fox implied that Fell was the Friends' officially designated representative at the Restoration, the lobbyist for an unpopular minority.[19] Although her social position and personal attractiveness undoubtedly helped gain her access to the king and court, other Quakers clearly assumed she was capable of arguing in the group's behalf on the spot. This was not a role that could be accomplished by prophetic inspiration; neither did Fell merely maneuver through the men behind the scenes for her own advantage, like Charles' mistresses. Ross says "it is a proof ... of

[16]Hill, 130.

[17]George Fox, *The Journal of George Fox*, rev., ed. John L. Nickalls (Cambridge: Cambridge University Press, 1952), 377.

[18]Kunze, 44.

[19]Fox, *Journal*, 1952, 343. Fell, "A Declaration and an Information from us the People of God called Quakers, to the present Governors, the King, and both Houses of Parliament...," 1710:202–10. Further citations in text.

the pioneering spirit and of the high position of Margaret Fell in the Quaker movement that hers was the first public statement" on Quaker pacifism. (128)

It is not clear how much influence Fell had on the policy of pacifism, but neither Fox nor any other man was the group's sole theologian. Rather, the proselytizing Friends seem to have been in continual consultation, shaping their own views while preaching them to outsiders. Some feminists, like Sara Ruddick, believe that pacifism is the only politics congruent with feminist values; interestingly, the seventeenth-century religious sect most egalitarian about women was also the champion of pacifism.[20]

We cannot know exactly what Fell said to the king in 1660, but we do have the written "Declaration" of 1660 and her later letter to King Charles of 1666. These documents demonstrate her use of familial, affective rhetoric for public purposes, as well as her fearless deployment of Biblical citations and rational argumentation based on principles of law, justice, and reason. "[T]he transformation of the Quaker ethos is connected with the social meanings of language itself," says Barbara Ritter Dailey, "[a]nd because language is the metaphor of experience that authorizes and legitimates our male and female identities, it simultaneously opens and closes possibilities for alternative behaviours."[21] At a time when public and private realms were becoming more separate and male and female roles more distinct, Fell's practice was to conflate familial and public language and to employ both gendered and generic usages to persuade the king, among others, that everyone should behave like a member of her religious family: "we ... are the people of god called Quakers, who are hated and despised, and everywhere spoken against, as people not fit to live," she begins the letter of 1660, emphasizing the power of language, or word of mouth, in the triumphs and also in the punishment of the group, which has been "stigmatized, bored through the tongue, gagged in the mouth, stocked, and whipped through towns and cities ... for conscience sake." (202–203) Depicting themselves as faithful to their word, the Quakers in 1660 are willing to say they trust "the word of a King" against all threats, as they try to hold him to his promises in their behalf. (209)

The Declaration addresses the king and "the present Governors" somewhat ambivalently. They "yet have not done us much wrong, in making any law against us, that we know of; and we do believe would not," if they rightly understood "our innocency and integrity, nakedness

---

[20]Sara Ruddick, *Maternal Thinking: Toward a Politics of Peace* (Boston: Beacon Press, 1989).

[21]Dailey, 68.

and singleness in our carriage towards all men." (204) Against the "prophane envious people" who want their lives and estates, the Quakers call upon the king's protection. Like other Protestant subjects of the nation, Fell claims, they deserve the rights of "liberty of conscience" and "our civil rights and liberties of subjects, as freeborn Englishmen" (205) because they are true patriots—peaceable people, not trouble-making revolutionaries as their slanderers allege: "treason, treachery, and false dealing we do utterly deny; false dealing, surmising, or plotting against any creature upon the face of the earth. Our weapons are not carnal, but spiritual" (209). Fell stresses the Quakers' innocence and passive courage, their ability to endure the false accusations against them without vindictiveness. She says the Quakers "speak the truth in plainness and singleness of heart, and all our desire is your good, and peace, and love, and unity, and this many thousands will seal with their blood, *who are ready not only to believe, but to suffer,* but only that the blood of the innocent may not come upon yourselves, through false informations." (210) "For no other cause but love to the souls of all people, have our sufferings been...." (209)

Fell concludes the document in behalf of its signatories, "we in the unity of the spirit." (210) After listing the signers, the document continues as though it is her oral presentation, which she speaks seamlessly for the group, merging her voice in the first person singular with her group's in the first person plural: "and now I am here to answer what can be objected against us on the behalf of many thousands, who are baptised with one spirit into one body, to bear my testimony, ... and to give an account of the hope that is in me to everyone that asketh according to the Scripture, who was moved of the Lord to leave my house and family, and to come two hundred miles to lay these things before you, who to the will of the Lord is committed. Margaret Fell." (210)

Fell's "Declaration" to the king is both intimate and authoritative, taking a tone we might call maternal. Her letter of 1666, written from prison, is even more maternal, though its note is one of betrayal and its intimacy chiefly attempts to induce guilt.[22] Feeling repudiated and betrayed by her only son, she speaks to the young king as though he too is a son who has treated her badly but may be induced to repent. "King Charles, I desire thee to read this over, which may be for thy satisfaction

---

[22]Fell, "A Letter Sent to the King from M.F." 1710:325–30. I have also examined a manuscript draft of this letter in Friends House Library, London, Spence MS. 3:120, somewhat blotted, which is shorter and omits some discussion of books previously sent to Charles and other matters. Quotations which follow in text are as in 1710 except as noted. I thank the Library of the Religious Society of Friends, London, for permission to use their collection, and the Newberry Library in Chicago.

and profit," she heads the letter colloquially, then admonishes: "In the fear of the Lord God stand still, and consider what thou and you have been doing these six years since the Lord brought you peaceably into this realm...." (325) During Charles' reign the state of the Quakers has worsened rather than improved, with "hundreds of God's people" sent "to their graves." The king should know better, Fell reminds him, since she herself had previously spoken with him on the Friends' behalf and received his personal assurances. "And before any of this was, when you first entered into this kingdom, ... I told thee, I was come to thee in behalf of an innocent, harmless, peaceable people: which words I would then, and ever since, and should at this day, seal with my blood, if I were put to it: and thy answer was to me, *if they be peaceable, they shall be protected.*" (326) In the holograph manuscript of this letter at Friends' Library, the last phrase is written in very large letters, as though Fell is shouting Charles' own faithless words back to him and as though he should be conscience-stricken hearing their reverberation. Despite his promises, her people have been "prosecuted to such a height of suffering without a just ground given" that God has punished the whole nation with his scourges of "pestilence and sword." (326) Fell alternates such guilt-inducing denunciations with professions of affection: "all this, with much more, I wrote to thee, ... in much love and tenderness to thee," she says to the king, turning from her people's fate to the personal relationship between him and herself. "And now I may say unto thee, for which of these things hast thou kept me in prison three long winters, in a place not fit for people to lie in; sometime for wind, and storm, and rain, and sometime for smoke...." (328) Like her son, the king has rendered her homeless and vulnerable to the elements. Emphasizing how long it has been since she has seen her home or children, she coaxes Charles, "let not the guilt of the burden of the breach of that word that passed from thee at Breda lie upon thy conscience, but, as thou promised when thou wast in distress ... in the fear of the Lord perform it, and purge thy conscience of it...." (329)

This last passage is not in the Friends' Library manuscript of the letter and may have been added later. In it she appeals most directly to the guilt she wishes to augment in the king by reminding him of his broken promises; at the same time, she does not want to overdo her denunciations to the point where the king finds it easier to close his ears against them. We might notice that this passage is highly oratorical. Fell heightens her appeal with sonorous rhythms, a roll of prepositional phrases, and pounding alliteration. Thus, in furthering the Quaker doctrine of pacifism, she utilizes a rhetoric of attentive care in which she addresses Charles as though he were an undutiful, ungrateful child and she an unjustly suffering mother. At the same time she tries to solicit in Charles a kind of parental concern that would include the despised Quakers as well as his more favored children. "I know it hath been often in thy heart to perform it," she placates and accuses, "and thou hast seen what fruit the want of it hath brought forth"; therefore he should "set open the prison doors, and let the innocent go free, and that will take part of the burden and guilt off you, lest the door of mercy be shut against you." (329–30) She signs herself ambivalently, and maternally, "a true lover of all your souls (though a sufferer by you)." (330)

Fell could modulate her tone and rhetoric considerably depending on her audience and purposes. When trying to persuade other Christians of the superiority of the Quaker approach to religious experience, she appealed to her readers with an intimate sense of equality, trusting them to agree with her after hearing her evidence. In "A True Testimony," published in 1660, she addressed the as yet unconverted reader as "Friend." "And so now, reader, these things being set before thee in love unto thee … slight them not…. Therefore search and examine the following treatise by the Scriptures, and the spirit of truth, and thou wilt find that in thy own bosom which will answer to the truth of what is here written."[23] Her models are the apostles who spoke according to the "spirit" against which even the Scriptures are to be tested. (241) Confident and colloquial in pressing her claims, she says, "now let any honest reasonable heart judge" (241); "and now reader, do but in soberness weigh these things according to the truth of the Scriptures, and this will take away the prejudice, and remove the objection which might arise in thy mind…." (263–64) At one point she anticipates that her "reader may judge it to be harsh or censorious" that Quakers speak against the established clergy as "ministers of darkness," so she justifies her complaints against them. (262, 263) Throughout her exposition, she is supremely self-confident that her interpretations of the Bible are correct and that these interpretations will persuade any genuinely pious and open-minded Christian reader: "this mystery I have endeavored in part to open, according to the Scriptures: and if any come to the key of David, which opens this mystery, they will see the truth of it…. Now let the reader, by what is here written, seriously search, examine, and try by the Scriptures and the measure of the spirit of God." (271) Such a prospective convert cannot help but agree with her as to "who are the true prophets and the false, and who are the true teachers, and who are the false." (270)

To enemies, those who had persecuted the Quakers, Fell could marshal a fierce denunciatory rhetoric, as in her tract "To Major General Harrison," published in 1660 but excluded from the 1710 collection of her

---

[23]Fell, "A True Testimony from the People of God (who by the World are called Quakers)" (1660), 1710:234, 236–37.

authorized publications, presumably because it is too vindictive.[24] "Now the desire of my heart is that you ... might see yourselves in the condemnation and feel the hand of [God's] justice and judgement," she tells Harrison, urging him to consider "what great mercy you have abused" by hurting innocent Friends through his "rotten deceitful profession." In another tract of 1660 that is also excluded from the 1710 volume, Fell lambastes "the city of London reproved for its abomination."[25] "Repent thou bloody city," she cries like a woman prophet, denouncing its accommodation to the changing times: "to every change of government, and every power that comes up to rule, thou can bow in thy deceitful flatterities ... for thy own ends." She catalogs the city's sins, including "chambering" and "wantoness," sins so great that even "heathens" would be "ashamed of your practices." Hypocrites and sinners as the Londoners are, they "make the name of a Christian ... odious." Repent immediately if you wish to be saved, she tells them, "and remember that you are once more warned."

Even to her enemies Fell could adapt her rhetoric as it proved valuable for the cause. Her self-assurance and ready wit are perhaps most evident in the published account of "The Examination and Tryall of Margaret Fell and George Fox" of 1664, in which she displays an image of herself as a wise, loyal, pious, and faithful citizen.[26] Richard Bauman refers to such incidents as "show trials," through which Charles' state tried to intimidate the sectaries.[27] The Quakers, in turn, used the proceedings as part of their own religious propaganda. Fell can be humble, adopting once again the position of injured innocent: "I am a widow, and my estate is a dowry, I have five children unpreferred, and if be the king's pleasure to take my estate from me, upon the account of my conscience, and not for any evil or wrong done, let him do as he pleases." But she is also willing to contend with the judge. "I appeal to all the country," she says, "what law have I broken for worshipping God in my own house." When the judge answers that she has broken the common law, Fell immediately corrects him, undermining his facade of inevitable authority: "I thought you had proceeded by statute." The sheriff tells the judge that Fell is correct. Then Fell argues that though in fact she has broken a law requiring an oath of allegiance, the oath was not intended for her or other

---

[24]Fell, "To Major General Harrison" (Aldersgate 1660), Friends Library Quaker Tracts, 51:5, p. 5.

[25]Fell, "The city of London Reproved for its Abominations..." (London: Robert Wilson, 1660), Friends Library Quaker Tracts: 51:6.

[26]*The Examination and Tryall of Margaret Fell and George Fox ... at Lancaster*, 1664.

[27]Richard Bauman, *Let Your Words Be Few: Symbolism of Speaking and Silence among Seventeenth-Century Quakers* (Cambridge: Cambridge University Press, 1983), 121.

loyal Protestants but for Papists, and she professes her allegiance to the king. As she continues her self-defense, according to the Quaker account, "the judge seemed to be angry and said she had an everlasting tongue." That is, the judge assimilates her to the image of the unruly and insubordinate woman, the scold, and she resists and defines herself as a loyal and well-informed citizen. Many historians have noted an apparent crisis of anxiety in the seventeenth century concerning the stability of English society, an anxiety played out in fears of witches, scolds, transvestites, and other supposedly domineering women. According to David Underdown, the civil war "renewed fears of female resistance to male dominance" as well as the fears of the propertied about economic expropriation by the Quakers and other radicals.[28] Clearly Fox's judge in this trial expressed such anxieties in his zeal to silence and punish Fell.

Apparently with no sense of either native incapacity or inadequate education for her tasks, Fell also argued over theology with the Anglican bishops and wrote pamphlets to convert the Jews, treating the former as intellectual equals but spiritual inferiors and the latter as misguided persons who might be persuaded to see the light. "Methinks I hear the bishops mutter, murmur, and contemn," she says, and she warned the king to beware of them. "I do hereby give" the bishops "my reasons," she challenges, "which reasons may satisfy them and the whole world, except they can, by as good or better, overturn them."[29] A writer of coherent, closely argued, if colloquial, even toughly humorous prose, Fell believed that the heart's intuitions might be misleading unless they were consonant with Scripture and with generally accepted standards of Christian conduct, though she also believed that the Scriptures were dry and potentially misleading without the interpretive guidance of the inner light of which she felt herself assured.

Fell assumes that her words will carry conviction simply because she is right. This powerful stance is strikingly unusual for a seventeenth-century woman; it is also ethnocentrically oblivious to other points of view. In her addresses to the Jews, for example, a group that she saw as outsiders like women, and to whom she showed unusual interest, she assures them that her love for them makes her wish them to avoid the damnation to which their wrong beliefs condemn them. To persuade them to believe in Jesus, she cites texts exclusively from the Old Testament and tailors her authorities, if not her attitudes, to accommodate her audience.

---

[28]David Underdown, *Revel, Riot, and Rebellion: Popular Politics and Culture in England, 1603–60* (Oxford: Clarendon Press, 1985), 209, 211.

[29]Fell, "'A Touch-Stone,' or A Tryal by the Scriptures..." (1667), 1710:357.

Although she is not usually considered an original theologian, it is important that she attempted such male-dominated rational discourses, for the more emotional expressions of religion supposedly characteristic of women and Quakers were stigmatized in the seventeenth century as they are in the present. For example, both Keith Thomas and Phyllis Mack claim that women's mystical and irrational religion lowered other people's opinions of them. "In the long run, the unconventional behavior of women prophets and their use of symbols of femininity as weapons of attack may have undermined the hierarchy of patriarchal authority within the family," Mack suggests. "But the immediate effect was surely to reinforce negative female stereotypes in the minds of their audience."[30]

If Fell could martial rational argument to dialectic and scriptural dispute, however, she also employed a familial, often maternal and empathic rhetoric to fellow believers and those she would persuade. The first enthusiasms of Quaker converts were often highly emotional and sexually tinged. The controversial and charismatic James Naylor, later purged from the Quaker movement, wrote to Fell, "thou art sealed in my heart my sister, thy care for thy babes is pleasant."[31] "I behold thy beauty dwell among the springs.... Dearly beloved this day I have received a letter from thee and verily it is joy to me when I hear thy voice.... My heart flows out with love to thee my sister, and chiefest of my father's daughters."[32] Fell addressed Naylor as "the fountain of life."[33] Fell wrote ecstatically to Fox in a melange of familial and erotic imagery: "my eternal brother in the eternal love ... my love meets thee ... and therein am I present with ye and have communion with thee my dear son whom the lord hath chosen."[34] Similarly, John Killom wrote his "dear sister" Fell that her "love toward me is great, and over me thou art tender as a nursing mother refreshing thy tender plant.... In the bowels of love I do thee greet ... and lie down in the arms of love embracing each the other

---

[30]Phyllis Mack, "Women as Prophets during the English Civil War," *Feminist Studies* 8.1 (Spring 1982):38. More recently, she describes the "infantile and apocalyptic imagery and the antisocial appearance" of early Quakers but also notes "the extent to which leading Quaker women succeeded in combining ecstatic prayer and public evangelizing with the more conventional activities of child rearing, charity work" and so on, in Phyllis Mack, "Gender and Spirituality in Early English Quakerism, 1650–65," in *Witnesses for Change: Quaker Women over Three Centuries*, ed. Elizabeth Potts Brown and Susan Mosher Stuard (New Brunswick and London: Rutgers University Press, 1989), 53, 54. Also see Keith Thomas, "Women and the Civil War Sects," in *Crisis in Europe 1560–1660*, ed. Trevor Aston (London: Routledge and Kegan Paul, 1965), 327–40.

[31]James Naylor, Swarthmore MSS, 2:895, Friends House Library, London.

[32]Ibid., 2:895. Such ecstatic language was edited out of later Quaker writings.

[33]Fell, Swarthmore MSS, 15:39.

[34]Ibid., 2:203.

where we cannot be separated."[35] Edward Burroughs called Fell, "oh thou daughter of God, and mother in Israel, and nourisher of our father's babes and children ... thou art comely in thy beauty clothed with the sun and the moon underneath thy feet ... by whom I am ravished with love which burnest in my breast."[36] From Boston prison Joseph Nicolson wrote to Fell, "oh thou fairest among women ... I am refreshed by night in my bed when I think of the sweet harmony that flows from thee."[37] Other women sometimes adopted a similar tone: "beholding thy beauty dear sister I was much refreshed by thy lines," Dorothy Howgill wrote to Fell.[38]

Although addressed as mother, daughter, sister, lover, and friend, and employing such familiar terms to others, Fell also shows a surprising ability to position herself as the speaker of an ungendered yet authoritative discourse, and she asserts an ethic of divinely familial caring that blurs conventional gender designations. Fell persistently challenges the assignment of gender to biology as well as the assignment of family categories only to biological relatives. She repeatedly states that Christ the spirit is the husband to his bride, the body of the church of believers. That is, the flesh and the human believer of either sex are metaphorically female in relation to Christ, who is male. God is not just a father in such usages but a loving or nursing parent.

Repeatedly Fell refers to Christ as the "seed of woman," a usage that may recall to us the rhetoric of that nineteenth-century American Quaker, Sojourner Truth, who claimed that Jesus was made by God and a woman and that man had nothing to do with him. "God sent forth his son, made of a woman," Fell writes.[39] She refers to new converts as like "new-born-babes desiring the sincere milk of the word, that ye may grow thereby." (197) In this image, God or the church or the scriptures are a nursing mother, and it sounds as though she herself can also be the maternal conduit for this healthful milk. God's relation to his people may be that of a mother to a child or of a husband to a wife in Fell's writing, which includes many intimate, affective, and gender-mixed metaphors of empathic dependence and protection. "My dear lambs," she addresses Friends, "... though a woman may forget the sucking child of her womb, yet cannot [God] forget such."[40]

[35]Quoted in Brown and Stuard, 66–68.
[36]Quoted in Hugh Barbour and Arthur O. Roberts, eds., Early Quaker Writings 1650–1700 (Grand Rapids: Wm B. Eerdmans, 1973), 477.
[37]Swarthmore MSS, 2:917.
[38]Ibid., 2:489.
[39]Fell, "A General Epistle to Friends (1658)," 1710:199, 197.
[40]Fell, "An Epistle to Friends" (1661), 1710:271–72.

Her rhetoric is richly empathic to those suffering for the faith. To prisoners at Lancaster Castle, before she was herself incarcerated, she wrote, in the paradoxes Cavalier poet William Lovelace used for love and imprisonment, "I am present with you.... Here is freedom, which the world knows not."[41] She signed letters of encouragement to Quakers in jail, "your dear Friend, that is one with you in all your sufferings."[42]

Fell not only preached and wrote, but she also argued in behalf of all other women to be guided by the spirit to speak and write, saying that God's inspiration must be allowed to overflow into speech. Her examples came primarily from the Bible, and not exclusively from women who were prophets. She cites Esther, Deborah, and the women to whom Christ appeared as precedents. Fell consistently argued that in Christ male and female were equal and that for those who were saved, the fallen condition of female subservience had already ended. Therefore, whatever [saved] men could do, [saved] women could do. Fell possessed a stunning self-assurance about her own ability to preach, theologize, or adjudicate equally with men, a real sense of herself as an equal that is very rare even in the most active seventeenth-century women. In contrast, for example, Margaret Cavendish, the notorious and prolific Royalist writer of mid-century, constantly reminds us that because she is a woman, her defects should be excused and her accomplishments admired. Even other Quaker women, though the most widely published and outspoken group of seventeenth-century women writers, relied on some traditional apologies to excuse their boldness in venturing before the public: God had bidden them to speak, they could not hide the truth revealed to them, and so on.[43]

In *Women's Speaking Justified*, 1667, Fell tells "how God himself hath manifested his will and mind concerning women, and unto women," and insists that "God hath put no such difference between the male and female as men would make."[44] Sex is less physical, less determinative in her view than in that of seventeenth-century society as a

[41]"An Epistle to Friends, that were Prisoners in Lancaster-Castle, by M. Fell, 1654." 1710:59.

[42]"An Epistle to Friends," 1710:274.

[43]For example, Elizabeth Bathurst writes, "neither have I fondly desired to get my name in print, for 'tis not an inky character can make a saint," *Truth Vindicated by ... Elizabeth Bathurst* (London: T. Sowle, 1695), B5v; E. Hincks, *The Poor Widow's Mite Cast into the Lord's Treasure*, 1671: "Now lest it should be counted a libel, or any should think I dare not own it in the world, I have subscribed my name," Quaker tracts 51:21.

[44]Fell, "Womens Speaking Justified, proved and allowed by the Scriptures," 1667. Reprint, with introduction by David J. Latt. Publication #194, William Andrews Clark Memorial Library (Los Angeles: UCLA, 1979), 3. This text is a reprint of the 1667 first edition. Pages in text are quoted from this accessible edition. Also 1710:331–50.

whole. Even if all flesh is metaphorically female, the spirit in either man or woman is genderless, transcending sexual difference. As Elaine Hobby notes, neither Fell's tract nor Fox's "The Woman Learning in Silence" of 1656 was the first Quaker defense of women's speech, and several of the earlier ones were more radical than that by Fell, who was notable for her logical approach, not for the direct evidence of enthusiastic inspiration.[45] Fox's treatise sought to distinguish the limited authority of the Law from the Spirit, which gives a Christian liberty. The liberation of women to preach and prophesy was for Fox subsidiary to the general point about Christian liberty: "that which usurps authority the Law takes hold of, but if you be led by the spirit, then you are not under the law." "Christ in the male, and in the female is one, which makes free from the law."

Fell's style is more colloquial than Fox's. She begins her tract abruptly, as though she were in the midst of the argument currently raging about women's speaking, both within the Quaker community and in terms of outside hostility to the practice: "whereas it hath been an objection in the minds of many, and several times hath been objected by the clergy, or ministers, and others, against women's speaking in the church.... But how far they wrong the apostles' intentions in these Scriptures, we shall show clearly." She speaks in the first person plural as though she represents the community of women, not in Fox's preacherly second person, and she uses metaphorical women and metaphorical roles of women in the Bible more than Fox does, while also expanding and elaborating on the roles of literal Biblical women. Her own emphasis is less on the difference between the spirit and the law and more on the indwelling nature of Christ as spirit in all people. She also stresses the metaphorical equation of the body with the female but extends this polarity to all persons, not just women. She insists that the Biblical verses are so clear that anyone, even an uneducated woman, can understand them: "let the reader seriously read that chapter," she instructs concerning the difficult passage 1 Corinthians 14, "and see the end and drift of the apostle in speaking these words"; "here the apostle clearly manifests his intent." (8)

Her proof for the holiness and acceptability to God of women is based heavily on reading the New Testament for examples of women in relation to Christ, as privileged to be present at the Resurrection, for example, when men are not. Thus she takes these Biblical examples not simply as historical facts but as God's deliberate lessons about women's roles. This tactic allows her to use Biblical examples in her favor but to

---

[45]George Fox, "The Woman Learning in Silence" in *Gospel Truth Demonstrated in a Collection of Doctrinal Books* (London: T. Sowle, 1706), 77, 78. Elaine Hobby, *Virtue of Necessity: English Women's Writing 1649–88* (Ann Arbor: University of Michigan Press, 1988), 43.

historicize all the Biblical strictures that appear to go against women as part of "the night of apostasy," a darkness that can be ignored by saved men and women since "the true light now shines." (11) She thus sees male dominance as part of a historical period that is benighted and of a spiritual condition that is fallen; neither is universal, and the Friends can separate themselves from these conditions. "Where He hath poured forth his spirit upon them, they must prophesy, though blind priests say to the contrary, and will not permit holy women to speak," she claims. (13) Citing the Biblical Ruth and Hulda, she taunts her opponents: "see if any of you blind priests can speak after this manner, and see if it be not a better sermon than any of you can make, who are against women's speaking." (14) Her adversaries "cannot make such a sermon as this woman did, and yet will make a trade of this woman and other women's words." (15)

All injunctions generally made to the church must automatically include women, Fell argues; otherwise the Bible would be contradictory to itself: "is not the bride the church? and doth the church only consist of men? You that deny women's speaking, answer...." (17) Her contrast between "a holy woman" and "blind priests" assumes the much greater determinative power of the adjectives over the nouns, of the spiritual condition over the relatively irrelevant physical situation. (16) Her position is not merely that women can speak, but that they must, should the spirit so inspire them. She cites Old Testament and Apocryphal women Esther and Judith as examples of holy, prophetic women, in contrast to "the false church, the great whore, and tattling women, and busie bodies" who are the only ones "forbidden to preach." (16) With statements like this, Fell shows the ease with which she separates herself and the community of female Friends from the categories of tattling women, busybodies, and scolds excoriated throughout seventeenth-century pamphlet literature, and also the ease with which she crosses metaphorical, allegorical, and real social categories of women.

Our records of seventeenth-century communal life in Britain show a great deal of petty rivalry, feuding, and bad feeling of the sort that led to witchcraft accusations and persecutions, rivalries over property, religion, and political allegiance, endemic family violence, and persecution of the poor and various outcasts, as well as the merry communalism of maypole and tavern.[46] The Society of Friends illustrates that the dichotomy between capitalist family and feudal community is too simple a way of

---

[46]See Underdown, 36–38; G. R. Quaife, *Wanton Wenches and Wayward Wives: Peasants and Illicit Sex in Early Seventeenth-Century England* (New Brunswick: Rutgers University Press, 1979), 158.

thinking about these social divisions, for Quaker affectivity is communal, not merely personal or familial. The Quakers were known for their rudeness, by the standards of their neighbors, because they did not greet non-Quakers or use other conventional gestures of respect, like doffing their hats.[47] Yet the Quaker use of family terms and of the intimate "thou" form across social class attempts to turn the larger community—or at least portions of it—into an affective family rather than insulating the family from it.

Lawrence Stone describes the seventeenth-century upper-class family as a cold one, characterized by distance, hierarchy, and even distaste. In contrast, the Puritan and/or middle-class family is seen as beginning the affective relationships that characterize modernity.[48] Marxist critics, in turn, see such a warm affective family structure as a harbinger of industrial capitalism, providing a female-dominated haven in a heartless world that allows the public sphere to be even more exploitative and indifferent to human needs. The Quaker rhetoric of the affective family coincides with that of the affective religious group, encouraging believers to persevere under persecution by the state, their neighbors, and also nonbelieving members of their own biological families. Thus this religious rhetoric served communal, not merely morcellizing processes. One can see it as a complex response to individualism and a variant development of it rather than an unequivocal embrace, adapting the authority of the family to a new, expanded familial grouping that might include people from a range of social classes and both genders, but exclude even close members of one's biological family. The very word "friend" denotes this ambiguity, since a "friend" in the seventeenth century could be an elective associate, a patron, a family member, or a lover. Moreover, male and female Friends may have stood in a different relation to the term and to individualism. Mack suggests that female Quakers did not reject family life in the same way as the earliest male converts did. Whereas the men might have found conversion to Quakerism more "liberating or cathartic" because they changed their prior roles so drastically upon conversion, the women behaved differently. "Far from being excessively undisciplined, extremist, or hysterical, women's predominant role in early Quakerism was to hold the movement together."[49]

According to some current theorists, linguistic forms shape our thoughts and so create human subjectivity. It is noteworthy, then, that the

[47]Bauman, 43.

[48]Lawrence Stone, *The Family, Sex and Marriage in England 1500–1800* (London: Weidenfield and Nicolson, 1977).

[49]Mack in Brown and Stuard, 56.

Quakers created a distinctive semiotic practice in dress and speech. Bauman reminds us that the first generation of Quakers learned new speaking habits as adults. Neither an inspired enthusiast nor a religious bureaucrat, Fell addresses even the king as though he were her own young son, and this rhetoric of intimate address implies a radical egalitarianism regarding gender as well as class. Margaret Fell spoke a language of wifely deference, yet she became a religious organizer against the earliest wishes of her first husband and, despite the gossip of her peers, largely independently of her second. She would not wear the grey clothing of the rest of her sect, and she used the advantages of her class position when it suited her purposes, at other times being more radically egalitarian. Although Mack contends that Quaker female authority was grounded in a "total rejection of self" for God, Fell, in contrast, assumed that her massive self-assertiveness was in the best interests of herself, her family, and all good Christians.[50] Unlike many publishing seventeenth-century women, she proudly signed her tracts and letters with her own name. Energetic, practical, and matriarchal, Fell helped shaped the Society of Friends into a community, an extended family, a society more flexible about class and gender than seventeenth-century English society as a whole and less enclosed than much of our contemporary historiography, both Marxist and feminist. She was indeed a role model for many of her peers and followers in the faith, but we can see her more fully as a historical actor at once unique, exemplary, and representative—a significant, if imperfect, religious and political leader, an effective organizer, a cogent and prolific writer, an important early pacifist, and one of the shapers, through her fluid language, of an affective familialism that did not divide the individual from her community.

---

[50] Ibid., 50. Phyllis Mack's comprehensive study, *Visionary Women: Ecstatic Prophecy in Seventeenth-Century England* (Berkeley, Los Angeles, Oxford: University of California Press, 1992), appeared after this essay was completed.

TWELVE

"Marrying that Hated Object": The Carnival of Desire in Behn's *The Rover*

Mark S. Lussier

As a woman successfully writing within a masculine economy of production, Aphra Behn has been one of those figures most fully recovered by revisionist approaches to the canon of English literature.[1] Although *The Rover* was controversial in Behn's day, it was generally well-received when it was first performed at the Duke's Theater in March 1677 and enjoyed a relatively long theatrical life during the eighteenth century, as Frederick Link has noted:

> Between 1700 and 1725 seventy performances are recorded…. In the second quarter of the century the play was equally popular, some eighty-eight performances being recorded between 1726 and 1760…. After performances at least once a season between 1703 and 1743, and revivals at Covent Garden in 1748 and 1757, the play was seen no more.[2]

Behn's libertine commitment to feminine sexuality generated increasingly hostile critical responses; finally, her writing was suppressed in an eigh-

---

[1]The impressive range of scholarship recently generated on Behn's *The Rover* is evident in the following studies: Elin Diamond, "*Gestus* and Signature in Aphra Behn's *The Rover*," *ELH* 56 (1989):519–41; and Catherine Gallagher, "Who Was That Masked Woman? The Prostitute and the Playwright in the Comedies of Aphra Behn," *Women's Studies* 15 (1988):23–42.

[2]"Introduction," in Aphra Behn, *The Rover*, ed. Frederick M. Link, Regents Restoration Drama Series (Lincoln: University of Nebraska Press, 1967), xiii. All subsequent citations are to this edition. The history of performance and publication are pithily outlined in Link's introduction to his edition of the play; he notes (xi–xii) that most of *The Rover*'s characters and plot devices are derived from Thomas Killigrew's closet drama *Thomaso, or, The Wanderer*, which was written in 1654 and published a decade later.

teenth-century drive, fueled by Dr. Johnson in particular, to establish a moral "canon" for English literature. According to Johnson, Behn was typical of Restoration playwrights who sought to please "their Age, and did not aim to mend."[3] Other critics describe *The Rover* as "very shocking," "one continued tale of bawdery," and "corrupt."[4]

The thrust of this essay, then, is to identify and examine those elements that render understandable both *The Rover*'s accessibility to audiences during Behn's time and its appeal to contemporary critics employed in recovering literary texts written by women. The play brings into dialogic exchange a series of competing discourses that variously address the conflict between the sexes, the clash of nationalities, the competition of conflicting idealizations of love, the friction between individuals and the state, and the constant association of venal interests with social relations. Calling attention to the interpenetration of literary and political concerns, Stephen Zwicker has observed that "[e]ven if we aim to elevate the literary above the political in this culture, we cannot fully appreciate what is literary without understanding the polemicized nature of literary language, literary subject, and literary authority."[5] Behn, a former royalist spy in Antwerp, was personally involved in Restoration politics, and her "Prologue" engages the overtly political climate within which any staged drama of the period was received.

Yet she was also a woman writing within and against a controlling social discourse that treated women as commodities. Several dramatic works by this remarkably insightful woman analyze what has been considered the foundation of capitalist patriarchal structure: the exchange of women to enhance male wealth, power, and position.[6] For Behn, this phallocratic social organization functions, to appropriate Frederic Jame-

---

[3]"Prologue Spoken by Mr. Garrick," *Prologue and Epilogue, Spoken at the Opening of the Theatre in Drury Lane 1747* (London: E. Cave for M. Cooper & R. Dodsley, 1747), 5.

[4]Citations are, in order, to William Oldys, "Behn (Aphara)," *A General Dictionary, Historical and Critical*, compiled by John Peter Bernard, et al., vol. 3 (London: J Betterham, 1735), 144; [Thomas] Wilkes, *A General View of the State* (London: J. Coote & W. Whetstone, 1759), 79; and Eric S. Robertson, *English Poetesses: A Series of Critical Biographies* (London, Paris & New York, 1883), 189.

[5]"Lines of Authority: Politics and Literary Culture in the Restoration," *The Politics of Discourse: The Literature and History of Seventeenth-Century England*, ed. Kevin Sharpe and Steven Z. Zwicker (Berkeley, Los Angeles, and London: University of California Press, 1987), 231–32.

[6]For a detailed reading of two such plays, *The Feign'd Curtezans* and *The City Heiress*, see my "'The Vile Merchandize of Fortune': Women, Economy, and Desire in Aphra Behn," *Women's Studies* 18 (1990):379–93.

son's terms, as a "political unconscious."[7] In other words, the prologue explores a literal politics while the play uncovers the symbolic ordering of the political unconscious, exemplifying in the process that "literature" in the Restoration cannot be "elevate[d] above the political."[8]

Criticism as Social Dis-Ease

The prologue directly addresses itself to what can be termed the politics of interpretation, comparing critics to doctors who diagnose the creative maladies of the stage:

> Wits, like physicians, never can agree,
> When of a different society.
> And Rabel's drops were never more cried down
> By all the learned doctors of the town,
> Than a new play whose author is unknown.
>
> (Prologue, 1–5)

These doctors of wit are defined by their cultural differences, a division which is heightened by the appearance of a "new play whose author is unknown." Behn directly confronts the increasingly acrimonious debate over the nature of the stage, uncovering the emotive rather than rational criteria at the foundation of most "objective" criticism: the "medical" parameters within which any new work is received are governed by "malice" and "pride" and defined by the author's status within the critics' "own cabal" (Prologue, 6–9). By the end of the century, a major metaphor emerged representing stage culture (aesthetically linked to the royal line of power) as a social disease. In 1695, Sir Richard Blackmore complained, in his Preface to *Prince Arthur*, that "The *universal* Corruption of Manners and irreligious Disposition of Mind that infects the Kingdom seems to have been in great Measure deriv'd from the Stage." Or, as Charles Gildon declared in *A Complete Art of Poetry*: "it is not less true, that Men often abuse the best Things, that which was design'd for a wholesome Remedy,

---

[7]*The Political Unconscious: Narrative as a Socially Symbolic Act* (Ithaca: Cornell University Press, 1981). My appropriation of Jameson's term intersects the debate over the interpenetration of literary and political culture that unfolds during and following the Restoration. For Behn, the reduction of women and feminine sexuality to the status of commodities provides "the absolute horizon of all reading and all interpretation" (Jameson, 17) of *The Rover*. This concept of social structure transcends partisan politics yet functions as its organizing principle. See also Jameson, 47–48.

[8]Zwicker, 232.

may in Time become a very dangerous Poison."[9] Thus, according to a more recent assessment, "Aphra Behn and her fellow wits infect one another."[10] Fellow poets, in this critical environment, act as inquisitors:

> Thus like a learned conclave poets sit,
> Catholic judges both of sense and wit,
> And damn or save as they themselves think fit.
> Yet those who to others' faults are so severe,
> And not so perfect but themselves may err.

> (Prologue, 17–21)

Although a royalist, Behn is not above addressing the religious prejudice that leads, finally, to the overthrow of James II, once Tory and Whig as political parties join forces to effect the "Glorious Revolution." She assumes the intertwining of literary and political cultures, yet the plumb line for both "camps" is based on the self-deception of critics who exist within an empowered discourse. I interpret these critical "cabals" to be an authorized manifestation of what postmodern psychoanalytic discourse has termed the "symbolic order." This political horizon for culture includes economies like theatrical production as well as the affairs of state, or what might be called the literal layer of political engagement. The variety of virulent responses to Behn's productions alluded to in the first half of the prologue can be read in light of this symbolic order, with censuring critics occupying the locus of critical standards to voice aesthetic laws.

The second half of the "Prologue" turns its attention to an anatomization of style and a consideration of those formal elements that delineate the shape of drama on the Restoration stage. Some writers, cognizant of the critical environment within which their efforts will be judged, "write correct" (Prologue, 22) yet without originality; others write "characters genteel and fine" (Prologue, 26), yet encounter conflict when they attempt

---

[9]Blackmore and Gildon are quoted in Andrew Bear, "Restoration Comedy and the Provok'd Critic," *Restoration Literature: Critical Approaches*, ed. Harold Love (London: Methuen & Company, Ltd., 1972), 5–6. Statements on the infectious nature of staged drama during the Restoration receive extended exploration in Bear's essay. He traces the clash between conflicting visions of the specular qualities of the stage, citing critics such as Collier and Steele who rail that "nothing has gone farther in Debauching the Age than the *Stage Poets*, and *Playhouse*" and that such representations directly impact "what Manners and Customs are transfused from the Stage to the World." (6–7) The resiliency of the attacked playwrights (Behn, Wycherly, and Congreve) derives from their ability to appropriate and invert the objections raised against them. Dennis, for example, replies to Steele's attack "by simply reversing the interpretation in order to show that the vices of characters are 'exposed' rather than 'recommended', so that the play functions to 'shew us what ought never to be done upon the Stage of the World.'" (8)

[10]Gallagher, 30.

to "mimic" what occurs naturally in social discourse. For this reason, art as it appears on the Restoration stage is defined mimetically, with the prescriptive "fashion" for success found in "the gleanings of good conversation." (Prologue, 35–36) In fact, in the estimate of Rose Zimbardo, such "gleanings" define Behn's achievement:

> Throughout the play Behn uses a new style in language (that is, simulation of real speech instead of declamation, heroic or satiric) and a new complex multidimensionality in character to build realistic overlays upon conventional types and stock situations.[11]

Although Zimbardo directly refers to *The Lucky Chance*, the same innovation of discursive exchange applies to *The Rover*, whose multidimensionality resides equally in the display of realistic language, which transcends the limitations of form, and the display of realistic relationships, which refutes the limitations of social convention.

Following this anatomization of the fashion of stage production, the "Person of Quality" who ushers in the play is called a "fool" by the play's author, since "you [the audience] came not here for our [the author's] sakes, but your own." (Prologue, 40–41) The audience comes to the theater seeking reification of its own values as these are manifest in "good conversation"; their critical standards are thereby grounded in a secondary narcissism, where empowered discourses continually marginalize new modes of discursive presence by regulating the arena within which artists traditionally push against the rigid strictures of society. Behn's stance against the controlling social matrix, which marginalizes women's desire and regulates wealth and power through adherence to the absolute rule of the name of the father, provides a mirror within which the audience can behold its own image, but this image is a conscious display of the unconscious structure of a society based upon the exchange of women rather than the conscious reflection of what Behn perceives to be a flawed social dynamic that privileges the masculine to the detriment of the feminine. Phrased another way (and as a way of returning to the prologue), Behn reveals that the "censure" of critics is governed by emotion, "love" and "hate" (Prologue, 16), despite claims to rationality. She also demonstrates that social relations like marriage are governed by rationality, in spite of claims for an emotional foundation. Behn discloses this paradox in order to confront, perhaps even correct, the "unconscious" structure that undergirds them both by bringing audiences to an awareness of disease at the foundation of social practice.

---

[11]Rose Zimbardo, *A Mirror to Nature: Transformations in Drama and Aesthetics, 1660–1732* (Lexington: University Press of Kentucky, 1986), 160.

Carnivalism and the Name-of-the-Father

The play is set in Naples at the time of carnival, and its structure depends, initially, on the role an absent father plays in determining social relations. The consummate skill with which Behn interrelates the notations of setting and structure, I argue, strengthens the revolutionary aspects of the work.[12] Although the father is never 'named' and never present on stage, the name-of-the-father governs the very structure of events in *The Rover,* as presented in the play's opening scene where the word "father" is invoked six times by male and female characters alike. The difference between these evocations of the function, as opposed to the name, is defined by gender, with the women, Florinda and Hellena, seeking to circumvent the father's desire to marry them off to secure wealth, power, and prestige for his family name, and the male, their brother Pedro, invoking the father's name to discourage their pursuit of objects of desire disconnected from economic considerations.

The play opens with an overt privileging of gender. The scene is set in a chamber, an enclosed space usually associated with the feminine, and the opening dialogue between Florinda and Hellena gives priority to the feminine voice. Florinda, whose "father" promotes her marriage to "the rich old Don Vincentio" (I.i.18–19), expresses the common despair confronting women in a masculine economy:

[H]ow near soever my father thinks I am to marrying that hated object, I shall let him see I understand better what's due to my beauty, birth, and fortune, and more to my soul, than to obey those unjust commands.

(I.i.21–25)

Florinda recognizes her status as commodity, since she knows "what's due to [her] beauty, birth, and fortune," and she seeks to subvert this status by pursuing designs that lead to emotional rather than venal recompense. Yet it is her desire to save her "soul" that motivates her stand against the "commands" of the father as articulated by Pedro: "I have a

---

[12]Behn's works point quite explicitly to modern analyses of the structure of social relations as built on the bodies of women. Elin Diamond argues that the carnival/masquerade setting for *The Rover* "threatens the Father's law (incest taboo) and all systems of representation." (540) Behn has anticipated both anthropological and psychological explorations of this cultural base. In her understanding of the function women play in stabilizing social structure, their status as objects of exchange between males, she foreshadows work done by Levi-Strauss in his classic *Structural Anthropology,* where social structure involves, in Jacqueline Rose's terms, a "notion of kinship in which women are defined as objects of exchange" ("Introduction II" to Jacques Lacan's *Feminine Sexuality,* Juliet Mitchell and Jacqueline Rose, eds., Jacqueline Rose, trans. [New York: W.W. Norton & Co., 1981], 45).

command from my father here to tell you ought not to despise him [Don Vincentio], a man of so vast a fortune." (I.1.62–63) The stage directions have Pedro put on a "masking habit" at this point, an action that matches his assumption of the voice of the father. To this end, Pedro enacts a central tenet in feminist critiques of patriarchal social organization: "Consider the exemplary case of *father-son relationships*, which guarantee the transmission of patriarchal power and its laws, its discourse, its social structures."[13]

Florinda immediately appeals to her brother to support her position against the father on the grounds of justice: "I would not have a man so dear to me as my brother follow the ill customs of our country and make a slave of his sister ... my father's will I'm sure you may divert." (I.1.66–9) Yet Pedro refuses to recognize the validity of Florinda's arguments, for he has absorbed the Father's venal conceptualization of social relations and shares his understanding of value:

> {Y}ou must consider Don Vincentio's fortune and the jointure he'll make you.... [Is it] a confinement to be carried into the country to an ancient villa belonging to the family of the Vincentios these five hundred years, and have no other prospect than that pleasing one of seeing all her own that meets her eyes...?
> (I.1.79–80;98–102)

Pedro suffers from an inability to place himself in his sister's situation; his judgment is clouded by the father's authority ("command") and the father's values (owning "all ... that meets her eyes"). To penetrate this veil of venal concerns, Florinda suggests that Pedro consider her obligations in the evening rather than the full light of day:

> And if these be her daily divertissements, what are those of the night? To lie in a wide moth-eaten bedchamber with furniture in fashion in the reign of King Sancho the First; the bed, that which his forefathers lived and died in.
> (I.1.107–10)

This more explicit evocation of the price her body must pay to secure Don Vincentio's fortune for the family makes little impact on Pedro at this point, yet he will, once he sees the machinations of his friends in vying for the favors of Angellica, alter his opinion.

The immediate dramatic context of "Carnival" (I.1.39), which has functioned as a culturally authorized breach in normal social codes from

---

[13]Luce Irigaray, *This Sex Which Is Not One*, trans. Catherine Porter (Ithaca and London: Cornell University Press, 1985), 193.

Shakespeare's *Romeo and Juliet* to the Restoration subgenre of "intrigues," provides the needed mechanism for the women to operate against the symbolic order itself. The carnival places the female protagonists—except for Angellica—in a position from which to read the phallocratic configurations of social reality and establishes a space from which to resist it. As Julia Kristeva has argued (following Bahktin): "Carnivalesque discourse breaks through the laws of language censored by grammar and semantics and, at the same time, is a social and political protest."[14] Certainly, carnival in Catholic countries is associated with an eruption of what Lacan, Kristeva, and others term *jouissance* prior to the advent of Lent, the period when the Church as primary social institution erected in the Father's name reasserts its authority over accepted behavior. Behn's use of carnival (etymologically linked to the carnal) inversely mirrors and thereby refutes symbolic codification. As Kristeva points out, carnival is a linguistic space in which "language escapes linearity (law) to live as drama in three dimensions ... where prohibition (representing 'monologism') and their transgression (dream, body, 'dialogism') coexist."[15] Interesting in this context is the anonymously written *Companion to the Theatre: or, A View of our most Celebrated Dramatic Pieces* (London, 1747), which attributes the carnival setting to Behn's desire "to give more Latitude to the Behaviour of the Characters." (256)

The phallus, according to psychoanalytic reading associated with Lacan, can play its role as the privileged signifier of culture only when it is veiled. When the female protagonists are allowed to assume veiled roles in relation to the controlling discourse of marriage marketeering and erotic speculation, they occupy a breach in this discourse to the end of unveiling the phallic foundation of culture.[16] For this reason, critics have seen in *The Rover* a "typical dramatic pattern" for Behn, where "a wild, witty heroine actively intrigu[es] to win the man she has chosen"

---

[14]*Desire in Language: A Semiotic Approach to Literature and Art*, ed. Leon S. Roudiez and Thomas Gora, trans. Alice Jardine and Leon S. Roudiez (New York: Columbia University Press, 1980), 36.

[15]Kristeva, 78–9.

[16]The nature of the symbolic order can be defined, according to Leon S. Roudiez speaking of its role in the work of Julia Kristeva, as "the establishment of sign and syntax, paternal function, grammatical and social constraints, symbolic law." (6–7) This places the secondary symbolic order in continual conflict with the "semiotic," which refers directly to "the actual organization, or disposition, within the body, of instinctual drives ... as they affect language and its practice." (18) As Lacan had argued prior to Kristeva, "It is in this symbolic register that the subject must be constituted before anything belonging to the order of desire can take on a structure for him [or her]" (*Feminine Sexuality: Jacques Lacan and the école freudienne*, ed. Juliet Mitchell and Jacqueline Rose, trans. Jacqueline Rose [New York and London: W.W. Norton and Company, 1982], 113). Thus, as expressed by Ellie Ragland-Sullivan, "Language

and where the aesthetic ethos is defined by "the domination and control of the women [over] the relative passivity of men."[17] This critique of social relations, then, introduces "a central formal disjunction that generates all the contingent terms of moral judgment," with Behn basing "her moral criticism of society, as does Wycherley, on its reduction of human relationships to economic exchange."[18]

Opposition to the feminine perspective established in the opening scene comes immediately in the second scene with the appearance of the male protagonists—Belvile, Willmore, Frederick, and Blunt—who wander the streets and discuss their own varied approaches to love. The minor characters, Frederick and Blunt, associate capital and sexual relations in predictable ways, which trope off the unconscious structure of society that Behn critiques; for Blunt, this language is one of literal consumption, where "our Cupids are like the cooks of the camp: they can roast or boil a woman." (I.11.34–6) For Frederick, the approach to women is defined by a more symbolic mode of consumption: women are "as troublesome to me i'th morning as they were welcome o'er night." (I.ii.41–2) Against this devouring approach to sexual relations, Belvile is defined by his constant love for Florinda and his fear that venal concerns will override emotional attachments:

> {T}he Viceroy's son ... has the advantage of me in being a man of fortune, a Spaniard, and her brother's friend; which gives him liberty to make his court, whilst I have recourse only to letters and distant looks from her window[.]
>
> (I,ii,26–30)

---

and human culture also arise out of identification with this differential Lacan called the symbolic order. So identity is learned as a gendered set of fictions which bear the truth of one's desire whose polymorphous perverse *jouissance* is carved up by the effects of language and taboos written on the body" ("The Sexual Masquerade: A Lacanian Theory of Sexual Difference," in *Lacan and the Subject of Language*, ed. Ellie Ragland-Sullivan and Mark Bracher [New York and London: Routledge, 1991], 51). Returning to Behn, it is clear that—as in Lacan, Kristeva, and others—the full authority of what Lacan terms the "paternal metaphor" (*Feminine Sexuality,* [1982] 39) is realized *in absentia*; Behn, perceiving this, finds within the body of desire, specifically women's desires, a means for overcoming the paradoxical situation mentioned above, where "love" (i.e. marriage) is governed by reason, and rational social organization is constructed from personal bias.

[17]Jacqueline Pearson, *The Prostituted Muse: Images of Women & Women Dramatists, 1642–1737* (New York: St. Martin's Press, 1988), 152.

[18]Laura Brown, *English Dramatic Form: An Essay in Generic History* (New Haven and London: Yale University Press, 1981), 61–2.

This group of foreign, that is to say English, intriguers is completed with the appearance of Willmore, a thoroughly recognizable rake, whose values are easily read: "Love and mirth are my business in Naples, and if I mistake not the place, here's an excellent market for chapmen of my humor." (I.11.76–8) Against the English rovers, who also function as emblems of the royal line set adrift upon the continent following the civil war and the establishment of the commonwealth, stand the continental males: Don Pedro (brother to Florinda and Hellena), Don Antonio (the Viceroy's son and Pedro's friend), Phillipo (a gallant), Stephano (servant to Don Pedro), and Biskey and Sebastian (two bravos to Angellica). The Englishmen, with the exception of Belvile, take a consuming approach to sexual and marital relations that can be defined by the gratification of lust; conversely, the continental men promote an altered form of consumption when they pursue attachments that reify their wealth and power.

Thus, the male protagonists define two varieties of masculine experience apparently opposed to each other but actually related in their view that the feminine is to be consumed as a commodity. By the end of the first two scenes, which comprise the first act, all the female and male protagonists, with one significant exception in the person of Angellica Bianca (a renowned courtesan), are introduced, and the primary conflict in the play, the clash between emotive relations pursued by the women and the venal and consuming vision of social relations pursued by the men, has been established. Yet, in the context of carnival and masquerade, the established order immediately undergoes subversion through the female protagonists' pursuit of loving rather than consuming relations. The intrusion of the feminine into the basically masculine configuration of the second scene, which parallels the intrusion of the masculine into the feminine that occurs at the end of the first scene, gives the opening of the play a highly structured context within which one can read a basic social foundation. The drive of The Rover can be measured in the degree to which feminine energy directed to the circumvention of custom re-forms masculine energy directed toward the realization of two conflicting yet related visions of social relations in which women are consumable commodities who circulate within a masculine economy of desire.

One layer of plot which has received fascinating treatment by several critics is that of "the famous Paduana Angellica Bianca" (I.i i.319–20), whose status independent from masculine "price-fixing" concerns the entirety of Act II. This disruption of the linear progression of the comic plot line—the bringing together of female and male protagonists in relationships based on love rather than money—allows Behn, in Catherine Gallagher's phrase, to juxtapose "the overlapping discourses of commercial, sexual and linguistic exchange."[19] As Elin Diamond points out, the whore's and author's initials are the same, intimating a commonality that can be read in Angellica's "unveiling" during the disruptive second act:

> Angellica's entrance is a complicated process of theatrical unveiling. She arrives first through words, then through painted representation, then through the body of the actress who appears on a balcony behind a silk curtain. She is also the site of a different politics, one that explores desire and gender not only in the text but in the apparatus itself.[20]

She provides a counterpoint to the virgins of the opening scene, since she exists outside the economy of male matrimonial desire, thus pointing to the irony of her name. Angellica, however, also reflects male values centered on the enhancement of wealth and the free play of erotic speculation. She sets her own price, "A thousand crowns a month," and this fiscal independence inspires Willmore to lament "this poverty, of which I ne'er complain but when it hinders my approach to beauty which virtue ne'er could purchase." (II,i,110–13) Yet the penniless rover Willmore victimizes Angellica when she embraces the "new" codes of values based in emotive rather than venal concerns, further cementing her status as counter-signifier in that her plot line is somewhat tragic rather than comic.

The second act closes with Willmore gaining entrance to Angellica's lodgings, following his appropriation of one of her representations, and their exchange reveals the complex intertwining of politics and representation. Willmore, "monarchy's representative,"[21] ascends to "rail" against Angellica's venal motives:

> I came to rail at you, and rail such truths too, as shall let you see the vanity of that pride which taught you how to set such price on sin. For such it is whilst that which is love's due is meanly bartered for.
>
> (II.ii.11–15)

Willmore argues against any interrelation of economy and desire, a rhetorical stance that plays upon Angellica's knowledge of her own alterity to accepted social convention, and he further rails that "Poor as I am I would not sell myself." (II.ii.56) In an enlightening response, Angellica asks, "are you not guilty of the same mercenary crime? When a lady is proposed to you for a wife, you never ask how fair, discreet, or virtuous she is, but

---

[19]Gallagher, 23.
[20]Diamond, 529.
[21]Ibid., 531.

what's her fortune." (I.ii.91–93) Willmore acknowledges her point but describes it as "a barbarous custom." (I.ii.97) Their verbal exchange evokes an emotional response from Angellica, for she seeks a consolidation of love beyond commerce. However, the word of warning is offered in the final speech of the act by her servant Moretta, who recognizes the inflexibility of the masculine economy of desire:

> Is all our project fallen to this? To love the only enemy to our trade? Nay, to love such a shameroon; a very beggar; nay, a pirate beggar, whose business is to rifle and be gone; a no-purchase, no-pay tatterdemalion, and English picaroon[.]
>
> (II.ii.160–64)

The virgins Florinda and Hellena assume masks of experience as gypsies, under the disruptive influence of carnival, to pursue their own designs, but Angellica, in unveiling her emotions, is no longer insulated by her representations or her high price. She has exchanged her basically masculine, venal views of sexual relations for those espoused by the virgins, attempting "to take herself out of circulation"[22] with disastrous results.

Over the final three acts, the virgins' attempts to secure emotional attachments grow more complicated, but Hellena emerges from the shadows of her sister and the nunnery to assume the pivotal role. Her desire "to love and to be beloved" (III.i.44) regardless of consequences is a matter of concern for her sister. Even her kinswoman Valeria, as early as the opening scene, chides Hellena that "a maid designed for a nun ought not to be so curious in a discourse of love" (I.i.32–3). Thus, the heart of conflict in the final stages of the drama finds its beat in the vacillation of Willmore between Hellena (the virgin desiring sexual experience) and Angellica (the experienced whore desiring love freed of commerce). Virgin and whore are one in their desire, and in Act IV Hellena, disguised as a man seeking to buy Angellica's favors, crafts a situation which brings the three—Hellena, Willmore, and Angellica—onstage together; furthermore, her disguise places her in a veiled position from which to observe Willmore's gestures of affection toward Angellica. Although the virgin and whore are one in their desires, they differ significantly in their responses to this situation. When she perceives that Willmore is doubly engaged with herself and Angellica, Hellena takes an active role in splitting their liaison through masking. When Angellica perceives that Willmore loves another and has used her purely for sexual gratification, she accepts the earlier judgment of Moretta that seeking love can only bring

---

[22]Ibid., 533.

emotional misery. The poignant scene is tragic and needs to be quoted at length:

> He's gone, and in this ague of my soul
> The shivering fit returns.
> As if the longed-for minute were arrived
> Of some blest assignation.
> In vain I have consulted all my charms,
> In vain this beauty prized, in vain believed
> My eyes could kindle any lasting fires;
> I had forgot my name, my infamy,
> And the reproach that honor lays on those
> That dare pretend a sober passion here.
> Nice reputation, though it leave behind
> More virtues than inhabit where that dwells,
> Yet that once gone, those virtues shine no more.
> Then since I am not fit to be beloved,
> I am resolved to think on a revenge
> On him that soothed me thus to my undoing.
>
> (IV.ii.398–414)

Angellica accepts a social stigma imposed from within a masculine double standard. The objects of vanity, personal charm, physical beauty, and fiery eyes prove "vain," and she pronounces herself "not fit to be beloved," the object of the alternative ordering based on emotions. The pain she feels is transmuted into a desire for revenge, a reaction more typical of males than females in the context of this play. The transitional stage between pain of rejection and desire for revenge is a remembering phrased as a forgetting: "I had forgot my name, my infamy." Nominalization and reputation in social discourse are under the sway of the symbolic; the patriarchal system is unforgiving and unforgetting. The ambiguities and frailties of a woman who plays the masculine game are straightforwardly presented: Angellica pays dearly for practicing sexual equality in the face of what Jacqueline Pearson terms "the sexual double standard."[23]

When Willmore and Angellica again meet, in Act V, she bears a pistol and threatens his death, and the dialogic exchange, laced with economic terms, anatomizes the structure of the masculine economy. The inversions are intriguing; Willmore has become the object of desire, and Angellica claims priority on his love through the repayment of vows. Angellica regrets not remaining in "innocent security" as a paid prostitute and further recognizes that she has lost her "richest treasure," her "honor."

---

[23]Pearson, 161.

(V.282, 288) Willmore responds from a feminine space, the alternative economy of emotions espoused by the virgins, when he argues that he will "be obliged for nothing but for love." (V.307) The conflict ends with Angellica being disarmed by Antonio, who immediately professes his love for her, and they depart. Thus, the stage is clear for Hellena's entrance and the concluding rhetorical exchange with Willmore.

Hellena has assumed two significant disguises during the drama, as a "gipsy" and as a male suitor; these disguises have allowed her to observe the authorized language of the phallocratic symbolic order, thereby gaining an admittance to this discourse that allows her to rebut Willmore's argument for "no vows but love." (V.443) Willmore's voice speaks against the structure that allows him free circulation in the distribution of his desire:

> Priest and Hymen? Prithee add a hangman to 'em to make up the consort. No, no, we'll have no vows but love, child, nor witness but the lover: the kind deity enjoins naught but love and enjoy. Hymen and priest wait still upon portion and jointure; love and beauty have their own ceremonies. Marriage is as certain a bane to love as lending money is to friendship.

> (V.441–47)

Willmore argues against the economic base of marriage, yet unbeknownst to him, Hellena brings with her "three hundred thousand crowns," which she suggests would "be better laid out in love than in religion." (V.523–25) He agrees to the marriage, and once Pedro, her brother and the voice of the father, acquiesces to the match, the young virgins win the day by erecting a counter-structure based on emotional rather than monetary gain. Pedro's sole concern, once Florinda, Hellena, and Valeria are successfully matched, is to "get my father's pardon" (V.541), and the play concludes with an evocation of the adventure of marriage: "Lead on; no other dangers they can tread, / Who venture in the storms o'th' marriage bed." (V.575–76)

The Politics of Interpretation

The play's "Epilogue" returns to the thematic established in the "Prologue," and critical judgment is again imaged as "a disease." (Epilogue, 9) The opening lines evoke "carnival" and "masquerade" to express the spirit of "our blessed times of reformation" (lines 2, 4) but then directly return to fallacious exercises of judgment based in "passions." (line 9) Behn abhors the "canting rules" which "refine" mimetic representations. (lines 14–15) For Behn, mimesis is defined in the articulation of the deepest political structure supporting social commerce: the status of women as a commodity exchanged by men for the enhancement of wealth and power. Behn's answer to the commodification of women, as expressed in *The Rover*, is to represent an opposing discourse invested with the authority of sentiment rather than the security of endowment and jointure.

Although the language of economic determinism in erotic relationships continually flows across Restoration stages, Behn's status as a woman writing within a basically masculine economy of literary production uniquely positions her to critique the "process" that invisibly exists to structure the individual subject in symbolic "communicative structures" authorized by empowered social discourses. For this reason, both Gallagher and Diamond link Behn's treatment of Angellica Bianca to her own status as writer. For Gallagher, "By literalizing and embracing the playwright-prostitute metaphor, Aphra Behn … becomes a symbolic figure of authorship for the Restoration, the writer and strumpet combined."[24] Diamond sees that "Behn was vulnerable to accusations of immodesty; to write meant to expose herself, to put herself in circulation; like Angellica, to sell her wares."[25] Furthermore, Behn's self-exposure unveils the symbolic ordering of culture in man's image, where Behn's acts of language simultaneously define a space in which "a woman enter[s] the symbolic order and at the same time calls it into question."[26] Read in this way, the assumption of pen and production is another masquerade, with Behn masking her intent to challenge the status of the phallus as privileged signifier of culture by appropriating and transmuting a metaphoric strain of economic language, as does Hellena at the conclusion of the play.[27]

[24]Gallagher, 31.

[25]Diamond, 536.

[26]Andrea Nye, "Woman Clothed with the Sun: Julia Kristeva and the Escape from/to Language," *Signs: Journal of Women and Culture* 12 (1987):665.

[27]See Lacan, 56, 79–93.

Courtesan Embracing a Man Impassioned by Wine
from *Drunkeness*, Jacob Matham. 93 X 157 *Rotterdam*

Contributors

CATHERINE LA COURREYE BLECKI, Professor of English at San Jose State University, is currently studying promptbooks, and engravings of *Carolianus*, concentrating on the various interpretations of Volumnia's role from the eighteenth through the early twentieth centuries. Her other publications have been in Quaker women's autobiography and in Restoration bibliography.

JEAN R. BRINK, Professor of English at Arizona State University, also serves as director of the Arizona Center for Medieval and Renaissance Studies. She is the author of *Michael Drayton Revisited* and articles on sixteenth- and seventeenth-century biography. She is currently working on a documentary biography of Edmund Spenser.

MARGARET DOWNS-GAMBLE, a doctoral candidate at The University of Texas, Austin, is currently finishing her dissertation, "John Donne's Monstrous Body," directed by Leah Marcus. The dissertation examines multiple seventeenth-century manuscript variants of John Donne's poetry to suggest that the artifacts of scribal culture are primarily argumentative transactions, and that the study of multiple versions can be facilitated by the alternative investigative environment of computerized hypertext.

MARY ERLER teaches in the English department at Fordham University. She has published in *Modern Philology, Studies in English Literature, The Library*, and *Medium Ævum*, and is coeditor of *Women and Power in the Middle Ages* (University of Georgia Press, 1988). She is currently working on a book about English womens' reading in the early modern period.

JULIET FLEMING is teaching English at the University of Southern California. Routledge will soon publish her book, *Ladies' Men, the Ladies' Text and the English Renaissance*, of which the essay in this volume forms a part.

DONALD W. FOSTER is Associate Professor of English at Vassar College. He is the author of *Elegy by W. S.: A Study in Attribution*. His published work also includes essays on literary theory, biblical narrative, and Shakespeare. He is currently editing *Women's Works: An Anthology of British Literature, AD 900–1640*, a collection of women's writing that has been culled largely from manuscript sources and little-known printed texts.

JUDITH KEGAN GARDINER is Professor of English and Women's Studies at the University of Illinois at Chicago. Her publications include *Craftsmanship in Context: The Development of Ben Jonson's Poetry; Rhys, Stead, Lessing, and the Politics of Empathy*. She also has published numerous essays on the English Renaissance, twentieth-century women writers, and psychoanalytic and feminist theory. Her essay on Margaret Fell contributes to her current project, *Add Women Who Stir: Rewriting Seventeenth-Century English Literary History*.

241

MARGARET P. HANNAY, Professor of English at Siena College, is the author of *Philip's Phoenix: Mary Sidney, Countess of Pembroke* (New York: Oxford University Press, 1990) and editor of *Silent but for the Word: Tudor Women as Patrons, Translators and Writers of Religious Works* (Kent: Kent State University Press, 1985). She is currently editing the *Collected Works of Mary Sidney Herbert, Countess of Pembroke* with Noel J. Kinnamon for the Oxford English Text Series.

JEAN E. HOWARD is Professor of English at Columbia University. Her new book, *Discourses of the Theater: The Stage and Social Struggle in Early Modern England*, is forthcoming from Routledge. She is completing, with Phyllis Rackin, a feminist study of the history play tentatively titled *Engendering a Nation: Shakespeare's Chronicles of the English Past.*

MARK S. LUSSIER is currently an Assistant Professor of English at Western Illinois University. He is the coeditor of *Perspective as a Problem in the Art, Literature, and History of Early Modern England* (New York and London: Edwin Mellen Press, 1992). His essays have appeared in the following journals: *1650–1850: Ideas, Aesthetics, and Inquiries in the Early Modern Era; Visible Language; Women's Studies; New Orleans Review; Arts Quarterly; RE;* and *Arts & Letters.* Three of his essays appeared in *Encyclopedia of Romanticism: Culture in Britain 1780–1830s* (New York and London: Garland Publishing, 1992), and he edited two special issues of *New Orleans Review*: "Feminist Literary Criticism: Theory and Politics," and "Reading Blake/ Blake Reading." He is currently completing a book-length study of economic language in Restoration drama.

PHYLLIS RACKIN, Professor of English in General Honors at the University of Pennsylvania, is Vice-President and President-Elect of the Shakespeare Association of America. Her articles on Shakespeare and related topics have appeared in such journals as *Shakespeare Quarterly, PMLA,* and *Theatre Journal,* and in various anthologies. Her most recent book is *Stages of History: Shakespeare's English Chronicles* (Cornell, 1990, and Routledge, 1991). She is presently working with Jean Howard on a feminist study of Shakespeare's English history plays, tentatively titled *Engendering a Nation: Shakespeare's Chronicles of the English Past.*

RETHA M. WARNICKE is Professor of History and History Department chair at Arizona State University. She is the author of *Women of the English Renaissance and Reformation, The Rise and Fall of Anne Boleyn: Family Politics at the Court of Henry VIII,* and many articles on women of Tudor and Stuart England.

Index